# The Beauty of the Triune God

# Princeton Theological Monograph Series
K. C. Hanson, Charles M. Collier, D. Christopher Spinks,
Robin A. Parry Series Editors

*Recent volumes in the series:*

Koo Dong Yun
*The Holy Spirit and Ch'i (Qi):
A Chiological Approach to Pneumatology*

Stanley S. MacLean
*Resurrection, Apocalypse, and the Kingdom of Christ:
The Eschatology of Thomas F. Torrance*

Brian Neil Peterson
*Ezekiel in Context: Ezekiel's Message Understood in Its Historical Setting
of Covenant Curses and Ancient Near Eastern Mythological Motifs*

Amy E. Richter
*Enoch and the Gospel of Matthew*

Maeve Louise Heaney
*Music as Theology: What Music Says about the Word*

Eric M. Vail
*Creation and Chaos Talk: Charting a Way Forward*

David L. Reinhart
*Prayer as Memory: Toward the Comparative Study of Prayer
as Apocalyptic Language and Thought*

Peter D. Neumann
*Pentecostal Experience: An Ecumenical Encounter*

Ashish J. Naidu
*Transformed in Christ: Christology and the Christian Life
in John Chrysostom*

# The Beauty of the Triune God
*The Theological Aesthetics of Jonathan Edwards*

KIN YIP LOUIE

☙PICKWICK *Publications* · Eugene, Oregon

THE BEAUTY OF THE TRIUNE GOD
The Theological Aesthetics of Jonathan Edwards

Princeton Theological Monograph Series 201

Copyright © 2013 Kin Yip Louie. All rights reserved. Except for brief quotations in critical publications or reviews, no part of this book may be reproduced in any manner without prior written permission from the publisher. Write: Permissions, Wipf and Stock Publishers, 199 W. 8th Ave., Suite 3, Eugene, OR 97401.

Scripture quotations, unless otherwise noted, are from THE HOLY BIBLE, NEW INTERNATIONAL VERSION®, NIV® Copyright © 1973, 1978, 1984, 2011 by Biblica, Inc.™ Used by permission. All rights reserved worldwide.

Pickwick Publications
An Imprint of Wipf and Stock Publishers
199 W. 8th Ave., Suite 3
Eugene, OR 97401

www.wipfandstock.com

ISBN 13: 978-1-61097-243-7

*Cataloguing-in-Publication data:*

Louie, Kin Yip

    The beauty of the triune God : the theological aesthetics of Jonathan Edwards / Kin Yip Louie, with forewords by David Fergusson and Samuel Logan.

    viii + 280 pp. ; 23 cm. Includes bibliographical references.

    Princeton Theological Monograph Series 201

    ISBN 13: 978-1-61097-243-7

    1. Edwards, Jonathan, 1703–1758. 2. Edwards, Jonathan, 1703–1753—Aesthetics. 3. Aesthetics—Religious aspects. I. Fergusson, David. II. Logan, Samuel T., 1943–. III. Series. IV. Title.

BX7260.E3 L794 2013

Manufactured in the U.S.A.

This work is dedicated to my wife Janet, in gratitude for standing by me as I pursued my studies, and for making my life so beautiful.

# Contents

*Foreword by David Fergusson* / ix
*Foreword by Dr. Samuel Logan* / ix
*Preface* / ix
*Acknowledgments* / ix

1　Introduction / 1

2　Definitions of Beauty / 17

3　Metaphysics of Beauty / 64

4　The Beautiful God / 94

5　The Beautiful Christ / 118

6　Eschatological Beauty / 142

7　Conclusion / 185

*Bibliography* / 219
*Index* / 227

# Foreword

*David Fergusson*
D. Phil., FRSE
Professor of Divinity, University of Edinburgh

THE FOCUS OF DR KIN YIP LOUIE'S WORK COMBINES TWO RECENT BUT quite different resurgences in theological study. These are the writings of Jonathan Edwards and theological aesthetics. Acknowledged as a preacher and scholar of high distinction, Jonathan Edwards has sometimes proved elusive to successive generations of scholars, the different aspects of his thought attracting the interest of diverse constituencies. Yet with the availability of the multi-volume critical edition of his works, both the unity and multi-dimensionality of his work are now increasingly apparent. Immersed in both Puritan and early Enlightenment thought, Edwards combines tendencies that have since become radically dissociated. Steeped in the history of Western thought and Christian theology, his work displays classical, Reformed, and modern influences, these being blended into a single theological vision that was preached with striking effects. This blend of historical awareness, intellectual rigor, and spiritual force surely explains much of his appeal today to a younger generation of theologians.

Although atypical of much earlier Reformed theology, Edwards' account of beauty is a persistent and pervasive theme in his writings. It is one that both reaches back into a classical aesthetic tradition and forwards into an era in which it has received concentrated attention from von Balthasar and others. Dr. Louie's study reveals the ways in which Edwards' account of beauty does not emerge as an epiphenomenon of his theological system or as a side-concern. It is neither an addendum to nor an excrescence of his theological work but quite integral to his vision of the world as created, redeemed and brought to eschatological fulfillment by the triune God. The embeddedness of beauty in the doctrines of the Christian faith, or more properly in that which they attest, is thus a central feature of Edward's theology, and one that is admirably displayed in this study.

*Foreword*

This is an important contribution not only to the burgeoning secondary literature on Edwards but also to recent literature in theological aesthetics. In exposing some of the tensions in Edwards' theology and bringing him into conversation with later studies of aesthetics, Dr. Louie points to the wider significance of his work. In doing so, he helps us to understand the persistent appeal of Edwards' theology in its articulation of the central convictions of the Christian faith as these bear upon the intellectual, emotional, and practical life of human beings.

# Foreword

*Dr. Samuel Logan*
International Director, The World Reformed Fellowship, www.wrfnet.org
September 22, 2012

Jonathan Edwards' *Treatise on Religious Affections* is surely one of the most important books ever written by a human being. This is true for many reasons, not least the fact that, in this book, Edwards does a masterful job of answering the question, "What makes a person a Christian?" And for those who would become Christians, or who would live like Christians, or who would seek to lead others to Christ, it is hard to imagine a more significant question.

Within the *Treatise on Religious Affections*, one of the fundamental of all of Edwards' ideas appears in Section Two of Part III where Edwards discusses this proposition: "The first objective ground of gracious affections is the transcendently excellent and amiable nature of divine things, as they are in themselves; and not any conceived relation they bear to self or self-interest." Here is what he says:

> Whereas the exercises of true and holy love in the saints arise in another way. They do not first see that God loves them, and then see that he is lovely, but they first see that God is lovely, and that Christ is excellent and glorious, and their hearts are first captivated with this view, and the exercises of their love are wont from time to time to begin here, and to arise primarily from these views; and then, consequentially, they see God's love, and great favor to them.[49] The saint's affections begin with God. [Emphasis added.]

Throughout this section (and, in fact, throughout all of Part III of the *Affections*), the words "beauty," "beautiful," "lovely," and their synonyms appear over and over again. And in every case, they appear as keys for identifying truly gracious affections. The unique "special grace" enjoyed by Christians is the gift of seeing God as "beautiful." Satan himself knows the truths about God, probably as well as or better than the most orthodox theologians. But God does not appear beautiful to Satan and that makes all the difference.

This aesthetic approach to understanding the fundamental nature of Christian experience carries over into many of Edwards' other works where the terms "fit" or "fitness" or "proportion," as well as "beauty," define critically important concepts. From his sermons on "justification," where Edwards uses "natural fitness" and "moral fitness" to define the essential difference between justification and sanctification to "The Nature of True Virtue," where Edwards uses "fitness" to describe "the last end for which God made all things," Edwards' approach to theology is decidedly aesthetic. Without an understanding and appreciation of the aesthetic dimension of Edwards' theology, the reader will inevitably miss or misunderstand the most important points that Edwards has to make.

This general point has been recognized by many scholars, as Dr. Louie points out in his "Introduction" below. But, as he also points out, the fully theological nature of Edwards' aesthetics has been largely ignored, a fact that would have been distressed Edwards himself. As stated in the quotation above, it is the perception of *God's* beauty, not the beauty of any created thing or person, that was uppermost in Edwards' mind. Without that dimension, the very reason and ground of the beautiful disappears.

Dr. Louie's work seeks to correct this lacuna in Edwards scholarship. And, in my opinion, he does a superb job.

I trust that those who read this book will find the incredible and majestic beauty of the God whom Edwards worshipped both clear and compelling.

# Preface

THIS IS A STUDY OF THE *THEOLOGICAL* AESTHETICS OF JONATHAN EDwards. Previous studies of Edwards' aesthetics tend to pass over doctrinal issues and address Edwards mostly within a philosophical context. In this treatment, the aesthetics of Edwards is examined within an explicitly doctrinal framework, including the doctrine of Trinity, Christology, and eschatology. Chapter 1 reviews previous scholarship on the theme of beauty in Edwards' theology. Chapter 2 gives the intellectual background to Edwards' discussion of beauty. Chapter 3 discuss how Edwards' metaphysics builds on his concept of beauty. Chapter 4 to chapter 6 shows how the theme of beauty is applied different doctrinal areas. It will demonstrate that many of his novel theological ideas come from a consistent application of his metaphysics of beauty into traditional doctrinal debates. Thus his theology is a combination of conservative doctrine positions and innovative speculations. The concluding chapter attempts to explain why his theology of beauty has a limited influence on subsequent American theology and how we can appropriate his insights today.

# Acknowledgments

IN ITS ORIGINAL FORM, THIS STUDY WAS A DISSERTATION FOR THE Doctor of Philosophy degree at University of Edinburgh. I would like to thank Dr. David Fergusson for his expert supervision and his timely response. I would like to thank Dr. Stanley Russell, my external examiner, and Dr. John McDowell, my internal examiner, for their valuable comments on a previous draft of this dissertation.

I would like to thank my longsuffering wife, Janet. She gladly accompanies me, moving from one continent to another, in those long years in the pursuit of my dream. When my previous doctoral program came to a standstill, she encouraged me to persevere in my calling and showed great confidence in me. She is my greatest treasure on earth. My gratitude goes to our three daughters, Simone, Janine, and Erin, for giving me so much joy.

I would like to thank China Graduate School of Theology, for providing me with the scholarship to come to Edinburgh, for trusting in me, as well as for their prayers. I would like to thank Christian International Scholarship Foundation for providing me with financial and prayer support.

Last but not least, I would like to thank our glorious and gracious God.

# 1

# Introduction

JONATHAN EDWARDS IS OFTEN REGARDED AS THE MOST IMPORTANT American theologian prior to the Civil War.[1] He has generated considerable attention in recent scholarship. Born in 1703, Edwards lived through a time of transition. The Puritan heritage still seemed vibrant at his birth. By the time of his death at 1758, the Puritan religion had lost significant ground to the "enlightened" Christianity in American culture. This "enlightened" Christianity rejected the complex dogmatic system of Reformed scholasticism and preferred the simplicity of Christian ethics.[2] His importance lies in his creative attempt to hold together old and new elements of his time. On the one hand, he is a staunch defender of the Reformed and Puritan heritage. His *Freedom of the Will* is famous (or notorious) as a formidable defense of the Reformed doctrine of predestination. On the other hand, he is remarkably familiar (as a pastor in New England) with contemporaneous British theologians and philosophers. Edwards made conscious efforts to get acquainted with the avant-garde thinking of his

---

1. "By many estimates, he was the most acute early American philosopher and the most brilliant of all American theologians." Marsden, *Jonathan Edwards*, 1. Ours is a theological study, and history is a peripheral concern. For historical concern, Marsden's *Jonathan Edwards* provides a comprehensive and excellent biography. We organize Edwards' material thematically rather than chronologically. The evolution of his theology over Edwards' lifetime is not our main concern. Partly this is due to the need to limit our research, partly to our belief that there is no major reversal or paradigm shift throughout his life. For a chronological study of Edwards' aesthetics, see Strader, *Chronological Development*. Strader thinks that Edwards' aesthetics is developed in three phrases in response to different needs. Early in his life, Edwards uses theological aesthetics to explicate his mystical encounter with God. In the middle period, aesthetics is used to defend the revival movement. In the later period, he uses aesthetics to engage in a dialogue with the Enlightenment (particularly Francis Hutcheson.) We shall address all three concerns in the dissertation, though not in a strict chronological order.

2. See Ahlstrom, *Religious History*, 350–59.

time. In both published works and private notes, Edwards wrote polemic works to defend Calvinism against liberal thinkers of his day. However, he is much more than just a defender of old traditions. Mostly in his private notes, he mused on the implications of Newtonian physics and Lockean epistemology. In this synthesis of the old and the new, Edwards' theology is almost unique among American theologians. It combines bold metaphysical speculations with strict adherence to traditional doctrines. It is this combination of the old and the new that makes Edwards so interesting to scholars. Is the new or the old that is the heart of Edwards' theology?[3] Is he the last Puritan or the first modern (or postmodern) American theologian?

It has long been recognized by scholars that aesthetics occupies a central place in Edwards' thinking. Delattre's *Beauty and Sensibility* has often been quoted in academic literature. It is often regarded as the standard work on this topic. Yet, *Beauty and Sensibility* hardly mentions anything about Reformed doctrines. In Delattre's study, Edwards is primarily the pioneer of new metaphysics and new theology. Is the Reformed heritage really tangential to Edwards' thinking, so that Delattre is justified in ignoring doctrines? Or has Delattre missed something important about Edwards' thinking on aesthetics? In this study, we shall study the aesthetics from an old and yet new perspective. It is old in the sense that we employ traditional theological topics such as doctrine of God and doctrine of Christ as organizing themes. It is new in the sense that no one yet has approached Edwards' aesthetics through this angle.[4] We hope to integrate Edwards the speculative philosopher with Edwards the Reformed theologian. Only with this integration can we see the true significance of the theological aesthetics of Edwards.

First, we need to explain the division between Edwards the philosopher and Edwards the theologian among scholars. As we shall see in the next section, aesthetics is at the center of this story. Before we can explain more about the uniqueness of our approach, we need to look at previous scholarship on Edwards' aesthetics. This is the topic of our next section.

---

3. As the survey below will indicate, Perry Miller is the prime advocate of the new thinking in Edwards. Gerstner's *Rational Biblical Theology* is a prime example of a scholarly work focusing on the traditional doctrines in Edwards.

4. Robert Jenson recognizes the importance of the Christian doctrine of God in Edwards' aesthetics. "The first: the God into whose beauty Edwards is led by the beauty of nature is no nature-God or God of natural theology, but from the very first and essentially the *triune* God." *America's Theologian*, 18. However, his book offers only scattered remarks on this theme. One can view our study as a systematic development of Jenson's remark.

*Introduction*

# Theological Aesthetics and Edwards—A Survey

It has long been recognized that aesthetics occupies a central place in Edwards' thinking. Delattre's work on this topic in the 1960s has often been quoted in academic literature.[5] In this section, we survey past studies of Edwards' theological aesthetics and offer motives for our new study.

The question of aesthetics, like so many academic questions about Edwards, begins with Perry Miller. Almost sixty years after its publication, Miller's intellectual biography of Edwards remains today unmatched in its wealth of provocative ideas and graceful prose. Its provocative power comes partly from Miller's attempt to separate the real Edwards from the superficial Edwards. In the introduction to his seminal work, he writes that "the student of Edward must seek to ascertain not so much the peculiar doctrines in which he expressed his meaning as the meaning itself."[6] For Miller, the Calvinistic doctrines expounded by Edwards are obsolete and boring. These doctrines are merely the husk that hides an original and brilliant kernel. According to Miller, Edwards' kernel is that: "As a Protestant, he protested against the tyranny of all formalism, especially of that which masquerades as sweet reasonableness. He preached a universe in which the nature of things will permit no interest to become vested."[7]

It is a startling conclusion because one can hardly find any explicit protest against formalism or human tyranny in Edwards' writings. On the surface at least, most of Edwards' publications and sermons are defenses of traditional Calvinism. They are not writings on general philosophy, even less about political philosophy. The way that Miller comes to such a startling conclusion is a long and winding road. We need to retrace this road briefly in order to understand the currents of contemporary Edwardsian scholarship. Moreover, aesthetics plays a central part in Miller's reinterpretation of Edwards.

We begin with the reading strategy of Miller. Miller gives a privileged status to the early writings of Edwards. When Miller introduces Edwards' 1933 sermon *A Divine and Supernatural Light* (when Edwards was thirty years old), he claims that "it is no exaggeration to say that the whole of Edwards' system is contained in miniature within some ten or twelve of the pages in this work."[8] He believes that Edwards' works are "statement

---

5. Delattre, *Beauty and Sensibility*.
6. *Jonathan Edwards*, xiii.
7. Ibid., xiv.
8. Ibid., 44.

3

and restatement of an essentially static conception, worked over and over, as upon a photographic plate, to bring out more detail or force from it clearer prints."[9] Miller often appeals to Edwards' early private notes in his creative interpretation of Edwards' later works.[10] For example, he claims that in Edwards' late work, *Freedom of the Will*, the question of the free will is really a masquerade for a deeper concern. "The *Freedom of the Will* is an immense cipher. Intellectually, the hidden meaning is 'Excellency.'"[11] We shall come shortly to the meaning of excellency. The issue here is that Miller believes that Edwards' doctrinal concerns should be deciphered for its deeper meaning. The key to decipherment lies in Edwards' early notes. These notes are the most speculative and explicitly philosophical among Edwards' works. This allows Miller to claim that Edwards' real concern is really philosophical rather than doctrinal. This interpretive strategy will cast a long shadow over subsequent scholarship.[12]

What are the central themes of these early notes (and in Miller's story, of all of Edwards' works)? The theme is the reconciliation of the Christian religion with the advancement of science: "Locke is, after all, the father of modern psychology, and Newton is the fountainhead of our physics; their American student, aided by remoteness, by technological innocence, and undoubtedly by his arrogance, asked in all cogency why, if the human organism is a protoplasm molded by environment, and if its environment is a system of unalterable operations, need mankind any longer agonize, as they had for seventeen hundred years, over the burden of sin?"[13]

According to Miller, Edwards learns from reading Locke that the old metaphysics no longer works. Locke claims that the only knowable objects in the human mind are ideas. And ideas are not the things themselves. "Locke amputated consciousness from things."[14] If we cannot know

---

9. Ibid., 45.

10. Many of these notes are published in *Scientific and Philosophical Writings*, the sixth volume of the Yale edition of *The Works of Jonathan Edwards*. Hereafter when we cite the Yale edition, we write *Works* followed by volume and page number. Occasionally, when we cite the Banner of Truth Trust's two-volume edition of *The Works of Jonathan Edwards*, we shall write *Works* (BT) followed by volume and page number.

11. *Jonathan Edwards*, 26.

12. There is another smaller stream of Edwardsian scholarship (e.g., Iain Murray) which interprets Edwards mainly as a revivalist preacher. It ignores Miller and assigns Edwards' philosophical writings to a peripheral role. Scholars in this tradition seldom address the questions of aesthetics explicitly, and they will not be our dialogue partners in this study.

13. Ibid., 72–73.

14. Ibid., 189.

things-in-themselves, then we can verify one idea only with other ideas. It is not a denial of the reality of the external world, since ideas are generated and conditioned by contact with the external world. But we cannot verify ideas by examining things unmediated. Therefore, "truth is a consistent supposition of relations among ideas, not because truth is separable from empirical test, but because only by a consistency of ideas can the mind participate in order and law."[15] If we know things only through ideas, and ideas come only from sensation, then how do we perceive bodiless objects such as God? If consciousness is amputated from things, then how is our mind related to the mechanical world of Newton?

According to Miller, Edwards learns from Newton that the universe is a gigantic web of cause and effect. The four causes of Aristotelian physics are reduced to one efficient cause. The Arminians deceive themselves in believing in human autonomy. "The notion that a man can cause whatever results he happens to prefer was not only bad theology, it was perverted physics."[16] Edwards recognizes that there is no such thing as substance; atoms are merely forces of resistance in this web of cause and effort. Seemingly, according to Miller, Edwards wants us to face the reality that our actions are also gears in the gigantic web of cause and effort. The Arminians clung to an outmoded metaphysics that has been refuted by Newtonian physics. "To Edwards' mind, the lesson of popular Arminianism was central: the modern era was committing itself to the delusion that experience is a congeries of ill-matched piece, of disjointed frames and discontinuous moments."[17] If autonomy is an illusion, then what is sin?

Miller claims that Edwards recognizes the profound implications of Locke and Newton for Christian religion before anyone in the New World (and arguably in the Old World too). For Miller, Edwards gives a brave new interpretation of the Christian faith as a total embrace of the Newtonian world mediated through Lockean psychology:

> Because the source of ideas is external, and yet every idea is a self's manner of conceiving, there must come a time when the redeemed self realizes that a sensation cannot be clutched to his bosom as a private luxury, but belongs to a system of impressions that has a logic deeper and more beautiful than any incidental advantages (or disadvantages) that accrue to him.

15. Ibid., 261.
16. Ibid., 122.
17. Ibid., 123.

> It is the love of the order, of divine things for their beauty and sweetness, arising out of perception of their "moral excellency." Not the perception of excellency within the soul, or of the idea of excellency suspended before philosophical contemplation, but of the excellency of the cosmic method, which contains cholera, burning tigers, the evil deeds of men, and death.[18]

Newton teaches us that the world is a web of cause and effect indifferent to our private wishes. Thus we must understand that reality has a logic deeper than our petty concerns. Locke tells us that we receive the world through subjective interpretations in the form of ideas. According to Miller, Edwards puts the two together and comes to the conclusion that the Christian faith is really a subjective appreciation of the gigantic web of cause and effect as beautiful. Cholera and death may not look pretty, especially when they happen around us. But this kind of perception comes from putting my existence or human existence as the center of the universe. This self-centered perspective is the essence of sin. Redemption requires us to adopt the right perspective: "It has meaning only when it also sees that all things are beautiful. . . . The sense of the heart enables the sight; without the sight, the universe remains the same universe, but 'unless this is seen, nothing is seen that is worth the seeing; for there is no other true excellency or beauty.'"[19]

According to Miller, this allows Edwards to be thoroughly materialistic (in the sense that the material world is a closed universe) while allowing for a subjective redemption.[20] Redemption is "a flash of experience" in which we perceive the simple idea that the totality of reality is good and beautiful.[21] Yet this subjective perception has important social implications. Edwards' vision is a denunciation of all justification of vested interest in the name of reasonableness. When dressed in millennial language, this vision challenges the complacency of the rising middle class of New England.

Francis Hutcheson had paved the way for Edwards by locating beauty within perception rather than in the things themselves. He also anticipated Edwards by claiming that we perceive morality in ways similar to

---

18. Ibid., 191–92.

19. Ibid., 192. The words in single quotation are supposedly quotation from Edwards. Miller, to the chagrin of all subsequent scholars, did all his reference only in an annotated copy of his book deposited in the Harvard College Library.

20. Ibid., 188.

21. Ibid., 154.

our perception of beauty. However, according to Miller, Edwards regards the inner sense of Hutcheson as only another form of animal instinct:

> So Hutcheson was correct when he identified morality with aesthetics. . . . But Hutcheson, and all utilitarians and humanitarians after him, failed to proceed from beauties to the beautiful, and so set up for perceiving beings a criterion applicable only to stones and planets. True virtue, therefore, is no law of inanimate things, but "is *that*, belonging to the *heart* of an intelligent Being, that is beautiful by a *general* beauty, or beautiful in a comprehensive view as it is in itself, and as related to every thing that it stands in connection with." The familiar process of perception still furnishes the distinction that a [*sic*] Hutcheson blurs: what sensation receives as the instigator of a reflex act is also received as a perception predetermined by the disposition of the agent, and according to the conception, not according to the thing, the motive compels the will.[22]

In other words, Hutcheson only explains why this flower or this house is beautiful. He never rises to the Edwardsian vision of the beauty of the total reality. Moreover, Hutcheson makes the sense of beauty a kind of reflex act. For Edwards, the vision of the totality is motivated by the will. It is a leap of faith, not a reflex action.

We have given a lengthy summary of Miller. In our opinion, Miller has given the most compelling (yet seriously flawed) vision of Edwards' aesthetics yet.[23] Miller reinterprets the whole corpus of Edwards' works through his thesis, putting aesthetics as the heart and soul of Edwards' thinking. He opens up questions that subsequent Edwardsian scholarship must wrestle with. Since Miller, the metaphysics and epistemology of beauty in Edwards have become central issues. No longer can scholars regard Edwards merely as a revivalist preacher. Edwards is henceforth regarded as engaging in a profound dialogue with Locke and Newton. These are all abiding contributions of Miller, and our work builds upon the path opened up by Miller.

22. Ibid., 290.

23. Our dissertation will draw out some of his flaws. As one example of his flaws that we will not go into any further, Miller refuses to take Edwards' concern for history with any seriousness (ibid., 313–30). For better or worse, Miller's direct influence tends to wear off after Delattre's work. For example, a recent doctoral dissertation on Edwards' aesthetics from Harvard (where Miller was a professor) mentions Miller twice only, on issues other than aesthetics (Mitchell in footnote 82). One of the consequences is that Edwards' relationship to British aesthetics of his time usually gets dropped out from the purview of Edwardsian scholarship.

On the other hand, Miller's slight treatment of doctrinal issues is controversial, to say the least. In Miller's portrait, Edwards is a modern philosopher dressed in the language of theology. Edwards becomes a new Eriugena disguised as a Puritan. The beatific vision of God is essentially a vision of the totality of reality.[24] This God is totally immanent within the web of cause and effect. It is so different from the God of Reformed and Puritan tradition that one wonders why Edwards continued to preach Reformed doctrines at all. Either he is a master of deception (as Miller believes) or he suffers some form of intellectual schizophrenia. What would happen if his doctrinal concerns are not merely the husk, but they are the central issues of his aesthetics? What would happen if we try to put Edwards' philosophical musings about excellency in an explicit doctrinal framework? Should we not allow his later doctrinal writings to have philosophical implications beyond his early private musings? We shall explore these questions rejected by Miller.

Having discussed the pioneer in details, we shall be more succinct with subsequent developments. Following Miller, Elwood claims that the Edwardsian vision is the sensibility of the divine immanence in the world:

> In mature years Edwards found increasing satisfaction in the view that God is known most surely and most convincingly by an immediate awareness of His creative beauty in and through all the things He has made. . . . For those who have the inner eyes to see, God may be found as present in the mystery of the familiar in our daily world of experience.
>
> The "otherness" of God is not to be interpreted as "otherworldliness," for the transcendent is not an otherworldly realm of being independent of this world, but a dimension of reality that underlies and penetrates all other dimensions.[25]

This vision is a mystical vision in the sense that it cannot be explicated or defended through ratiocination. We simply see (or fail to see) divine beauty permeating all creatures. God and the world are not separable, as they are two dimensions of the one reality. Like Miller, Elwood interprets Edwards as a philosopher of intuition while pushing doctrinal issues to the side. He thinks that Edwards' vision is similar to that of Whitehead and

---

24. "Yet this beauty is not a Platonic idea. . . . It arises by discoverable processes out of motion and perception. Critics like Chauncy and Whittelsey never understood Edwards, but their instinct was not far wrong when they accused him of atheism—except that they would not conceive an atheism more profoundly conscious of God than they could experience." Ibid. 292.

25. Elwood, *Philosophical Theology*, 16, 18–19.

*Introduction*

Schelling.²⁶ According to Elwood, they are great philosopher-theologians because they pursue to the limit of human language the ineffable divine dimension of reality.²⁷

Following a similar approach, Delattre has given the fullest exposition of Edwards' aesthetics to date.²⁸ Delattre addresses the relation between beauty and other important concepts such as being, goodness, God, Christ, and the Holy Spirit. While Miller paints with a broad brush, Delattre gives a detailed account of how beauty is related to various important philosophical and theological topics in Edwards. The result is an impressive digest of the then unpublished notes of Edwards, but also a rather diffuse discussion of various topics.²⁹ Delattre differs from Miller in emphasizing the objectivity of beauty. Beauty is not just a certain inner sight; it is the structure of reality itself. Delattre claims that Edwards "finds that beauty provides the first and fullest and most adequate way of filling in the right-hand side of the equation 'being is x' or 'being consists in x.'"³⁰ While Miller separates use (the physical world) from pleasure (our perception), Delattre separates pleasures from objective relations: "Beauty is objective in that it is constituted by objective relations of consent and dissent among beings, relations into which the subject (or beholder) may enter and participate but the beauty of which is defined by conformity to God (consent to being-in-general) rather than by degree of subjective pleasure."³¹

However, the focus on objectivity is not meant to be a denial of the importance of perception. Delattre emphasizes that perception and existence of beings are two sides of the same coin. Being is manifested as existence and encountered as beauty.³² Consent and dissent are the operation of the will. Thus it is objective in the sense that the operation of the

---

26. Ibid., 9, 17.

27. "Doubtless Jonathan Edwards' chief fault lay in trying to express, without a poet's imagination, ideas so profound that they can be expressed adequately only in the language of poetry" (ibid. 159). If Elwood is right, then perhaps the song *Colors of the Wind* from the Disney movie *Pocahontas* expounds a better theology than Edwards.

28. *Beauty and Sensibility*. Delattre explicitly expresses his debt to Miller and Elwood on p. 4.

29. My frustration with Delattre is perhaps shared by Farley, who says that "if his work has a simple thesis, it is probably that Edwards has an objective notion of beauty" (Farley, *Faith and Beauty*, 49–50).

30. *Beauty and Sensibility*, 28.

31. Ibid., 22.

32. Ibid., 31.

will is real in some metaphysical sense. Yet it is subjective also in the sense that it is the operations of a subject.[33] Perhaps Delattre is portraying Edwards as having a philosophical system similar to the natural philosophy of the early Schelling, where thinking subjects and perceived objects are two sides of one reality of being.[34] Beauty is not determined by our private perception, but it is determined by the structure of reality.

We shall return to Delattre at various points of our dissertation. Here we may summarize Delattre's work as an attempt to develop a metaphysics of being in which beauty is the primary transcendental quality of being.[35] Thus half of *Beauty and Sensibility* is devoted to metaphysical problems, where he lays out the relationship between beauty and other transcendental qualities (existence, oneness, and goodness, etc.). When Delattre comes to theology, the first half of that section is devoted to so-called natural theology. When he finally comes to Christian doctrines such as the Trinity and redemption, the treatment is much too brief. In Delattre's interpretation, Edwards is primarily an expert metaphysician with little interest in Puritan doctrines. One is again left to wonder why Edwards continued to preach the old doctrines. Is Edwards' theology primarily a philosophy of being? Does Edwards use beauty mainly to explain the nature of being? Is Edwards a Puritan version of Pseudo-Dionysius? We suspect that Delattre is reading into Edwards an alien agenda.

The latest major contribution along the tradition of Miller is Sung Hyun Lee.[36] While Miller paints in bold and broad strokes the relationship between the Enlightenment and Edwards, Lee is meticulous and focused. Lee believes that Newton has delivered a daunting challenge to traditional metaphysics. According to Lee, Edwards' answer is a new depositional metaphysics. Edwards denies that there is something called substance underlying the interactions between an object and the world. The interactions, taken as a whole, constitute the object itself. The laws of nature are not the accidents of physical objects; they are the essence of the object. Therefore, if the harmonious working of the universe is defined as beauty,

---

33. Farley, *Faith and Beauty*, 49–50, points out this ambiguity of Delattre.

34. Bowie, *Schelling*, ch. 2.

35. "Edwards' philosophy is a philosophy of being. Nothing, not even God, is beyond being. . . . The concept of beauty is the one with which Edwards makes the first decisive move; it is the concept he joins to that of being for the development of his philosophy of being." *Beauty and Sensibility*, 104.

36. *Philosophical Theology*.

*Introduction*

to perceive the beauty of the universe is to perceive the essence of the universe.[37]

From Locke, Lee focuses on the question: What is the role of the mind's own activity in the cognitive process? According to Lee, this question is crucial to the epistemology of Locke, yet Locke never provides a satisfactory answer. Edwards advances beyond Locke in identifying habit as the active principle of cognition. By means of the habits in the mind, we join sensible data into a coherent whole in our mind. Thus the visual data of a rectangular white object becomes the idea of a door. Therefore, "the mind's sensation of beauty then is in its essence an active exerting of the mind's habit."[38] For example, the mind habitually associates an act of kindness with beauty and act of cruelty with ugliness. Instead of the mystic vision of Miller or the metaphysical doctrine of Delattre, Lee helps us to understand aesthetic sensibility of Edwards in the vocabulary of Lockean psychology. In our opinion, Lee's interpretation represents a real advance in scholarship.

Along the line of philosophical appropriation of Edwards, Stephen Daniel provides an original and idiosyncratic reading of Edwards. Like Miller, Daniel believes that Edwards is opening up some bold new understanding of deity. Instead of accentuating the importance of Locke and the Enlightenment, he thinks that Edwards develops a metaphysics of divine semiotics based on Ramist and Renaissance logic. Enlightenment philosophy focuses on the subject who interprets reality. Daniel interprets Edwards' philosophy as a postmodern metaphysics, where the message or the communication process is reality itself. We become reconciled with this ontology through our aesthetic vision. As we shall see in the next chapter, the definition Edwards gives to beauty is the consent of being to being. According to Daniel, "consent to being is the acknowledgment that being consists in the activity of substitution or displacement of individuality with some other."[39] This aesthetic vision "recognizes that the intelligibility of individual existence consists in being related to others in virtue of a divinely established harmony."[40] It recognizes that *to be* is the same as *to be intelligible*. *To be intelligible* is to be related to a web of meaning. The essence of language is that it is a system of mutual references. The epistemology of Locke is the epistemology of fallen, sinful human-

---

37. Ibid., 81–82.
38. Ibid., 150.
39. Daniel, *Philosophy of Jonathan Edwards*, 179.
40. Ibid., 184.

ity, because it assumes a dichotomy between the sign and the signified.[41] Edwards claims (according to Daniel) that we need a "sense of the heart" where we recognize that signs and suppositions are the essence of reality. *To be* is to defer oneself to others. That is true both for a person and for God. The interpreting subject of the Enlightenment is an illusion.

Daniel represents the most radical reinterpretation of Edwards since Miller's work. If Daniel is right, then most scholars have missed the heart of Edwards' philosophy completely. In this case, we think that the majority is not mistaken. We differ from Daniel in many points of interpretation. For example, we believe that the interpreting subject is an important element in the theology of Edwards. His doctrine of Trinity, his Christology, and his eschatology all rely on the concept of a knowing and willing subject. We think that Daniel has mistakenly applied Edwards' understanding of the material world to spiritual reality as well. He ends up with an Edwards who is completely foreign to seventeenth-century New England.[42]

Mitchell has taken an alternative approach to Edwards' aesthetics by concentrating on the manifestation of beauty in Edwards.[43] Mitchell is interested in a comprehensive summary of Edwards' employment of aesthetic vocabulary. Building upon the works of John Smith and Lee, Mitchell regards aesthetic experience as a specifically religious experience. Mitchell's conclusion is that aesthetic vocabulary underlies much of Edwards' writings, such as narratives of the Great Awakening, his spiritual biographies and autobiography, and his theology of sanctification. While Mitchell opens us to the variety of ways in which Edwards applies aesthetic vocabulary, he does not break new ground in our theological or philosophical understanding of Edwards.

Scholars in Miller's tradition study Edwards mainly for his innovative development of Enlightenment philosophy. They tend to dismiss or ignore the Calvinist doctrines in Edwards. In recent years, there is a renewed interest in Edwards the theologian. For example, McClymond situates Edwards' dialogue with the Enlightenment within the context of a defense of Reformed theology.[44] Instead of dressing up Enlightenment metaphysics in Christian jargon, McClymond shows that Edwards ingeniously diffuses the challenges of the Enlightenment to the Puritan vision. Holmes has pro-

---

41. Ibid., 186.

42. Just to give one example, can a Puritan like Edwards really believe that "sin is the loss of this sense of immanent meaning within discourse" (ibid., 22)?

43. Mitchell, *Experience of Beauty*.

44. McClymond, *Encounters with God*.

vided an excellent summary of Edwards' theology, paying close attention to Edwards' continuity with and innovations in the Reformed tradition.[45] These works have shown us that Edwards the theologian is neither a bore nor a great pretender. There are also specialized studies on his doctrine of Trinity, Christology, and pneumatology, which we shall encounter later in our study. It is time to build on these studies and to re-examine Edwards' aesthetics systematically as a theological enterprise.

Not many Protestant theologians have made beauty a central theme of their theology. Naturally, recent writers on Christian theological aesthetics have turned to Edwards as a valuable resource from the Protestant tradition. They tend to stand apart from the influence of Miller. Edward Farley emphasizes self-transcendence as the central theme of Edwardsian aesthetics. Beauty is the perception of the global good, in contrast to our private good. For Farley, the main significance of Edwards' aesthetics is that it points to the affective side of ethics. Ethics is not just a matter of rules; it is also an affective delight in the beauty of our actions.[46]

Much closer to our concern is the discussion of Sherry. Sherry points to the central significance of the doctrine of Trinity in Edwards' aesthetics.[47] He points out that Edwards follows the Western tradition in his doctrine of Trinity. In this tradition, the Spirit is regarded as the bond between the Father and the Son. This bond creates harmony within the Trinity, and it is also the role of the Spirit to create harmony in the universe: "Edwards derives the Holy Spirit's mission as beautifier from his role within the Trinity (and also the Son's, as image of beauty, likewise), and he explains that both the role and the mission in terms of harmony, consent and agreement, in that the Holy Spirit, being the harmony and beauty of the Godhead, has the particular function of communicating beauty and harmony in the world."[48]

Sherry recognizes that divine beauty in Edwards is a doctrinal issue. It should not be reduced to general philosophical concepts. However, Sherry does not grasp fully the complexity of Edwards' thought. Sherry thinks that Edwards never addresses why the Spirit should be uniquely associated with beauty: "We may ask why the harmonies found in the world should be taken to derive from the harmony of the Trinity itself; for a

---

45. Holmes, *God of Grace*.

46. E. Farley, *Faith and Beauty*. See especially ch. 3 and ch. 7.

47. Delattre discusses beauty in the Holy Spirit and Jesus in *Beauty and Sensibility*, ch. 7 and pp. 171–73. But he interprets these metaphysically and does not address the issue of the immanent Trinity.

48. Sherry, *Spirit and Beauty*, 93.

weaker position is available to us here, namely that there is an analogy between the Holy Spirit as the harmony of the Trinity and beauty as the harmony of the world, but that the former plays no special causal role with regard to the latter."[49]

Actually Edwards has a profound answer for Sherry's question: the Holy Spirit bestows his own beauty upon the saints, which enables the saints to perceive the beauty of the world. The other major criticism of Sherry is that Edwards fails to explain why beauty should be limited to the concept of harmony.[50] Sherry takes no account of the tradition of Miller, which emphasizes harmony as the essence of reality.

Dyrness also shares our agenda in trying to locate Edwards' aesthetics within the Reformed heritage.[51] He considers Edwards as the culmination of Puritan thinking on the imagination. Dyrness thinks that Edwards' main contribution to Reformed aesthetics is his claim that after sensing the glory of God in their hearts, the saints will have a new sense of the beauty of the world. For Dyrness, the main weakness of Edwards' aesthetics is that there is a dichotomy between the sensibilities of the saints and non-Christians. Consequently, it cannot serve as a mandate for culture in general. Dyrness' criticism raises the question of the purpose of a Christian theological aesthetics, a question which we shall return to in our conclusion.

Last, but definitely not least, we shall comment briefly on an authoritative and comprehensive treatment of Edwards' theology—*The Theology of Jonathan Edwards*.[52] It contains a short chapter on the theology of beauty, and we have little to disagree with.[53] However, owing to the nature of that work, it cannot lay out in detail the implications of the theme of beauty for the rest of Edwards' theology. For example, it does not address the relationship between divine beauty and the psychological model of the Trinity.[54] In general, this study gives an excellent account of the theocentric idealism of Edwards.[55] We are grateful that our understanding (particularly chapter 3) of Edwards is congruent with this important monograph.

---

49. Ibid., 96.
50. Ibid., 95.
51. *Reformed Theology*, 274–87.
52. McClymond and McDermott, *Theology of Jonathan Edwards*.
53. Ibid., chapter 6, 93–101.
54. It seems to be influenced by Pauw, *Supreme Harmony*, and advocates more of a social model of Trinity than our discussion in chapter 4. See ibid., 197–200.
55. Ibid., chapter 7 and 8, 102–29.

*Introduction*

## Our Agenda

It is time to summarize our survey and lay out the agenda of our study. We have indicated that there are three different approaches to Edwards' theological aesthetics. One focuses on Edwards' relationship to the Enlightenment; another approaches Edwards through the heritage of Reformed theology; and the third addresses Edwards within the context of a search for a Christian theological aesthetics. We hope to integrate these three approaches in our study. In the next chapter we shall follow Miller's agenda by comparing the definition of beauty proposed by several English Enlightenment thinkers and by Edwards. Then we shall depart from Miller by arguing that Edwards' theological aesthetics is inseparable from his Christian doctrine. We allow his theological writings and sermons to have equal weight to his early philosophical musings. In the third chapter, we look at how the concept of beauty serves as the cord that binds God, human beings and the material world together. This chapter will answer Sherry's criticism of Edwards. It will also argue that Edwards is building on Puritan spiritual theology. Miller, Delattre and Daniel have interpreted Edwards as a bold metaphysician with a bold new concept of divinity. Chapter 4 will look specifically at divine beauty. We claim that the doctrine of the Trinity and the attribute of infinity play central roles in Edwards' doctrine of God and aesthetics. In the fifth chapter, we point out that Jesus Christ exhibits a uniquely human beauty inapplicable to the pre-incarnate Son. This human beauty of Christ points to a kind of beauty different from the Trinitarian beauty. We shall see how both kinds of beauty are consummated in the eschaton in chapter 6. Then we conclude our study with some remarks regarding Edwards' relationship to his theological heritage, to the aesthetics of the Enlightenment, and to the project of theological aesthetics today. Throughout the discussion, we attempt to examine the philosophical implications or presuppositions of his doctrines, without overwhelming his doctrines with philosophical speculations.

We hope to show that theological concern is central to the Edwards' aesthetics. Edwards is not constructing metaphysics for its own sake, but he is laying out aesthetics as a channel for the perception of and communion with a personal God. The material world is not merely a giant web of impersonal cause and effect. It is rather a metaphor for spiritual reality beyond this material world. The beauty of this world is intended to induce us into divine life. The intra-Trinitarian life of God is the archetype of beauty. We participate in divine life when God reveals this beauty to us in sensible form. The world may speak the metaphor of divine beauty, but only the Holy Spirit can enable one to be sensible of divine beauty. This sense of the heart is neither the mystical vision of Elwood nor the leap of faith of Miller. Thus Edwards' aesthetics is an extension of the spiritual theology of the Puritans. On the other hand, Edwards develops the Reformed vision of the majesty of God into a specifically aesthetic vision. The perception of this aesthetic vision will be infinite joy for the saints and infinite pain for the damned. The tension between the Trinitarian beauty and the majestic beauty of God brings out the inherent tension and richness of the Christian theology. Edwards' ideas find their counterparts in the distinction between beauty and sublimity in philosophical aesthetics. Thus both theological aesthetics and philosophical aesthetics indicate the importance of the sensible perception of nonconceptual knowledge of supersensible reality. The analysis of such sensible perception of divine reality is the task of theological aesthetics that Edwards bequeaths to us.

# 2

## Definitions of Beauty

IN THIS CHAPTER, WE INTEND TO SET OUR STUDY WITHIN THE HISTORY OF Western theological aesthetics. We begin by looking at the history of theological aesthetics before the Enlightenment in a rapid fashion. It shows us what kind of questions theologians and philosophers have raised about the nature of beauty. It will serve as a general background to our study. We shall return to some of these issues in our concluding chapters.

As we have seen in the last chapter, much of Edwardsian scholarship has focused on Edwards' relationship to the Enlightenment.[1] Our second section will take a detour from the history of aesthetics, and we shall examine the major themes in the English Enlightenment that are crucial to understanding the aesthetics of Edwards. Miller has already suggested the science of Newton and the philosophy of Locke. We like to suggest the twin themes of reason and empirical observations. These themes are championed as foundation of scientific knowledge of the physical world and the mental world. Edwards, along with many Puritans, embrace these themes as their own. In the second section, we shall give a brief introduction of these themes in old England and in New England.

Following that, we shall return to aesthetics and examine the concept of beauty in three English Enlightenment thinkers: Shaftesbury (1671–1713), Joseph Addison (1672–1719), and Francis Hutcheson (1694–1746).[2] The importance of Hutcheson for Edwards' aesthetics has

---

1. For Edwards' engagement with the Enlightenment beyond the theme of aesthetics, see McClymond, *Encounters with God*, Chai, *Limits of Enlightenment,* and Zakai, *Philosophy of History.*

2. A succinct treatment of the importance of these three philosophers for the origin of modern aesthetics is in Guyer, *Value of Beauty*, 8–28. Our focus is different from Guyer because he treat these philosophers as precursors to Kant. The development of English aesthetics in the seventeen and eighteenth century is laid out in Ernest Lee Tuveson, *Imagination as a Means of Grace.*

long been recognized and debated.³ However, Hutcheson represents only one view of beauty in the English Enlightenment. We need the other two to give a more complete picture of the aesthetics of the time. All three writers are explicitly referred to in Edwards' *Catalogue*.⁴ While we cannot know for certain how each might have contributed to Edwards' thought, together they form the "modern opinions" that Edwards was eager to enter into a dialogue with.⁵

After discussing these philosophers, we shall give a preliminary definition of beauty according to Edwards. Lastly, we shall offer some comparisons.

## Aesthetics from Plato to the Puritans

Viladesau suggests that there are three inter-related but distinctive meanings of the word *aesthetics*:

> 1. The general study of sensation and imagination and/or "feeling" in the wider sense of nonconceptual or nondiscursive (but nevertheless "intellectual") knowledge
>
> 2. The study of beauty and/or "taste."
>
> 3. The study of art in general and/or of the fine arts in particular.⁶

In modern philosophical discussion of aesthetics, the focus is usually on the third meaning of the term.⁷ Perhaps it reflects the gradual decline in confidence in defining beauty with philosophical rigor.⁸ However, Puritan New England is not known for its cultivation of fine arts, and Edwards

---

3. See especially Paul Ramsey, Appendix II, *Works* 8:689–705 and A Owen Aldridge, "Edwards and Hutcheson." Ramsey and Aldridge come to opposite conclusion regarding Hutcheson's influence on Edwards. We are close to Ramsey in believing that the direct influence of Hutcheson is minimal.

4. MSS 151, box 15, folder 1202, in Beinecke Library, Yale University. The *Catalogue* is a small manuscript containing an annotated list of books that Edwards was interested in. Edwards might not have read all the works in the list. This manuscript has not been published yet when the research for this book was done. Since then it has been published as the 26th volume in the Yale edition.

5. Edwards mentions the fashionable and erroneous "modern opinions" of Shaftesbury, Hutcheson, and Turnbull on the nature of virtue in Letter 222, *Works* 16:696

6. Richard Viladesau, *Theological Aesthetics*, 7.

7. For example, the majority of essays in two recent handbooks of aesthetics deal with different aspects of the fine arts: Gaut and Lopes, eds., *Routledge Companion*, and Kivy, *Blackwell Guide*.

8. See Stolnitz, "Beauty."

*Definitions of Beauty*

shows little interest in aesthetics in the third sense. Moreover, the concept of fine arts developed gradually only in the eighteenth century. Literature, paintings and other art forms have always been present, but they are not gathered together in philosophical discourse until the Enlightenment.[9] Edwards may not even know the modern concept of fine arts.[10] We shall return to the question of the fine arts briefly only in our conclusion.

Aesthetics, in the sense of the study of beauty, has a much longer history in philosophy and theology. Sometimes, if beauty is understood as nonconceptual in that particular theory, the study of the theory of beauty will lead to epistemological questions of non-conceptual knowledge. Edwards conceives beauty as part of the essence of God. To become a Christian is to become sensible of and to partake in divine beauty. In this study, we shall take aesthetics both in the first and second sense. A brief historical survey of the theological aesthetics will help us to understand Edwards in a broad perspective.

We begin our story with Plato. Plato is famous for his advice to banish poets. His main objection is that poets invoke in us behavior that we would disdain in real life:

> I think that you know that the very best of us when we hear Homer or some other of the makers of tragedy imitating one of the heroes in grief, and is delivering a long tirade in his lamentations or chanting and beating his breast, feel pleasure, and abandon ourselves and accompany the representation with sympathy and eagerness, and we praise as an excellent poet the one who most strongly affects us in this way.
>
> But when in our own lives some affliction comes to us, you are also aware that we plume ourselves upon the opposite, on our ability to remain calm and endure, in the belief that this is the conduct of a man, and what we were praising in the theater that of a woman.[11]

Why do we enjoy being "womanish" in theater and recommend being "manly" in real life? In real life, we recognize that we must face calamities rationally. Emotions merely interfere our thinking process and they should be suppressed. Our suppressed emotions hunger for release in a

---

9. This story is told in P. Kristeller, "Modern System."

10. As practitioners of fine arts, both Edwards and his wife Sarah enjoyed singing. Cf. Marsden, *Jonathan Edwards*, 106.

11. *Republic* 605c-d. All quotations of Plato from Hamilton & Cairns, *Completed Dialogues*. Our discussion is based on Janaway, "Plato," in *Routledge Companion*, 3–14 and, Beardsley, *Aesthetics*, ch. 2.

good cry, when we can sympathize with sufferers from the safe position of an observer. The problem is that "after feeding fat the emotion of pity there, it is not easy to restrain it in our own sufferings."[12]

For Plato, real beauty is eternal and impassionate. In the dialogue *Symposium*, Plato discusses how a person should progress from enjoying the beauty of a particular human to human bodies in general, then to the beauty of laws and institutions, then to the beauty of knowledge in general. Finally, "turning his eyes toward the open sea of beauty, he will find in such contemplation the seed of the most fruitful discourse and the loftiest thought, and reap a golden harvest of philosophy, until, confirmed and strengthened, he will come upon one single form of knowledge, the knowledge of the beauty."[13]

This single form of beauty "is neither words, nor knowledge, nor something that exists in something else . . . but subsisting of itself and by itself in an eternal oneness."[14] True beauty is imageless, since beauty is the same as goodness, and goodness has no image: "It is only when he discerns beauty itself through what makes it visible that a man will be quickened with the true, and not the seeming, virtue—for it is virtue's self that quickens him, not virtue's semblance."[15]

The problem with poetry is that it necessarily remains at the level of dealing with imagery. It is the job of philosophy to train people to reach this vision of the eternal beauty and the ultimate goal of human life. "If a man's life is ever worth living, it is when he has attained this vision of the very soul of beauty."[16]

Having answered the nature of beauty, we are still left with the question of criteria. For example, how do we distinguish a beautiful body from an ugly one? Plato has much less to say on this question. He does tell us that the qualities of measure and proportion invariably constitute beauty and excellence.[17]

This short summary of Plato already shows that Plato has laid out the agenda of much subsequent philosophical and theological aesthetics. What is the role of emotions in our appreciation of true beauty?[18] Does true

---

12. *Republic* 606b.
13. *Symposium* 210d.
14. Ibid. 211a-b.
15. Ibid. 212.
16. Ibid. 211d.
17. *Philebus* 64e.
18. We note in passing that Aristotle deliberately refutes Plato in *Poetics* by

beauty reside in the rational and universal, or the sensible and particular? If beauty is ultimately one, how is Beauty related to particular manifestations of beauty? How does a person go from particular beauties to Beauty itself? Are beauty and goodness merely two descriptions of one reality? In theological terms, what is the relationship between divine beauty and creaturely beauties? How can we rise from particular beauties to the appreciation of divine beauty? Plato's theory of proportion also becomes the theory of beauty with which later aestheticians had to wrestle.[19] Plato's theory is further developed into Neoplatonism in the writings of Plotinus and others. It is Neoplatonism that is most important for the medieval concept of beauty.

From Plato we shall go to the church fathers. The Fathers do not give systematic treatment to the beauty of God. There is no major controversy about divine beauty in the early church; so there is no need for the Fathers to reach maximal clarity. Nonetheless, there are some common themes. First, they think that the best kind of creaturely beauty is the spiritual beauty of the saints. Second, they believe that Christ is the manifestation of the beauty of the Father. Third, they believe that the beauty of this world is created by God. God is the source of all beauty and God is most beautiful. Fourth, the Holy Spirit is the mediator of the knowledge of divine beauty to the saints and the beautifier of the souls of the saints. The Spirit also mediates the divine ability of creativity to the servants of the Lord.[20]

Augustine, the most important church father for the Western church, has given only scattered remarks about the nature of beauty. He subscribes to the view that the beauties of particular things are informed by the indivisible Beauty of God. Beauty is manifested by unity, proportion and order.[21] Far more important than his occasional remarks on beauty is the question that he bequeaths to subsequent theologians: "If I were to ask first whether things are beautiful because they give pleasure, or give pleasure

---

claiming that tragedy helps to purify our emotions. Rather than suppressing our emotions, we should train them to take delight in what is good and to be repelled by what is bad. (See Pappas, "Aristotle," in *Routledge Companion*, 15–27) Though Aristotle has a colossal influence on medieval theology, *Poetics* has made little impact on medieval theological aesthetics.

19. Plato may have been influenced by the Pythagoras school. On some texts on the beauty of numbers in the Pythagorean school, see Eco, *Aesthetics*, 72–74. For Greek and medieval fascination with the aesthetics of numbers, see Eco, *On Beauty*, ch. 3.

20. See Sherry, *Spirit and Beauty*, 4–7.

21. See Beardsley, *Aesthetics from Classical Greece*, 92–98; Joseph Margolis, "Medieval aesthetics," in *Routledge Companion*, 29–40.

because they are beautiful, I have no doubt that I will be given the answer that they give pleasure because they are beautiful."[22]

In modern vocabulary, Augustine is asking whether beauty is an objective reality or a subjective reality. Augustine assumes that beauty is obviously objective. For others, the answer turns out to be much more complicated.

Within the early church, Pseudo-Dionysius provides the most important and systematic exposition of the Neoplatonic theory of beauty. On addressing the relationship between Beauty and beautiful objects, Dionysius writes:

> But the beautiful which is beyond individual being is called "beauty" because of that beauty bestowed by it on all things, each in accordance with what it is. It is given this name because it is the cause of the harmony and splendor in everything . . . and gathers everything into itself.
>
> From this beauty comes the existence of everything, each being exhibiting its own way of beauty. For beauty is the cause of harmony, of sympathy, of community. Beauty unites all things and is the source of all things. . . . And there it is ahead of all as Goal, as the Beloved, as the Cause toward which all things move, since it is the longing for beauty which actually brings them into being.
>
> The Beautiful is therefore the same as the Good, for everything looks to the Beautiful and the Good as the cause of being, and there is nothing in the world without a share of the Beautiful and the Good.[23]

In Dionysius, beauty is portrayed as the mechanism in which all beings are engaged in a journey of process and return. God is the superperceptible and ineffable Cause of everything, and God is the eternal and one Beauty. Insofar as all things proceed from God, they partake in the beauty of God. God bestows being along with goodness and beauty to all things. In other words, beauty is a transcendental property of beings. If Beauty is the origin of all things, it is also the goal of all things. It is a form of metaphysical striving, in which both conscious and inanimate beings

---

22. Augustine, *De Vera Religione*, cited in Eco, *Aesthetics of Aquinas*, 49.

23. *The Divine Names* 4.7, 701c–704b. All quotations of Dionysius from Pseudo-Dionysius, *Pseudo-Dionysius*. We give the chapter and sections number, and the column and line numbers in the Migne edition of Dionysius (given on the margin in the Luibheid translation).

*Definitions of Beauty*

are constantly returning to God at the same time as they proceed from God.

Like Plato, Dionysius adopts harmony as the criterion for discerning beauty. However, this is given a distinctly metaphysical interpretation. All things must be harmonious because they come from a single Cause. There is an innate togetherness of everything because the Cause is not divided or confused. In emanation, the Cause creates all diversity and gives each being its appropriate rank and movement. All beings return in a harmonious way back to the one Cause.

The Neoplatonic account of beauty is not the only theory of beauty in the medieval age, but it is the most prominent one. One particular development is that of John Scotus Eriugena. Eriugena interprets the beauty of the universe as a web of signs: "Eriugena taught the Middle Ages to look upon things with a penetrating eye, to read the universe, to read nature, as if it were a vast store of symbols. For him, the relations between God and things were not solely causal, but were also like the relations between sign and signified. . . . It is a theophanic vision which is openly profoundly aesthetic."[24] Eco calls this kind of vision *pankalia*, the beauty of all things. It projects an optimistic universe in which the reality of evil becomes problematic.

In the writings of Thomas Aquinas, the Neoplatonic theory of beauty comes to its most systematic treatment.[25] However, his Neoplatonism is heavily modified by Aristotelianism. One particular passage in Aquinas becomes the standard definition of beauty in the high medieval period: "For beauty includes three conditions, 'integrity' or 'perfection,' since those things which are impaired are by the very fact ugly; due 'proportion' or 'harmony'; and lastly, 'brightness' or 'clarity,' whence things are called beautiful which have a bright color."[26]

Eco has shown us the complexity of Aquinas' definition.[27] Out of the three criteria, proportion is the most basic and important. For Aquinas, proportion is not merely or primarily a matter of quantitative ratio. It means all kinds of fitness or harmony found in reality. Eco lists seven kinds of proportion in Aquinas: matter and form; essence and existence;

---

24. Eco, *Aesthetics*, 24.

25. Dionysius' influence on Aquinas is shown by Aquinas' important commentary on *The Divine Names* of Dionysius, in which he developed his ideas on beauty and other metaphysical concepts.

26. *ST* I.39.8. All quotations of *Summa Theologica* come from the translation by the Fathers of the English Dominican Province.

27. See Eco, *Aesthetics*, 64–121, on which we base our exposition of Aquinas.

sensible and quantitative ratio (e.g., in music); rational coherence in our intellect; an object and its function; the totality of reality and its individual parts; sense organs and their corresponding objective quality (e.g., between eye and light). In each case, the seemingly different domains (e.g., form and matter) in fact cohere together in a harmonious whole. These are important examples of harmony, but they are not an exhaustive list. Eco explains: "The fact is rather that proportion, because it is constitutive of beauty and thus coextensive with it, has its own transcendental character. Proportion therefore has an infinity of analogues. Every existent, beautiful in that it possesses existence, can present us with new and unsuspected types of proportion."[28]

In other words, since proportion is the content of beauty, and beauty is a transcendental character of being, proportion is also a transcendental property of being. To call it a *transcendental* property means that beauty is a property of all beings. Truth, goodness, and beauty are commonly regarded as the transcendental properties. Since proportion is a transcendental property, every existent has proportions unique to itself. Therefore, the types of proportion are potentially infinite.

Medieval metaphysics is sometimes regarded as a static metaphysics of substance. It is important that we understand proportion in a *dynamic* sense: "[Proportion] does not signify something static and crystallized in a motionless perfection, but rather a dynamic unity. It is a dynamic unity because it involves a combining of living forces which do not annul or rigidify themselves when they combine; rather, they confer life upon a type of activity whose value derives from their several vigorous and operative energies."[29]

For example, the harmony between objective quality and sense organs happens when some operations of the physical world interact with a particular living organ (e.g., red color reflecting from a piece of paper hitting our eyes). The universe consists of constant interactions of different activities. It is the harmonious coherence of this web of activities that constitutes beauty.

The meaning of integrity is indicated by Aquinas' understanding of perfection: "The 'first' perfection is that according to which a thing is substantially perfect, and this perfection is the form of the whole; which form results from the whole having its parts complete."[30]

28. Ibid., 97.
29. Ibid., 95.
30. *ST* I.73.1.

*Definitions of Beauty*

An object has the perfection of integrity when it corresponds to the form of the object as a whole. For example, a handicapped person does not have bodily integrity of a human being because she has some limbs missing. In Aquinas' theology, beauty is based on the metaphysics of form. But form is not some kind of productive force, as (maybe) in the case of Plato. The form of an object is the idea of it that preexists in the mind of God.

The most ambiguous term in Aquinas' three criteria for beauty is *clarity*. The two terms *proportion* and *clarity* reflect two different traditions in the understanding of beauty. While proportion derives from the conception of a harmonious universe, clarity derives from the imagery of light.[31] Light is almost universally regarded as beautiful, yet it is most simple and does not seem to contain any mixture or proportion. Medieval aesthetic theories are put to test in their attempt to reconcile the two traditions. Aquinas' solution is to subsume clarity under form. "Clarity is the fundamental communicability of form, which is made actual in relation to someone's looking at or seeing of the object."[32] Proportion refers to the objective orderliness of form; clarity refers to the perception of the form by a human subject. An object achieves clarity for a human subject when she sees beyond the physicality into the form of the object, the ontological and divine ground of that object. What then is the beauty of physical light? Aquinas regards light as the form of the sun and other celestial bodies. Hence light is subsumed under a particular kind of form, even when it is the form of some exalted objects.

If Aquinas builds his aesthetics on form, does he have an objective theory of beauty? The answer is not simple. Aquinas provides an indirect answer when he distinguishes beauty from goodness: "The beautiful is the same as the good, and they differ in aspect only. For since good is what all seek, the notion of good is that which calms the desire; while the notion of the beautiful is that which calms the desire, by being seen or known. Consequently those senses chiefly regard the beautiful, which are the most cognitive, viz. sight and hearing, as ministering to reason; for we speak of beautiful sights and beautiful sounds."[33]

Both goodness and beauty are transcendental property of beings. They differ in their relation to the knowing subject. Goodness is the desirability of the object and it is related to our appetitive faculty. Beauty is the form of the object and it is related to our cognitive faculty. Therefore

---

31. On medieval aesthetic appreciation of light, see Eco, *On Beauty*, ch. 4.
32. Eco, *Aesthetics*, 119.
33. *ST* IIa.27.1.ad.3.

beauty is based on the objective property of objects, but it is inseparable from the human perception of it.[34] Beauty, for Aquinas, is essentially a cognitive perception of the super-sensual form that subsides in particular objects. While Pseudo-Dionysius identifies beauty as a metaphysical process, Aquinas grounds beauty on the cognitive power of the human subject. Thus Aquinas can be seen as moving one step towards a modern theory of beauty. On the other hand, his emphasis on the cognitive nature of beauty runs contrary to the Enlightenment.

The cognitive aspect of Aquinas' theory contains a fatal inconsistency. If I want to appreciate the form of an object in all its integrity, I have to know its relationship with everything else in the universe. Therefore, I must start with knowledge of the whole universe in order to know a particular object. However, I can learn about the universe only by studying particular objects. There seems to be no humanly possible mechanism for me to appreciate the beauty of any particular object.[35] While Edwards also regards beauty as knowledge, he arrives at a different epistemology which circumvents this inconsistency.

We have spent considerable time on Aquinas because he presents perhaps the most sophisticated philosophical aesthetics in the West until the rise of modern aesthetics. It serves as a good reference point for comparison with the theological aesthetics of Edwards. We have one last question for Aquinas: in what sense is Aquinas' aesthetics a *theological* aesthetics? To answer this question, we must remember that the passage on the three criteria of beauty actually occurs in a question about the nature of the Trinity. The question is what attributes we should appropriate to the three persons of the Trinity. Aquinas answers: "According to the first point of consideration, whereby we consider God absolutely in His being, the appropriation mentioned by Hilary applies, according to which 'eternity' is appropriated to the Father, 'species' to the Son, 'use' to the Holy Ghost. For 'eternity' as meaning a 'being' without a principle, has a likeness to the property of the Father, Who is 'a principle without a principle.' Species or beauty has a likeness to the property of the Son."[36]

Immediately following the above quotation, Aquinas gives the definition of beauty as proportion, integrity, and clarity. Then he argues that the Son, being the image of the Father, is the archetype of beauty. In

---

34. According to Eco (*Aesthetics*, 118), this is the major difference between Aquinas and his teacher Albert the Great. Albert thinks that beauty resides in the form irrespective of any knowing subject.

35. Eco points out this *aporia* in ibid. 203.

36. *ST* I.39.8.

other words, beauty should be understood first of all as an attribute of the eternal Son. The Son has both integrity and proportion, because he is the perfect express image of the Father. "The Son, as the Word, which is the light and splendor of the intellect,"[37] is the archetype of clarity. As the Son is the Word and the intellect of the Father, he is the originator of all the forms of reality.[38] All things are beautiful only because they participate in the life of the Son. To appreciate the beauty of any particular object is to see it grounded in the source of its existence—God.

We do not have space for other theories of beauty in the medieval age or the demise of the Thomistic synthesis in the hands of Duns Scotus and William of Ockham. Similarly, we have to pass over the Renaissance with a few remarks. One excuse is that "there was no great philosopher to turn his mind to the problem of aesthetics, and no single thinker made systematic contributions to its progress."[39] In general, as the Renaissance scholars go back to classical Greek and Roman thought for inspiration, a Neoplatonic understanding of beauty prevails in philosophical discourses. Humanists such as Marsilio Ficino contrast the real beauty of the forms with the superficial beauty of physical appearance. On the other hand, the theoretical practitioners of that time open the door for future development. Painters such as Lenonardo da Vinci emphasize that we learn to create beauty in art by careful observation of real life objects. If we want to paint beautiful portraits, we start by looking at people around us. We do not begin with philosophical theory about the essence of humanity. We should especially observe their emotional expression so that our portraits will be filled with the emotions of living people.

More relevant for our study is the place of beauty in Reformation theology. Unlike the medieval theologians, Reformers like Luther and Calvin had neither the time nor the intention to develop a comprehensive account of reality. They do not have an explicit theology of beauty. Nonetheless, they do give some indications of their perspective.

Luther believes that all created things are really masks of God (*larvae Dei*).[40] They are media through which God can speak to us. He has no objection to the use of images *per se*. For Luther, the crucial dichotomy is between faith and works, not the physical and the spiritual. As long as

---

37. *ST* I.39.8.

38. On the relationship between forms and God in Aquinas and its historical background, see Boland, *Ideas in God*.

39. Beardsley, *Aesthetics*, 117. Our discussion is based on ch. 6 of his book.

40. Dyrness, *Reformed Theology*, 52. Our discussion of Luther and Zwingli is based on pp. 51–62 of his book.

the images proclaim the centrality of the Word, Luther allowed the use of images in worship. Zwingli, owing to his fear of superstition, banned the use of images from worship. However, he also allowed simple images in his printed works for illustration of the gospel. In both Luther and Zwingli, the pursuit of artistic beauty is not denied. However, beauty should not become a focus in and of itself. Its only purpose is to serve the gospel. Since neither regards the category of beauty as important to the gospel story, they do not develop any theory about divine beauty and its relation to earthly beauty.

Calvin regards nature as a most beautiful theatre of God's work.[41] God makes the world beautiful so that we can enjoy it.[42] In describing the world as beautiful, Calvin adopts a common sense usage of the word without giving an exact theory of the nature of beauty. The important theme for Calvin is that the orderliness of nature shows us the wisdom and the goodness of God.[43] If we accept that the world is created, then natural beauty exhibits the glory of Creator. Unlike Aquinas, there is no ontological link between natural beauty and divine beauty. The manifestation of divine glory is not the product of metaphysical reasoning. It is the result of seeing the beauty of the world within the Christian narrative of creation and redemption. Non-Christian and Christian can both appreciate natural beauty. The non-Christian does not see the glory of the Lord in natural beauty because they do not look at the world with the right spectacles—the perspective of the Bible.[44] In other words, they do not read the world within the gospel narrative.

For Calvin, the primary image of divine glory is our ethical life. The material world does not hold the sacramental function of the medieval worldview. As Dyrness puts it: "In serving our neighbor, wife, child, friend, we are serving God and creating a world—making images—which in some way can reflect the splendor that belongs to God. The world then is given a new, and radically different importance. Our work can point to God; but it is not enchanted with God's presence."[45] In other words, God's presence is not engraved in the essence of being. God's glory is manifested in our stewardship of the material world and our lives.

---

41. *Institutes of Christian Religion* I.14.20.

42. Dyrness, *Reformed Theology*, 73. Our discussion of Calvin is based on ibid., 72–84.

43. Cf. Schreiner, *Theatre of His Glory*, 22–28.

44. *Institutes* I.6.1

45. Dyrness, *Reformed Theology*, 84.

## Definitions of Beauty

From Calvin we move to the immediate context of Edwards—the Puritans. Like the Reformers, the Puritans seldom reflect on beauty explicitly. Yet they all agree that the joy of the Christian is to behold the glory of God. Yet how do we perceive the glory of God? According to Dyrness, Puritans tend to answer along two different traditions: intellectualist and affective.[46]

William Perkins and William Ames are prominent theologians in the intellectualist tradition. Following the Reformation hostility to icons, they emphasize that the visible cannot be grasped by the invisible. They advise against the use of both physical images and mental images. Moreover, they have an intellectualist understanding of the natural world as the theatre of God's glory. To appreciate the beauty of the world, they advocate organizing knowledge of the world according to some rational schemes. One of the most important works in this tradition is Ames' *Technometry*. In this treatise, Ames arranges the content of the arts curriculum (which is another name for the totality of human knowledge at that time) according to a Ramist bifurcation method. His theology textbook, *The Marrow of Divinity*, exhibits a similar Ramist organization. For Ames, grasping the structure of the knowledge correctly is to appreciate the glory of God's wisdom.

Richard Sibbes and John Cotton are representative theologians of the affective tradition. These theologians emphasize the taming of imagery in our mind rather than avoidance: "Imaginations, however, though it is a "windy thing," does have real effects. It stirs up affections, which move spirits and humours and thus the whole person. The remedy is to bring these risings of our souls under the obedience of God's truth and spirit, rather than led by appearance."[47]

For these theologians, the danger is not in imagery *per se*, but in failing to perceive the spiritual truth behind the images. The image of gold is idolatrous if it leads to the worship of gold. It is not idolatrous if it is understood as a metaphor for the glory of heaven. They use various imageries in their sermons to depict the grace of God. The most famous example of such imaging of grace is probably Bunyan's *Pilgrim's Progress*. The purpose of these imageries is to invoke holy affections. These theologians employ imagery of earthly things in order to purge our devotions to earthly objects. Thus gold may be used to illustrate heaven so that we may

---

46. Ibid., 148. Dyrness builds on the work of Knight, *Orthodoxies in Massachusetts*. Our discussion of the two traditions is based on *Reformed Theology*, ch. 5 and ch. 7. Medieval spirituality has a similar division of focus. See McGinn, "Love, Knowledge."

47. Dyrness, *Reformed Theology*, 169

learn to love heaven instead of gold. For these theologians, the glory of God is beheld more by affections than by reasoning.

The two traditions should not be considered as contradictory to one another. Perkins and Ames do not denounce the use of all imagery in sermons, and Sibbes and Cotton do not deny the importance of doctrines. It is a difference in focus. One may even attempt to combine both perspectives. John Owen, for example, writes about our affections for God in the form of scholastic theology.[48] As we shall show in this study, Owen proves to be an interesting dialogue partner in assessing the significance of Edwards' theology. We may approach Edwards' theological aesthetics as engaging both traditions by giving a theological and reasonable account of the religious affections. Moreover, both traditions emphasize the subjective act of interpretation. In the intellectualist tradition, human beings recognize the wisdom of God through its organization of the knowledge of earthly realities. In the affective tradition, earthly things are interpreted as imageries of divine things. Edwards will follow this focus on the interpretative act of the subject in his appreciation of beauty.

Edwards works out his aesthetics through the concepts developed in the Enlightenment. The aesthetics of the Enlightenment should be the next topic in our survey. We shall turn to this topic in later sections, allowing us to go at a slower pace. For our purpose, we have given a sufficient historical background for Edwards in the area of theological aesthetics. We can summarize the story and bring out the significant issues faced by Edwards. Plato identifies beauty as form and gives beauty an intellectualist interpretation. He adopts harmony and proportion as criteria for beauty. The church fathers regard God as the source of all beauty without giving a rigorous theory of beauty. Pseudo-Dionysius gives a Neoplatonic account of emanation in which beauty is a metaphysical principle of generation. This beauty is objective and human being can grasp its principle through the use of reason. Aquinas develops this tradition into a systematic account of beauty as one of the transcendental properties of being. He also modifies this tradition by emphasizing the inseparability of beauty from human cognition. He gives a theological account for identifying the Son as the archetype of beauty. The Reformation disavows any attempt to correlate God and the world in some form of natural theology. The beauty of the world declares the beauty of the Lord only in the context of the gospel narrative. Orderliness is still considered beauty, but it is a sign of divine beauty only from the perspective of a Christian doctrine of creation.

---

48. See especially his *Communion with God* and *Pneumatogia*.

*Definitions of Beauty*

Following this tradition, Puritans emphasize that the beauty of the world needs to be interpreted through holy affections or orthodox doctrines. Otherwise it may lead to idolatry. Yet the Puritans have not developed any rigorous theory to explain their perspective. For example, how are holy affections related to knowledge? Is beauty a description of emotion or a form of knowledge? How does one integrate the doctrine of creation with the use of earthly things as spiritual images? In what sense is God beautiful? Is God beautiful only in the sense that he is the Creator of earthly beauty, or is there some analogous relationship between divine beauty and earthly beauty (as in the case of Aquinas)? In what sense can we attribute proportion and harmony to the Godhead? Edwards' theology will provide answers to some of these unresolved questions of the Puritan heritage.

While we began our survey with Plato and went through the medieval age to the Puritans, we are not suggesting that Edwards writes his aesthetics in conscious dialogue with this whole heritage. Edwards probably has very limited first-hand knowledge about Greek philosophy as well as the early and medieval church. His acquaintance with the early and medieval church comes through reading the Reformed schoolmen such as Mastricht and Turretin. He is acquainted with Neoplatonism through reading the works of the Cambridge Platonists and, perhaps, Malebranche. Edwards develops his theology mainly in dialogue with his contemporaries. In our exposition of Edwards, we shall concentrate on his relationship with the Reformed heritage and the Enlightenment. However, we need a wider context to access the significance of Edwards' aesthetics. We shall return to this wider context in our chapter 7. There we shall explore in a preliminary way how Edwards may contribute to theological aesthetics today.

## The Enlightenment and New England

Before we can address the significance of aesthetics in the Enlightenment period, we need to understand the questions posed by the Enlightenment. Before we ask the relationship of Edwards' aesthetics to the Enlightenment, we need to ask how the Enlightenment was perceived by New England in Edwards' time. This section provides brief answers to these questions. We begin this section with a brief remarks on empiricism. For people of the seventeenth century, the astronomical laws of Kepler and the gravitational laws of Newton ushered human knowledge into a new era. These laws were considered the product of exact reflections based on careful empirical observations. They are not deductions based on *a priori* principles. While the progressive European philosophers of the seventeenth century are not unified in their paradigms, they are unified in their hostility towards Aristotelianism.[49] For them, Aristotelianism represents vain speculations based on useless first principles. Only by careful observations can we arrive at true knowledge. In the words of Newton, the analysis of difficult subjects should "consist in making experiments and observations, and in drawing conclusions from them by induction, and admitting of no objections against conclusions, but such as taken from experiments, or other certain truths."[50] For Newton, general induction from phenomena produces knowledge that is almost certain.[51] In the analysis of the human mind, the philosophers of the English Enlightenment intended to be "the Newton of moral science."[52] They would use induction method to study scientifically the human psyche. In the article on *moral philosophy* in the first edition of the *Encyclopedia Britannica* (1771), the author calls moral philosophy "a science, as it deduces those rules from the principles and connexions of our nature, and proves that the observance of them in production of our happiness."[53] The article then draws on Shaftesbury, Hutcheson, and Butler for a discussion on moral senses and other principles of realities.

In this new science of the mind, John Locke (1632–1704) is the most important thinker in setting the agenda. Locke rejects the existence of innate ideas, and emphasizes that all knowledge comes from experiences. These experiences begin with ideas that external objects imprint in our mind. Knowledge is now defined as "*the perception of the connexion and agreement, or disagreement and repugnancy of any of our Ideas.*"[54] Locke pushes aside metaphysical principles, which supposedly are self-evident axioms independent of experiences, as unproductive speculations. The science of the mind is the study of how our ideas function together.

Progressive thinkers such as Shaftesbury, Addison, and Hutcheson are eager to develop the empirical studies of the mind. These studies begin with the analysis of our experiences. Unlike physical events, outside

---

49. Menn, "Intellectual Setting," 67.

50. Cited in Peter Dear, "Method," in Garber and Ayers, *Cambridge History*, 166.

51. Ibid., 168.

52. Broadie, "Human Mind," 62.

53. Cited in Emerson, "Science and Moral Philosophy in the Scottish Enlightenment," 26.

54. Locke, *Essay*, 525.

observers cannot have direct experimental observations of psychic events. In other words, I cannot directly observe what your mind is thinking about. I can only observe your behaviors, or listen to what you tell me about your thoughts. Though they seldom ponder the question directly, these philosophers would probably hesitate to conduct experiments on human beings as if the people were chemical compounds. Mental introspection, analysis of the testimonies of others, and historical researches are three primary ways to conduct empirical research on the human soul.[55] While David Hume (1711–76) prefers the historical method, Shaftesbury and others often appeal to our introspection. Whatever the preference, they are participants in a common project creating the science of morals.

On the other hand, Edwards is a pioneer in his milieu. Seventeenth-century New England did not lack a tradition in empirical science. The Puritans believe that the creation is the embodiment of divine art. In studying nature, we are also studying the divine mind. Therefore, the creation is a form of divine discourse. They employed the dialectic method of Ramus to study the divine discourse. "Detailed empirical observation of nature now became a duty; new discoveries were sought and prized as revelations of the divine wisdom."[56] Technologia were produced as encyclopedia of knowledge.[57] Jonathan Edwards' father, Timothy Edwards, contributed some observations of a peculiar prolific pumpkin vine that evolved into a paper published in the *Philosophical Transactions of the Royal Society* in old England.[58] Cotton Mather (1663–1728), the leading minister and spokesman for New England of his generation, was elected member of the Royal Society in 1713 based on his writings in natural history and medicine.[59]

As the eighteenth century arrived, New England aspired more and more to the learning of old England. On religious purity, the New Englanders still prided themselves. On the other hand, "for New England elites, England supplied the standards of urbanity, sophistication, and broadmindedness to be emulated for both intellectual and social reasons."[60] *Philosophical Transactions* was a coveted sign of recognition. Cotton

---

55. Broadie, "The Human Mind," 63–65.

56. Flower and Murphey, *History of Philosophy*, 1:23.

57. On the genre of technologia and its philosophical presuppositions, see ibid., 1:20–40.

58. *Works* 6:151–52.

59. Ibid., 6:38; Flower and Murphey, *History of Philosophy*, 1:75.

60. Stout, *New England Soul*, 128.

Mather popularized the teachings of Newton's *Principia Mathematica* in his work *The Christian Philosophy*, published in 1721. However, Mather had neither the mathematical skills nor the patience to learn the equations in *Principia*. The important point for Mather is that the laws of motion demonstrate empirically the wisdom of God by which God directs the creation towards its decreed ends.[61]

The scientific interests of the New Englanders were mostly observations of nature, not construction of theoretical systems. "Edwards appears to be nearly unique among colonial scientists in the early eighteenth century, in that while their contributions were overwhelmingly in the fields of natural history, agriculture, and medicine, his primary interests and efforts were directed to the problems in physics."[62] Following the example of Newton, Edwards approaches physics as a series of theoretical constructions based on observable phenomena. As a student of Yale at in 1716–22, Edwards was educated mainly in scholastic science.[63] Yet Edwards dug into the writings of Newton in the Yale Library. For example, Edwards' paper "Of the Rainbow,"[64] probably written in 1722, reflects his effort to build upon the foundation of Newton's *Optics*. In the paper, citing the work of Newton on "different reflexibility and refrangibility of the rays of light," Edwards tries to explain the convex shape of the rainbow. Like his fellow scientists in New England, Edwards is interested in empirical observations, as indicated by his "Spider" letter.[65] However, observation is just the starting point for Edwards. Edwards also wants to explore the structure of reality that makes the observations possible. Unlike Mather, he recognizes that the new physics requires a new metaphysics. On the question of beauty, he will push into theoretical constructions far more complex than any of his predecessors in either the English Enlightenment or among the Puritans.

In the new science of the human mind, Edwards is a pioneer in New England too. The Puritans have built a complex psychological theory of faith;[66] they do not have a common paradigm on the theory of the mind. What constitutes knowledge? How does the mind acquire knowl-

---

61. Flower and Murphey, *History of Philosophy*, 1:77.

62. *Works* 6:39.

63. Anderson discusses in detail the education received by Edwards at Yale in *Works* 6:7–27.

64. In *Works* 6:298–301; on dating of the manuscript, see 6: 296–97.

65. In ibid. 6:163–69.

66. Cf. Cohen, *God's Caress*.

edge? The New Englanders did not entangle themselves with this kind of speculations. When Locke published his *Essay* in 1689, it created no ripples in New England. The Yale Library possessed the first known copy of Locke's *Essay* in New England.[67] Edwards probably studied Locke intensively during the years when he was a tutor at Yale in 1724.[68] According to Hopkins, Edwards "was as much engaged, and had more satisfaction and pleasure in studying it [*Essay*], than the most greedy miser in gathering up handsful of silver and gold from some new discover'd treasure."[69] He was set onto the road of defending the orthodox theology of the Puritans with the new science of Locke. Like the English philosophers, Edwards adopted partially to the agenda of Locke. Their aesthetics all builds on Locke, yet each develops it in a different and creative way.

We shall now address briefly on the role of reason in relation to faith in the English Enlightenment and New England. Unlike the French Enlightenment, the English Enlightenment was not anti-clerical. The English spokesmen for the new sciences—Francis Bacon and Robert Boyle—distinguished between reason and faith. They placed characteristic Christian doctrines, such as the Trinity, as "truths above reason."[70] These advocates of using reason as arbitrator in matter of faith are often clergymen themselves. The clergymen of the Anglican Church employed reason to defend themselves against the Puritan radicals and the Popish church.[71] Richard Hooker (1554–1600), for example, used natural laws as argument for the Elizabeth settlement against the biblicism of the separatist Puritans.[72] In other words, reason was seen as a tool of stabilization in the post-Reformation war of religions.

Gradually in the seventeenth century, the use of reason shifted from defending the *via media* to defending the essential goodness of human beings.[73] Benjamin Whichcote (1609–83), father of Cambridge Platonism,

---

67. *Works* 6:17

68. According to Samuel Hopkins, Edwards' first biographer, Edwards read Locke at the age of 13. Anderson has provided good evidence that this is highly improbable (*Works* 6:17–26). Marsden (*Jonathan Edwards*, 63), based on the research of Claghorn, believes that Hopkins' date is possibly true. Here I follow Anderson's dating.

69. *Works* 6:17.

70. Beiser, *Sovereignty of Reason*, 16.

71. Ibid., 10–12.

72. Ibid., 62–77.

73. According to Beiser (ibid., 140–55), the Cambridge Platonists developed their theology in reaction to the psychological anxiety raised by Puritan practical syllogism of salvation. (If I am truly saved, I will have a reformed life. Therefore I must examine

believes that "where the demonstration of the spirit is, there is the highest purest reason; so as to satisfie, convince, command, the mind."[74] The Cambridge Platonists reject the dualism between reason and "truths above reason." Reason contains not just the antidote to extremism, but it is also the judge of truthfulness in religious issues. In particular, reason gives us a better guide to salvation than the introspection of conversion experience. Through reason we grasp the eternal moral rules that even God must abide by in the final judgment.[75] However, the Cambridge Platonists were not against their Protestant tradition. Rather, they saw reason as the best means of defending Protestantism against atheism and papism.[76]

Shaftesbury and Addison share in this confidence in the harmony between faith and reason. As we shall see in the next section, Shaftesbury develops his aesthetics as a defense of the essential goodness of human nature and the power of reason in leading to goodness. For him, enthusiasm, or blind devotion to obscure doctrines, is the primary enemy of true religion. Similarly, Addison paints a Puritan as someone with a morbid obsession with death. For him too, reason clearly shows us the existence of a reasonable God.[77] In particular, beauty is one of the evidences of the goodness of God.

The Scottish Enlightenment follows the pattern of the English Enlightenment in its endorsement by the clergymen. Though the Scottish church was staunchly Calvinistic in theology in the seventeenth century, it was not opposed to science or the right use of reason. Hutcheson studied theology at the University of Glasgow. Hutcheson and other liberal and learned clergymen of his generation (Patrick Cumming, George Turnbull) used reason to retard the growth of fanaticism in the first half of the eighteenth century. Hutcheson represents the transition generation between the seventeenth century orthodoxy of the church, and the moderate and urbane Presbyterian ministers of the mid-eighteenth century who defended infidel philosophers such as Hume and Kames.[78] Hutcheson shares

---

myself for evidence of reformed life in order to assure myself of my salvation.) Beiser's account can alternatively be interpreted as a revolt of the intellectual elite against Calvinistic pessimistic view of human bondage to sin.

74. Ibid., 136.

75. Ibid., 149

76. Ibid., 139

77. For Puritans, see article No. 494, in Addison, *Selections from Addison's Papers*, 201–3; rejection of atheism, see No. 186, 164–67; reasonableness of theism, see No. 531, 204–7.

78. Sher, *Church and University*, 152–54.

*Definitions of Beauty*

the ethos of his time in believing in the harmony of the reason and faith. Hutcheson believes that his aesthetic theory is the delivery of reason, and significantly it also confirms the reasonableness of the theistic worldview. Even if Hutcheson had not in fact hindered Hume from obtaining the chair of moral philosophy at University of Edinburgh, he would not approve of the agnosticism of Hume.

New England is no stranger to the use of reason either. For Cotton Mather, reason "was the faculty for apprehending truth as truth exists in objects, it was master of the passions."[79] Reason is considered by Mather and other New England preachers as tools to strengthen true religions against the passions and foolishness of humankind. Mather thinks that the progress of reason will make those "pitiful Cries of Priestcraft" no longer credible. He welcomed the importation into New England of books by Scottish moralists, by Ferguson, Buchanan, and above all by Hutcheson, "who has taught us how to gather the Delicious things that grow on the Tree of Life."[80]

The New England divines are aware of the dangers of reason too. In *A Man of Reason*, Mather argues against the foolish opinion that all right and wrong are arbitrary conventions of human society. We know innately what is right or wrong. Mather insists that, in matter of morality, "the Voice of Reason, is the Voice of God."[81] Indirectly Mather is arguing against the empiricism of Locke. The divines are also aware of the threat of deism, though deism never gained much popularity in the seventeen and eighteenth century New England. To counter the threat of deism, the divines assert the Bible as divine testimonies. Mysteries of faith have to be accepted based on the authority of the Bible.[82]

Edwards follows his peers in trusting in both the authority of Scripture and the reasonableness of faith. During the 1730s and 1740s, Edwards worked from time to time on the "Outline of 'A Rational Account of the Main Doctrines of the Christian Religion Attempted.'"[83] This is one among many evidences of Edwards' interest in the rational defense of the Christian faith. While Hutcheson proposes his aesthetic theory as a defense of the goodness of human nature, Edwards constructs his aesthetic theory as a rational defense of Calvinism and a meditation on the glory of God. For

---

79. Miller, *Colony to Province*, 420.
80. Ibid., 426.
81. Ibid., 427.
82. Ibid., 422.
83. *Works* 6:394–97.

Edwards, "holiness is a most beautiful and lovely thing."[84] In joining his aesthetics to the glory of God, he follows the example of other New England divines in joining the discovery of science with the wisdom of God. On the other hand, Edwards does it in a sophisticated and metaphysical system that has no parallel among the other divines.

Having laid out the larger agenda of the aesthetic theories in the seventeenth century, we now turn to an exposition of those theories.

## Shaftesbury

The importance of Shaftesbury for modern aesthetics is a debatable issue.[85] The influence of Locke on him is also debatable.[86] He is important for our story because Edwards seems to be familiar with his thinking and his aesthetics bears striking similarities to Edwards.'

In 1711, the third Earl of Shaftesbury, Anthony Ashley Cooper, published his only major work—*Characteristics of Men, Manners, Opinions, Times*.[87] This clumsy title reflects the untidy content of the book, which includes texts of different genre written over a period of time. There are two open letters, a soliloquy, a short treatise on virtue, a Socratic dialogue on morality, and commentaries on the previous treatises in the book. Given the way Shaftesbury develops his ideas, we have to piece his aesthetics together from scattered remarks throughout the book.

Shaftesbury was partly responding to the perceived negativism of Locke: "Twas Mr. Locke that struck at all fundamentals, threw all order and virtue out of the world, and made the very ideas of these (which are the same as those of God) *unnatural*, and without foundation in our minds. *Innate* is a word he poorly plays upon; the right word, though less used, is *connatural*."[88]

For Shaftesbury, Locke has asked the wrong question. The real question is not whether people are born with concepts of right and wrong.

---

84. Ibid.13:163.

85. See Stolnitz, "Significance of Lord Shaftesbury."

86. See Tuveson, *Imagination* and Dabney Townsend, "Lockean Aesthetics," for Locke's influence on Shaftesbury, Hutcheson and others.

87. All quotations of Shaftesbury are from *Characteristics*. We give the name of the treatise within the book, its section number, and page number in Klein's edition. See Klein's introduction on the history of composition and the intellectual background for this work.

88. Letter to Ainsworth, 1708/9, cited in Tuveson, *Imagination*, 51–52. All italic emphasis is original to the text.

## Definitions of Beauty

The important question is whether people are by nature meant to develop certain order and virtue in their mind. The fact that we are not born with the ideas of order in our mind does not imply that there is no proper order inherent to human nature. The fact that we are not born with concept of right and wrong should not lead us to the conclusion that morality is arbitrary.

In a nutshell, this natural order of our mind is the real beauty of the world. Thus Shaftesbury concludes his *Characteristics* with these words: *"It has been the main scope and principal end of these volumes to assert the reality of a beauty and charm in moral as well as natural subjects, and to demonstrate the reasonableness of a proportionate taste and determinate choice in life and manners."*[89]

Our exposition will unpack this summary phrase by phrase. Let us start with the distinction between natural and moral subjects. For Shaftesbury, both the existence of natural beauty (i.e., beauty of physical objects) and spiritual beauty are self-evident: "The case is the same in the mental or moral subjects as in the ordinary bodies or common subjects of sense. The shapes, motions, colours and proportions of these latter being presented to our eye, there necessarily results a beauty or deformity, according to the different measure, arrangement, and disposition of their several parts. So in behaviour and action, when presented to our understanding, there must be found, of necessity, an apparent difference, according to the regularity or irregularity of the subjects."[90]

Following the Platonic tradition, Shaftesbury believes that beauty is a judgment of reason. When reason comes across visible objects, it will naturally judge the beauty of those objects according to the arrangement of shapes and colors in those objects. Similarly, reason will judge actions and behavior according to their conformity to the regularity of reason.

Not only do we reflect on our actions, we also reflect on our affections. This ability of reflection is what makes us a rational being: "In a creature capable of forming general notions of things, not only the outward beings which offer themselves to the sense are the objects of the affection, but the very actions themselves and the affections of pity, kindness, gratitude and their contraries, being brought into the mind by reflection, become objects. So that, by means of this reflected sense, there arises another kind

---

89. "Miscellany V," ch. 3, 466.

90. "An Inquiry concerning Virtue or Merit," (hereafter just "Inquiry") Bk 1 Pt. 2 Sec. 3, 172.

of affection towards those very affections themselves, which have been already felt and have now become the subject of a new liking or dislike."[91]

As we perceive physical objects by external senses, we perceive our affections in our reflection. We are rational creatures who can form "general notions of things." Therefore we can reflect notionally on our affections. If our affections accord with the ordering of reason, if we like and hate the things we should like and hate, then we possess inward beauty.[92]

Shaftesbury writes his aesthetics not as a detached observer. He regards inward beauty much superior to outward beauty: "Who can admire the outward beauties and not recur instantly to the inward, which are the most real and essential, the most naturally affecting and of the highest pleasure as well as profit and advantage?"[93] Shaftesbury believes that we can modify and cultivate our taste for beauty by studying philosophy—"the study of inward numbers and proportions."[94] His writings are meant to encourage the readers to cultivate this inward beauty: "It is we ourselves create and form our taste. If we resolve to have it just, it is in our power. We may esteem and resolve, approve and disapprove, as we would wish."[95]

Why should we cultivate this inward beauty? The reason is that this beauty is "of the highest pleasure as well as profit and advantage." This inward beauty is nothing more than the manifestation of true human nature. If we live according to our true nature, we will naturally find life pleasurable and fulfilling.

For Shaftesbury, beauty lies in living according to the natural function of the object. Truth, beauty, and utility are variations of the same reality: "The truth or the beauty of every figure or statue is measured from the perfection of nature in her just adapting of every limb and proportion to the . . . life and vigour of the particular species or animal designed. Thus beauty and truth are plainly joined with the notion of utility and convenience."

Thus to live truly as a human being is to live beautifully and to function fully as a rational being. This inward beauty is obligatory because this is our true destiny. Therefore, beauty and goodness are "one and the

---

91. Ibid., Bk 1, Pt 2, Sec 3, 172.

92. This makes Shaftesbury closer to Aristotle than to Plato. See chapter 1 of our study.

93. "Miscellany III," ch. 2, 416

94. Ibid., 416.

95. Ibid., 417.

## Definitions of Beauty

same."[96] Truth, beauty and goodness all refer to living out the true nature of human beings.[97] The other side of the coin is that *"to be wicked or vicious is to be miserable and unhappy."*[98] One cannot be truly happy if one goes against its nature.

How do we know the human beings have a common true nature? Shaftesbury suggests that a moment of reflection will convince us of this truth is acknowledged universally: "The standard of this kind and the noted character of moral truth appear so firmly established in nature itself, and so widely displayed through the intelligent world, that there is no genius, mind or thinking principle which, if I may say so, is not really conscious of the case."[99]

How can we discern that we are acting according to nature? Shaftesbury suggests, in a cryptic way, that we all have a sense of right and wrong. We can do wrong habitually only if we take away our "natural and just sense of right and wrong," substitute it with a wrong sense, or are carried away by "contrary affections."[100] How is this sense different from reason? Is this sense just a special case of our reasoning power? Shaftesbury gives us few clues to these questions.

How does this sense of beauty manifest itself? Shaftesbury spends more time arguing for the existence of such sense than in describing the content of it. The main feature of such taste seems to be disinterestedness. For example, when we truly appreciate the beauty of the ocean or the hills and woods, we will not fantasize about owning it or mastering it. We simply engage in a "rational and refined contemplation of beauty."[101] Similarly, when we act beautifully, we do not act for any reward we may reap from such actions: "If the inclination be right, it is a perverting of it to apply it solely to the reward and make us conceive such wonders of the grace and favour, which is to attend virtue, when there is so little shown of the intrinsic worth or value or the thing itself."[102]

---

96. "The Moralists," Pt. 3, Sec. 2, 320.

97. Are the three terms the same? It seems that Shaftesbury, similarly to Aquinas, makes beauty refers to perception of affections. Goodness is a quality of actions or affections themselves, while truth may refer to the propositions of reason. Shaftesbury is not precise about his terms.

98. "Inquiry," Conclusion, 229.

99. "Miscellany V," ch. 3, 466

100. "Inquiry," Pt. 3, Sec. 1, 177.

101. "The Moralists," Pt. 3, Sec. 2, 319.

102. "Sensus Communis, " Pt. 2, Sec. 3, 46.

Therefore, we have developed a sense of inward beauty when we learn to appreciate virtues for its own sake, instead of any rewards brought by acting virtuously. Similarly, a virtuous person learns to seek the common good rather than private good. He is not satisfied with finding beauty in individuals. He will seek beauty in the society, rising to the good of mankind, and finally to the supreme beauty.[103] A primary obstacle in developing our sense of true beauty is the lure of selfish gains.[104]

How is earthly beauty related to the supreme beauty—God? In one of his most Platonic passage, Shaftesbury differentiates three kinds of beauty:

> First, *the dead forms*, as you properly have called them, which bear a fashion and are formed, whether by man or nature, but have no forming power, no action or intelligence.
> The second kind, *the forms which form*, that is, which have intelligence, action, and operation.
> [T]hat third order of beauty, which forms not only such as we call mere forms but even the forms which form.[105]

In other word, Shaftesbury differentiates between material beauty, spiritual beauty, and divine beauty. Material beauty is only passive; inanimate objects cannot create or perceive beauty. Spiritual beings can create beauty as well as be beautiful. For Shaftesbury, forms are proportions in an object. Since human beings can design and make objects according to proportions, they can form forms. These forms are not eternal Platonic forms. The highest beauty is the One who can form spiritual beings. Shaftesbury claims that all material beauty is a shadow of spiritual and divine beauty: "For if we may trust to what our reasoning has taught us, whatever in nature is beautiful or charming is only the faint shadow of that first beauty."[106]

How does reason teach us that beauty of nature is a shadow of divine beauty? Shaftesbury claims that material beauty lies not in the material itself, but on its form. For example, the beauty of an alabaster statue lies not in the stone, but in the design and the sculpturing. A piece of alabaster lying on the ground is not beautiful at all. He concludes that *"the beautiful, the fair, the comely, were never in the matter but in the art and design, never in body itself but in the form or forming power."*[107] Though he

103. "The Moralists," Pt. 1, Sec. 3, 243–44.
104. "Sensus Communis," Pt. 2, Sec. 2, 44.
105. "The Moralists," Pt. 3, Sec. 2, 323.
106. Ibid., 318
107. Ibid., 322.

never explicitly claims it, he probably assumes that greater forming power is equivalent to greater beauty. Human beings can only form forms, but God can form the forms which form other forms. So God is the supreme beauty. Natural beauty is a shadow of divine beauty in that it indicates a power that can form forms. In other words, nature is a shadow of the divine in a teleological sense.

We shall now briefly indicate the importance of Shaftesbury for our study. Shaftesbury is both a pioneering and a transitory figure in modern aesthetics. His focus on reason and forms as foundation of aesthetic experience will be rejected by subsequent aestheticians as well as Edwards. His gradation of beauties will be rejected by other aestheticians but embraced by Edwards. Unlike Neoplatonism, God, human beings and nature stay as three separate entities in Shaftesbury. His aversion to speculations means that he avoids constructing a metaphysical system that unites God, spiritual beings and material things. Edwards will go where Shaftesbury hesitates. While Shaftesbury takes nature as a shadow of the divine in a teleological sense, Edwards takes it in a metaphysical sense. Other themes in Shaftesbury will be picked up by both British aestheticians and Edwards. Shaftesbury brings out the importance of affections in aesthetic experience for both Hutcheson and Edwards. Edwards, however, will react strongly against the optimism of Shaftesbury in our power to shape our affections. Disinterestedness will also become a major theme.[108] While Hutcheson will emphasize the part about not motivated by private gain, Edwards will emphasize the part about rising to the beauty of the whole. As an alternative to Hutcheson, Shaftesbury provides interesting parallels to Edwards. While we do not claim that Edwards consciously built on Shaftesbury, undoubtedly Shaftesbury was part of the milieu from which Edwards developed his aesthetics.

## Addison

Joseph Addison wrote a series of remarkable essays on the "pleasures of the imagination" in *The Spectator* in June and July of 1712. Just before Addison began his series, there is an article in the *Spectator* in which the author argues for the balance of passions and reason: "For as nothing is produced without a cause, so by observing the nature and course of the

---

108. This is Shaftesbury's main contribution to modern aesthetics, according to Stolnitz, "Significance of Lord Shaftesbury." We think that disinterestedness is not so uniquely central to modern aesthetics as claimed by Stolnitz, and Shaftesbury's contribution is more multifaceted.

passions, we shall be able to trace every action from its first conception to its death . . . for the actions of men follow their passions as naturally as light does heat, or as any other effect flows from its cause; reason must be employed in adjusting the passions, but they must ever remain the principles of action."[109]

According to the article, reason is too lazy and needs the drive of passions. Passions are easily corrupted and need the guidance of reason. The articles on beauty can be approached as an exercise in "passions seeking understanding." The starting point of Addison is that people have some natural pleasures of imagination. The articles seek to explain how these pleasures function.

Addison defines the pleasures of imagination as those pleasure that "arise from visible objects, either when we have them actually in our view, or when we call up their ideas into our minds by paintings, statues, descriptions or any the like occasion."[110] Addison conceives of imagination in terms of imageries. The pleasures of the imagination apply primarily to visible objects. They are applied to other kinds of objects only by metaphorical use. For Addison, these pleasures "are not so gross as those of sense, nor so refined as those of the understanding."[111] Refinement in the taste for these pleasures is easier to acquire than those pleasures of the understanding, and they are good for our health. We discern here that Addison's positive evaluation of the pleasures of the passions is mixed with a certain elitist pride in the intellect.

For those pleasures that arise from real objects actually present with us, Addison classifies them into greatness, newness and beauty. Natural scenery is offered as an example of greatness. The pleasure of greatness is to our imagination "as the speculations of eternity or infinitude are to the understanding."[112] There is a natural tendency in our psyche that disdains confinement, whether in imagination or in understanding. Newness creates pleasure because it gratifies our curiosity.

For beauty, Addison does not provide a uniform answer. A beautiful object is that which "immediately diffuses a secret satisfaction and complacency through the imagination." He believes that "there is not perhaps any real beauty or deformity more in one piece of matter than another,

---

109. No. 408, 45. For this section, we give the article number in *The Spectator* and the page number in *The Spectator*. No. 408 is signed "T.B." Whether the article is penned by Addison or not, it represents the opinion of Addison.

110. No. 411, 56.

111. Ibid., 57

112. No. 412, 60.

## Definitions of Beauty

because we might have been so made, that whatsoever now appears loathsome to us, might have shewn it self agreeable."[113] In other words, beauty is whatever pleases our imagination. There is no absolute standard for beauty. Instead of an objective standard, Addison gives the two common classes of beautiful objects. The first is the opposite sex of our own specie. The second class contains objects with a certain pleasant look. "This [pleasant look] consists either in the gaiety or variety of colours, in the symmetry and proportion of parts, in the arrangement and disposition of bodies, or in a just mixture and concurrence of all together."[114] Addison is probably aware of the long tradition of joining proportion and beauty together. However, he does not regard proportion as holding the unique key for beauty. It is just one among many possibilities. An equilateral triangle may be beautiful, but so may a young girl to most men. Addison is not interested in giving a unified theory to explain why such different objects may all be beautiful.

Addison believes that fine arts are in general inferior to nature in these primary pleasures of the imagination. Yet the superiority is not absolute. Nature appears more beautiful when it resembles works of arts in some way (e.g., a meadow in which the flowers of different colors are seemingly coordinated in a certain geometric pattern). On the other hand, works of arts are more beauty when they can copy the beauty of nature.[115]

Fine arts can provide us with the secondary pleasure of imagination by arousing in our mind the imagery of the original objects.[116] Thus a painting of my wife gives me pleasure when I notice the striking similarities between the painting and the image of my wife in my mind. It will be particularly pleasurable if such representations are accompanied by strong feelings.[117] A picture of any of my acquaintance may give me pleasure, but a picture of my wife will be especially pleasurable.

Why do human beings enjoy such pleasures of imagination? Addison attributes these to the wisdom of the Creator. These pleasures are indicators of divine truth. Our pleasure for greatness reminds us that everything in this world is too small for our heart. "The Supreme Author of our being has so formed the soul of man, that nothing but himself can

---

113. Ibid., 61.
114. Ibid., 62.
115. No. 414, 66–67.
116. No. 416, 74.
117. No. 418, 82.

be its last, adequate, and proper happiness."[118] Our pleasure in newness encourages searching into the wonders of God's creation. Our pleasure in beauty renders the whole creation delightful. It is a sign of the goodness of the Creator. Addison appeals to Locke to support his theological interpretation. According to him, Locke has shown that colors and light are only ideas in our mind. They are not objective properties of things themselves. Why should God set up the rules so that things in this world will arouse such pleasing imageries in our mind? For Addison, these pleasing imageries serve "imaginary glories of heaven."[119]

Why then does God give us the secondary pleasure of imagination? The reason is that God wants to encourage us in searching after truth: "The final cause, probably of annexing pleasure to this operation of the mind, was to quicken and encourage us in our searches after truth, since the distinguishing one thing from another, and the right discerning betwixt our ideas, depends wholly upon our comparing them together, and observing the congruity or disagreement that appears among the several works of nature."[120]

Following Locke, Addison regards truth as the agreement of ideas. The search after truth involves careful comparison of ideas. Secondary pleasure comes from comparing the ideas aroused from the object immediately in front of me (the painting of my wife) and the ideas already stored in my mind (my mental image of my wife). Since such comparison induces pleasure in me, it will encourage me to be more diligent in comparing of ideas in general.

Let us summarize our exposition of Addison and compare him to Shaftesbury. While Shaftesbury has an objective and intellectualist understanding of beauty, Addison builds a subjective and emotional theory of beauty. By locating beauty in our mind alone, Addison is a crucial figure in the development of modern aesthetic theory.[121] Beauty ceases to be some grand principle of reality. It is just one of three pleasures of imagination. The strength of Addison's position is that he can address a variety of aesthetic experiences. In particular, greatness, or sublimity, would soon become an important theme in aesthetics.[122] Addison has declared the in-

118. No. 413, 63.
119. Ibid., 64.
120. No. 416, 75.
121. Stolnitz, in "Beauty," argues that the distinguishing factor of modern aesthetic theories (as opposed to medieval theories) is the shift to a subjective perspective.
122. Monk, *Sublime*, treats the theme of sublimity in English aesthetics before and after Edwards' time. Edwards is seemingly oblivious to such discussions.

*Definitions of Beauty*

dependence of aesthetic experience metaphysical and moral theories. Our pleasure is the yardstick of beauty.

The main weakness of Addison is that his shrewd observations are not backed by a vigorous theoretical framework. His classification of the three pleasures of the imagination seems rather arbitrary. Nothing in his framework will hinder us from giving more examples of the pleasures of imagination. How do we know that greatness, newness and beauty are the only, or even the most important, of the pleasures of the imagination? His definition of beauty seems to be a potpourri of items. Why should the attraction of opposite sex, the gaiety of colors, and proportions all put under the category of beauty? Can these be listed as separate pleasures, just like greatness and newness? Is there any coherence to these pleasures beyond mere coincidence?

Addison blazes another new trail by distinguishing between the pleasures of the imagination from the pleasures of the senses and the pleasures of the understanding. It occupies a kind of middle ground between mere sensations and reasoning. These pleasures appeal to passions. They engage the mind without engaging in a reasoning process. Yet Addison is vague on the nature of this middle. For example, does not the comparison of ideas involve understanding? How does Addison differentiate between a non-conceptual pleasure of proper proportions in object and an intellectual pleasure in understanding such proportions? Moreover, by limiting his theory to visual objects, Addison has severely limited the applicability of his aesthetic theory. His theory, rich in suggestions, cries out for more vigorous formulation and extension to non-visual beauty. Hutcheson's theory provides the next stage of such developments.

## Hutcheson

Hutcheson is almost contemporaneous with Edwards. He gives the most sophisticated British aesthetic theory that Edwards can respond to. His major work in aesthetics is *An Inquiry concerning Beauty, Order, Harmony,*

## The Beauty of the Triune God

*Design*.[123] This is the first English work on philosophical aesthetics. He builds upon the works of Shaftesbury and Addison.[124]

The starting point of Hutcheson's aesthetic theory is empirical observation. By carefully analyzing how people use *beautiful* and similar words, Hutcheson believes that he can discover the essence of the concept of beauty. His first main thesis is that beauty is an inner sense. The definition of the word "*beauty* is taken for *the idea raised in us*, and a *sense* of beauty for *our power of receiving this idea*."[125] So what is "sense" or "sensation"? "Those ideas which are raised in the mind upon the presence of external objects, and their acting upon our bodies, are called *sensations*."[126] Hutcheson does not explain further the meaning of an idea. The vocabulary of "ideas" and the focus on sensation are both Lockean. However, Hutcheson extends Locke's framework by including internal sensation as a source of idea.[127]

Hutcheson's definition reflects his psychological interest. He wants to know how ideas operate in our mind, rather than how external objects cause ideas in our mind. It is assumed that certain ideas inevitably arise in our mind when coming into contact with external objects. The agent is passive, as these ideas arise involuntarily. For example, someone has made a candy incredibly like a piece of bread. Yet when I put the candy in my mouth, the idea of sweetness immediately arises in my mind. I do not need to anticipate it beforehand, nor do I need to engage in any discursive thinking. Similarly, when presented with a beautiful object, the idea of beauty (according to Hutcheson) will spontaneously arise in our mind.

---

123. It was first printed in 1725 together with *An Inquiry concerning Moral Good and Evil*, under the title *An Inquiry into the Original of our Ideas of Beauty and Virtue*. It will be cited as *Beauty*, followed by section and subsection number, and page number from the (slightly abridged and readily accessible) version in Hutcheson, *Philosophical Writings*. The abridged materials are mostly illustrations and examples. The Downie edition reprints the 4th ed. of 1738.

124. He recommends Shaftesbury in the Preface to *Beauty*. We shall see his reference to Addison.

125. *Beauty* 1.9, 10.

126. Ibid. 1.1, 7.

127. See Chappell, "Locke's theory of ideas," for an introduction to Locke's theory of ideas. Townsend, "Lockean Aesthetics," 351–52, argues that Hutcheson has a different concept of idea from Locke. For Locke, ideas are simple building blocks (e.g., redness, roundness, etc.). Reflection of ideas produces knowledge. Hutcheson's idea of beauty is not a simple attribute of an external object. Instead of merely passive, the idea of beauty already involves subjective interpretation. However, this interpretation is not reflection because no reasoning is involved. Strictly speaking, the framework of Locke does not allow something like the internal sense of Hutcheson.

## Definitions of Beauty

Hutcheson calls the sense of beauty *internal sense*.[128] External senses like sight and hearing are tied to a specific bodily organ. Internal senses can be aroused by more than one of the external senses. For example, there is beautiful sight as well as beautiful music. Hutcheson regards his internal sense as the same as Addison's "pleasure of the *imagination*."[129] These internal senses can be aroused just by the imagination of certain objects, without that object physically present to our external senses. How many internal senses are there? In *Beauty*, he lists the senses of beauty, regularity, and harmony.[130] In later writings, he lists beauty, imitation, harmony, design, grandeur, and novelty.[131] Hutcheson probably has no rigorous classification of the internal senses. Moreover, Hutcheson believes that there are more than two senses: external sense, internal sense, public sense ("our determination to be pleased with the happiness of others, and to be uneasy at their misery"), moral sense, sense of honor.[132] He claims that "decency, dignity, suitableness to human nature in certain actins and circumstances" and others may also be distinctive classes of perception.[133] Common to all these senses is the fact that they are all natural powers in the human mind. For Hutcheson, the perception of beauty, moral goodness, honor and other qualities are all spontaneous actions of the mind. If I see a pretty picture, I spontaneously enjoy the sense of beauty. If I see a murder scene, I spontaneously feel the evilness of the act. By this proliferation of senses, Hutcheson emphasizes that human beings are by nature disposed to certain standards. Beauty, morality, honor, and other standards do not arise arbitrarily; they are connatural to us.

However, will there be too many kinds of senses? If I see my child, there is also a spontaneous joy in me. Does that mean that there is also a parental sense too? Likewise, is there a humorous sense too? In that case, does sense become just synonymous with feelings? In defending that beauty is really a sense, Hutcheson gives us some clues for the demarcation of a sense.[134] First, the pleasure of beauty does not involve knowledge. One does not need to study musicology before she can appreciate a beautiful

---

128. *Beauty* 1.10, 10

129. *An Essay on the Nature and Conduct of the Passions and Affections* 1.1, in *Philosophical Writings*, 115. Hereafter cited as *Passions and Affections*, originally published in 1728.

130. *Beauty* 1.8, 10.

131. Kivy, *The Seventh Sense*, 35–36.

132. *Passions and Affections* 1.1, 116.

133. Ibid., 1.1, 116

134. *Beauty* 1.12–14, 11–13.

piece of music. Second, beauty is a necessary idea. When I listen to Bach's *St. Matthew Passion*, there inevitably arises the idea of beauty in my mind. You may bribe me to lie about my true feelings, but I cannot force myself to feel terrible about the music. Third, beauty is an immediate idea. We feel that something is beautiful without first calculating whether such feeling is advantageous to us. "Nay, do not we often see convenience and use neglected to obtain beauty, without any other prospect of advantage in the beautiful form than the suggesting the pleasant ideas of beauty?"[135] Our enjoyment of beauty is disinterested. The pleasure comes from beauty alone, not depending on or for the sake of something else. Presumably the other senses, such as moral sense, also will have these three properties.

In comparison with external sense, there is an obvious difficult with calling beauty a sense. While few people will fail to agree on whether something is red or blue, beauty seems to be often controversial and subjective. Assuming that *St. Matthew Passion* is indeed beautiful music, why do so many people find it boring? Hutcheson attributes this difference to taste: "It is plain from experience that many men have in common meaning the senses of seeing and hearing perfect enough. . . . And yet perhaps they shall find no pleasure in musical compositions, in painting, architecture, natural landscape, or but a very weak one in comparison of what others enjoy from the same object. This greater capacity of receiving such pleasant ideas we commonly call a *fine genius* or *taste*."[136]

The difference between internal and external sense is that inner sense requires something called taste, which is lacking in brute animals and weak in some people. External ideas are the product of bodily organs. Eyes will automatically give us sight. Internal sense is a response to complex ideas about external objects.[137] According to Hutcheson, not all people are equipped to perceive these complex ideas. The mind's power in this area varies from person to person. But what is taste? How is it formed? What explain for the differences in people's taste? How can we discern that someone has taste, other than using the circular definition that a tasteful person is someone who can discern beauty? Hutcheson does not address these issues in any of his works.[138] As we shall see, this creates insurmountable problems for his aesthetic theory.

135. Ibid. 1.14, 12.
136. Ibid. 1.10, 10–11.
137. Kivy, *Seventh Sense*, 260–65, discusses the issue whether beauty is a simple or complex idea in Lockean sense. Kivy concludes that beauty is an idea about other ideas.
138. Broadie, "Art and Aesthetic Theory," 284. Little did Hutcheson anticipate that

## Definitions of Beauty

Having explained internal sense in general, let us turn to the definition of beauty. What gives unity to the sense of beauty? While it is easy to see the commonality in the concept of novelty, such as a new shirt, a new song or a new idea, it is not obvious if there is commonality among a beautiful picture, a beautiful song, and a beautiful idea. What is the class of ideas unified by the word *beauty*? Hutcheson distinguishes two kinds of beauty: absolute (original) and relative (comparative) beauty. The two are quite different concepts.

We shall begin with absolute beauty. This is beauty that we find in an object in itself. For Hutcheson, the scenery of sunset has absolute beauty because it gives pleasure without requiring us to compare it with another object. For absolute beauty, "the figures which excite us the ideas of beauty seem to be those in which there is *uniformity amidst variety*."[139] Hutcheson gives a variety of examples, beginning with geometric figure. A square is more beautiful than an equilateral triangle, because the former has more variety than the latter within equal level of uniformity. Equilateral triangle is more beautiful than isosceles triangle because the former has more uniformity within the equal level of variety. A scientific theory is beautiful because it gives uniform explanation for a variety of particular case. Therefore beauty tempts us to the impossible task of explaining everything with one simple principle. In Hutcheson's opinion, Descartes, Leibneiz, and Puffendorf have all fallen into this trap.[140] Hutcheson applies the same principle to music, architecture and other areas of art.

Relative beauty "is apprehended in any object commonly considered as an *imitation* of some original. And this beauty is founded on a conformity, or a kind of unity between the original and the copy."[141] The original need not be beautiful by itself. Thus a novel about a villain can be quite beautiful, though a real villain would not be beautiful. In fact, a book about a perfect person would be rather boring, because we find it hard to identify with such a beautiful person.[142] Hutcheson takes all examples from fine arts (literature, painting etc.). Though he does not explicitly say so, Hutcheson here is suggesting a norm for good art works. Art should copy life exactly.

---

the variation in taste would soon become a major theme in aesthetics, epitomized by David Hume's essay "Of the Standard of Taste."

139. *Beauty* 2.3, 15
140. Ibid. 2.5, 22.
141. Ibid. 4.1, 23
142. Ibid. 4.2, 24.

## The Beauty of the Triune God

We should note that the definitions of absolute and comparative beauty are not intended to be normative. Hutcheson's intention is not to prescribe a standard of beauty. His intention is the positive task of analyzing what is the idea of beauty in humankind. Presumably, we can test the validity of Hutcheson's theory by asking whether most people throughout different ages use the word *beauty* to express the pleasure of perceiving uniformity amidst variety and conformity to the original.

As an empirical theory, the diversity of taste among people is a major challenge to his theory. The concept of uniformity amidst variety suggests an almost mathematical precision in the grading of beauty, as illustrated by his discussion of geometric figures. In fact, people's taste about a lot of things belies such variety that any uniformity in the standard of beauty seems questionable. One person's ideal of beauty may be another person's nightmare. How does one account for such variety?

Hutcheson's answer has two parts. The first is to say that uniformity is much more important than variety. "But in figures, did ever any man make choice of a trapezium, or any irregular curve, for the ichnography or plan of his house, without necessity, or some great motive of convenience?"[143] For Hutcheson, it is sufficient proof for his theory that ordinary folks like neither chaos nor monotony. It is just common sense that only the orderly can be beautiful.

Second, Hutcheson claims this: "Associations of ideas make objects pleasant and delightful which are not naturally apt to give any such pleasure; and the same way, the causal conjunction of ideas may give a disgust where there is nothing disagreeable in the form itself."[144]

Though the standard of uniformity among variety is universally recognized, it is often distorted in individuals by the wrong kind of associations. For example, many people have irrational fears about swine and serpents. Accordingly, Hutcheson recommends that one of the goals of education is to eradicate these prejudices so that people can enjoy real beauty. For example, people should learn to dissociate fear from dark places, or dissociate illness from eating meat.[145]

Before we go into the theological significance of Hutcheson's theory of beauty, let us take a short digression into sublimity. Hutcheson applauds Addison for bringing out the importance of sublimity: "The ingenious Mr. Addison, in his treatise of the pleasures of the imagination, has justly

---

143. Ibid. 6.4, 33.
144. Ibid. 6.3, 32.
145. Ibid., 7.2, 39.

*Definitions of Beauty*

observed many sublimer sensations than those commonly mentioned among philosophers: he observes, particularly, that we receive sensations of pleasure from those objects which are great, new, or beautiful."[146]

Hutcheson is obviously familiar with Addison's discussion in *The Spectator*. The interesting aspect is that Hutcheson seems to think all the pleasures of the imagination are sublime. Here sublimity is probably contrasted with selfishness. Hutcheson does not have an aesthetic theory specifically for sublimity.

We return to the theory of beauty. Assuming that Hutcheson has proven this case, what is the significance of his definition? First, it is the rejection of a purely subjectivist theory of beauty. For such kind of theory, beauty is separable from the pleasure of beauty. In other words, beauty is just another word for our delight in a certain object. Calling something *beautiful* is the same as saying "Wow!"[147] In Hutcheson's theory, beauty and pleasure are distinct concepts. Beauty represents a recognizable pattern of ideas. Both uniformity and variety are ideas that supposedly reflect objective characteristics of the external objects. Just as novelty has objective meaning, so does beauty in Hutcheson's theory. Uniformity amidst variety is an objective quality without the intonation of almost mathematical precision. As we shall see, Hutcheson argues that the fact that beauty causes pleasure serves as a theistic proof.

Secondly, beauty transcends social convention. Hutcheson argues against a narrow understanding of the human mind, where it has no inherent qualities. "Nothing is more ordinary among those, who, after Mr. Locke, have reject *innate ideas*, than to allege that all our relish for beauty and order is either from prospect of advantage, custom, or education, for no other reason but the *variety* of fancies in the world."[148] If we can find universal standard for beauty, then it is more plausible that the sense of beauty is a natural power of humankind.

What difference does it make to claim that beauty is a natural power? The answer is that it gives a positive picture of human nature, and it gives credibility to the existence of a benevolent Creator. If beauty is merely a subjective feeling or a social convention, then beauty has no inherent purpose. If beauty has an objective basis, then we can ask if the existence of beauty points to a higher purpose.

---

146. *To the Author of the Dublin Journal, Philosophical Writings*, 52. The intent of the letter is to refute Hobbes' account of laughter as a product of our self-love.

147. Kivy, *Seventh Sense*, 63 calls this the non-cognitive understanding of beauty.

148. *Beauty* 6.8, 35.

Hutcheson proposes beauty as evidence affirming the existence of God: "There seems to be no necessary connection of our pleasing ideas of beauty with the uniformity or regularity of the objects, from the nature of things, antecedent to some constitution of the Author of our nature, which has made such forms pleasant to us."[149] Beauty is a sign of God's benevolence towards humanity; it seems that beauty serves no other purpose than making us happier. It is particularly a benevolent act towards rational human beings. As rational but finite, we yearn to simplify reality with general principles. Moreover, we find it easier to understand and remember objects that agree with general laws.[150] Were people to delight in deformity and irregularity, their affections will conflict with the tendency for understanding to search for general principles.[151]

The second question raised by Hutcheson is why there are so many regularities in the world. The answer is that the world is a product of intelligent design. In God's benevolence, the world is full of uniformity for the enjoyment of humankind.

The third question is why God chooses to order the universe according to general laws, a special form of uniformity amidst variety. Hutcheson is alluring to the success of Newtonian science. Hutcheson suggests that this is the way we finite beings can enjoy more the diversities of the universe. Had God chosen to order the universe with particulars all the time, the human mind would be baffled and left in misery. Moreover, morality would suffer because our actions would carry no regular consequences.[152]

We shall now evaluate the significance of Hutcheson for our study. As an empirical theory to explain the origin and meaning of the concept of beauty, Hutcheson's theory is incomplete because of its inherent ambiguities.[153]

We begin with internal sense. Hutcheson advances beyond Addison by giving criteria for demarcating an internal sense. Yet the criteria are not perfect. For example, the first argument—independence from knowledge—has obvious problems. As a counter-example, my pleasure of listening to Bach's *St. Matthew Passion* will suffer without understanding

---

149. Ibid. 5.1, 27.

150. Ibid. 8.2. This comes from a section omitted by Downie. It can be found in the reprint of the 1726 edition, 101–2.

151. Ibid. 8.2, 43.

152. Ibid. 8.3, 44.

153. Kivy is harsh on Hutcheson: "Viewed in the light of this progressive aesthetic empiricism, Hutcheson's aesthetic theology seems like deplorable backsliding." (*Seventh Sense*, 123) Kivy offers other criticism from the perspective of modern aesthetics.

## Definitions of Beauty

the theological message and its correspondence with the music. Moreover, someone with no background in classical music is unlikely to appreciate the *Passion*. Therefore, is knowledge required in taste? We need a clearer distinction between rational knowledge and aesthetic experience.

The criterion of disinterestedness would become a major issue in later aesthetic theory. Hutcheson brings out more clearly than Shaftesbury and Addison that disinterestedness is specifically associated with aesthetic experience. Can this disinterestedness be explained? As we shall see, Edwards thinks so, and so does Kant. Modern aesthetics tends to shrink away from explaining it. .

The definition of *uniformity amidst diversity* has its problems. In real life, uniformity and diversity are often hard to define or measure. For example, if one (like me) is bored by the paintings of Jackson Pollack, should the reason be too much diversity (too many colors randomly mixed together) or too much uniformity (drippings all look the same)? Moreover, there are examples of natural beauty that seems difficult to be explained with uniformity amidst diversity. For example, the beauty of sunset or vast landscape seems to appeal to us for different reasons. The relationship between uniformity amidst diversity and other aesthetic experience is left unexplored. On the other hand, Hutcheson's attempt to explain diversity of taste by means of association seems to be too successful. For example, people who like the pictures of hills and lakes usually associate these with serenity. Yet there is arguably nothing inherently serene about hills and lakes, where Darwinian struggles go on everyday. Take away all associations, and we are left with a very poor concept of beauty. One way out is to suggest that the formal properties of an object become beautiful only when they become symbols of some reality. Again, Edwards and Kant will go along this road, though with very different reality in mind.

The theological message of Hutcheson is similar to Addison. It is basically a teleological argument. The design of the human psyche suggests a designer.[154] The teleological argument is probably the most popular theistic argument in the English Enlightenment.[155] The design argument agrees

---

154. Kivy (*Seventh Sense*, 115–16) asserts that Hutcheson's arguments are all varieties of the God of the Gaps theory, and we know better in this post-Darwinian age. Besides being anachronistic, he seems to misunderstand Hutcheson too. Natural selection does not give a full answer to the existence of the sense of beauty or our instinctive search for orderliness. Unlike the joy we get from food or sex, the joy we have from beauty seems unrelated to any essential task of survival. Rather, beauty seems to be an integral part of our perception of reality, often without functional necessity for the propagation of the species.

155. Stewart, "Religion and Rational Theology," 32–41.

well with the contemporaneous emphasis on empiricism. Hutcheson follows this ethos in presenting the sense of beauty as theistic evidence.

For Puritans, the problem with this kind of argument is that it gives only the benevolent God and the affable humankind. These English philosophers never dream that aesthetic experience can represent either the condemning or the saving act of God. Their God is too reasonable to hold humankind responsible for anything beyond the deliverance of reason. Edwards will give a radically different interpretation of aesthetic experience.

## Edwards

In developing Edwards' aesthetics, one must make a choice on how to organize the material. Edwards never wrote an explicit treatise on aesthetics, and his most important treatment of aesthetics is contained in a work on the nature of virtue.[156] One can follow Edwards in that treatise by starting on the fundamental connections between beings and beauty.[157] One then moves down the scale of beauty until one reaches beauty in inanimate object. Alternatively, one can start with the beauty in inanimate or sensible objects. Then she will demonstrate how the need for completeness gradually leads one to fundamental questions about the nature of beings. In order to facilitate comparison with other British aestheticians, I shall employ the second approach.

Edwards calls the beauty perceived by our physical senses "secondary beauty." This is in contrast to spiritual beauty, which is "primary beauty." Sensible beauty is defined by Edwards as "a mutual consent and agreement of different things in form, manner, quantity, and visible end or design; called by various names of regularity, order, uniformity, symmetry, proportion, harmony, etc."[158] Following this definition, Edwards claims that his definition is "the same that Mr. Hutcheson, in his treatise on beauty, expresses by uniformity in the midst of variety."[159] Edwards has probably read Hutcheson's work,[160] but he offers no other comments about the aes-

---

156. *The Nature of True Virtue*, Works 8:537–627. To be precise, this is the second half of his two-part treatise. *Concerning the End for which God Created the World* (8:403–536) is the first half.

157. This is the approach adopted by Delattre.

158. Works 8:561.

159. Ibid. 8:562.

160. Edwards developed his concept of beauty before his discovery of Hutcheson. According to Anderson (*Works* 6:326), Edwards wrote *The Mind* No. 1 (6:332–38), on

thetics of Hutcheson. It is not clear whether Edwards quotes Hutcheson as supporting authority just on the wordings of the definition, or Edwards truly regards his theory as similar to that of Hutcheson.

In fact, there are significant differences between Hutcheson and Edwards. Let us begin with the similarities. Both use geometrical figures as the simplest illustration of beauty. Squares and equilateral triangles are cited as examples of uniformity amidst diversity.[161] If there are two circles lying between two parallel lines, Edwards claims that the most beautiful form will have both lying midway between the parallel lines. Hutcheson claims that square, having greater diversity, is more beautiful than triangle. Edwards does not compare the relative beauty of geometric figures.

For Hutcheson, the geometric examples are paradigmatic examples. They express beauty in its clearest form, and other examples of beauty are seen as opaque extension of this simple beauty. The association of ideas with specific object is regarded as a cause of distortion and prejudice.

For Edwards, the geometric examples serve as illustration of the simplest kind of mutual consent. They are the most obvious examples, but they are also the most simplistic example. For Edwards, mutual agreement is pleasant because it expresses design. It is not simply the quantity of uniformity amidst diversity that determines the level of beauty, but the sophistication of the design expressed by such mutual agreement that carries the degree of beauty: "Thus the uniformity of two or more pillars, as they may happen to be found in different places, is not an equal degree of beauty as that uniformity in so many pillars in the corresponding parts of the same building. So means and an intended effect are related one to another."[162]

To use a terminology not employed by Edwards, we may call the regularity of geometric figures "brute beauty," because geometric figures alone do not serve any purpose. When we use geometric figures to design and build a house, the beauty is multiplied because the uniformity of shapes is employed to achieve a harmonious result—the house. On the other hand, the house becomes more beautiful if it is built in harmonious geometric figures and proportions. The means and end come together in a harmonious design, which manifests to our mind as beauty.

---

the topic of excellency and beauty, in 1723. The first edition of Hutcheson's *Beauty* was published in 1725. According to Ramsey (8:562), Edwards' own copy of the *Inquiry* is the fourth (1738) edition. *True Virtue* has the same framework as *The Mind* No. 1.

161. *Beauty* 2.3, 15; *Works* 8:562.
162. *Works* 8:563.

The importance of design is also brought out by Edward's distinction between simple beauty and complex beauty.[163] Simple beauty is strict equality (e.g., a square), while complex beauty is proportion. In a complex design, we may have to give up simple beauty for the sake of complex beauty. Consider the two sets

$A = \{1, 3, 4, 9\}$

$B = \{2, 6, 8, 18\}$

Judging A or B by itself, the numbers in them are chaotic and without beauty. Putting A and B together, we see the proportion between the two sets and chaos turns into beauty. Should we change B to $\{2, 6, 8, 9\}$, a kind of proportion is established within the set B; but we lost the proportion between A & B. For Edwards, the complex beauty of the totality takes precedence over the simple beauty of the elements.

In Edwards, uniformity cannot be measured by mere equality of the parts. The parts joined together in harmonious proportion for a singular purpose gives it an extra dimension of beauty. In the case of paintings by Jackson Pollack, if one can discern a unitary purpose that somehow harmonizes the drippings with certain purposes (symbol of artistic freedom?), then one can call them beautiful by Edwards' standard.

Then Edwards goes where Hutcheson and Addison (along with modern aesthetics) avoid: extending the definition of beauty to immaterial entities. "If uniformity and proportion be the things that effect, and appear agreeable to, this sense of beauty, then why should not uniformity and proportion affect the same sense in immaterial things as well as material, if there be equal capacity of discerning it in both? And indeed *more* in spiritual things (*ceteris paribus*) as these are more important than things merely external and material?"[164]

Harmonious society, harmonious thinking or wisdom, harmonious acting or justice, are examples of spiritual beauties.[165] For example, in the case of justice, it requires that "he which from his will *does* evil to others should *receive* evil from the will of others."[166] There is a spiritual equality in justice. A clear self-consciousness is another form of spiritual beauty, as it implies an equality between who a person actually is and what she thinks she should be.[167]

163. Ibid. 8:333–34.
164. Ibid. 8:568.
165. Ibid. 8:568–69.
166. Ibid. 8:569.
167. Ibid. 8:589.

Though inanimate objects can be arranged according to purpose or intent, the objects themselves do not have intention. They do not consciously arrange themselves in a purposeful way. From this perspective, we understand why Edwards call beauty in material objects secondary beauty. Only beings with intentions, i.e., spiritual beings, can self-consciously adhere to some purpose. This joining of the will of spiritual beings is primary beauty.

For Edwards, the end of secondary beauty is to lead us to primary beauty: "God has so constituted nature that the presenting of this inferior beauty, especially in those kinds of it which have greatest resemblance of the primary beauty, as the harmony of sounds, and the beauties of nature, have a tendency to assist those hearts are under the influence of a truly virtuous temper, to dispose them to the exercises of divine love, and enliven in them a sense of spiritual beauty."[168]

Hutcheson has emphasized that beauty is a sense of delight. Why should uniformity amidst diversity lead to pleasure? His answer is that God set up such rules in our psyche. God wants to make the task of understanding this world a pleasure. Beauty is a property of this world designed to make this world pleasant. For Edwards too, the pleasure of secondary pleasure is also a rule set up by God: "The *cause* why secondary beauty is grateful to *men* is only *a law of nature*, which God has fixed, or an *instinct* he has given to mankind; and not their perception of the same thing which *God* is pleased to have regard to, as the ground rule by which he has established such a law of nature."[169]

God makes secondary beauty pleasurable so that it may enliven people to spiritual beauty. In seeing harmonies in the material world, we are supposed to be enlivened to the harmonies of the spiritual world. But people often stop at the pleasantness and fail to appreciate the true nature of beauty. Therefore, they enjoy beauty without reflecting on the Creator of beauty.[170] For Hutcheson, it is the essence of beauty to be non-reflective. For Edwards, it is a failure of our mind if beauty does not lead to intellectual reflection. Beauty comes from proportion, and proportion is a construction of the mind. For Edwards, the focus on proportion should lift us from the confinement of material reality to spiritual reality.

If secondary beauty is the harmonious arrangement of material objects for a unitary purpose, then primary beauty is the consent of minds

---

168. Ibid. 8:565.
169. Ibid. 8:565–66.
170. Ibid. 8:567.

on a common purpose. However, not any kind of consent is beautiful. Suppose two people consent to go on a killing spree in St. Andrew Square, it would be an ugly act. Edwards would argue that their consent may have a particular beauty (in respect to the two people only), but it does not have general beauty (in respect to all people).[171] Considered in its most comprehensive context, beauty is consent to all beings. "And if every intelligent being is some way related to Being in general, and is a part of the universal system of existence; and so stands in connection with the whole; what can its general and true beauty be, but its union and consent with the great whole?"[172]

In other words, general beauty is the union and consent of all intelligent beings with the great whole. While Shaftesbury and Hutcheson focus beauty on the proportions of individual objects, Edwards wants us to ask about proportions on a global scale. Each level of beauty is related to a bigger context. A knife may be beautifully crafted, but it becomes an ugly tool in the hand of a murderer. From Edwards' perspective, we cannot know anything is really beautiful until we have a picture of the totality of beings.

But what is the purpose of the great whole, or the totality of beings? Does the totality of beings have a purpose? We are driven by Edwards' theory of beauty to the concept of God again. If the totality of beings can have a purpose, then either this totality is in some sense intelligent,[173] or the Creator of this totality gives it a purpose. If the world is created by God, then we cannot truly appreciate the beauty of this world unless we know God's purpose for the world. As we shall see, Edwards argues that the glory of God is the purpose of the world. It turns out that the theory of beauty in Edwards can only be completed in a theistic worldview. The beauty of a flower can be fully appreciated only when we behold the glory of God. Yet how do we know God's glory? How does the world exhibit divine glory? We shall address these questions in the following chapters.

## Some Comparisons

The British aestheticians and Edwards are all writing in response to the empiricism of the new science and the search for a reasonable faith. On the question of empiricism, there are different understandings of its implication for aesthetics. For Addison and Hutcheson, it means theorizing

---

171. See ibid. 8:540, for the distinction between general and particular beauty.
172. Ibid. 8:540.
173. This is Hegel's perspective.

as closely as possible with observable data and sensible objects. Addison's pleasures of the imagination and Hutcheson's internal sense are both attempts to ground beauty on our perception process of sensible objects. Beauty is portrayed as part of the structure of human psyche that is verifiable by simple reflections. For Shaftesbury and Edwards, they start their theories with sensible objects. However, they soon turn their attention from the perception of sensible objects to the self-perception of one's own affections. If we can analyze the perception of external objects, then we can analyze the perceptions of affections too. For Addison and Hutcheson, beauty is applied only to external objects. Shaftesbury and Edwards apply beauty to internal affections too. Just as there are beautiful objects, so there are beautiful souls where the affections are well-proportioned. Though all four writers subscribe to the empiricism of Locke to some extent, they differ on what can be taken as the raw data (the ideas in a Lockean sense). In particular, they differ on whether our affections can be taken as a form of raw data for higher level of synthesis.

These writers also differ on the role of reason in shaping our sense of beauty. Shaftesbury believes that we can change and shape our sense of beauty by the study of philosophy. For Addison and Hutcheson, the sense of beauty is aroused spontaneously without the use of reasoning. For Addison, we improve our taste by spending more time with recognized examples of beauty. For Hutcheson, reason has a negative function of training us to disassociate unhealthy associations (e.g., darkness with fear). For Edwards, the picture is more complicated. With his focus on overall purpose, it seems that beauty cannot be separated from the reasoning about purpose. However, as we shall see on the next chapter, Edwards emphasizes that God—the final purpose of everything—cannot be grasped by reason. It can only be perceived passively through spiritual sense.

While all four writers adopt some of the Lockean perspectives or vocabulary, none of them is slavish in following Locke. The pleasures of imagination or the sense of beauty are natural abilities of our psyche not readily explainable in a strictly Lockean framework. For these writers, people naturally develop a sense of beauty. This sense is not further explained by certain associations of simple ideas. For Shaftesbury and Hutcheson (probably for Addison too), this indicates a richness and goodness of human nature not strictly verifiable under Lockean scheme. For Edwards, this sense of beauty is a clue for a higher reality beyond our physical senses.

## The Beauty of the Triune God

We now turn to the relationship between beauty and God. All four writers regard beauty as a doorway to God, though in different ways. Shaftesbury focuses on the issue of design: if human can design material beauty, there should be a designer who designs human beings. All beauties or designs remind us the great Designer. For Addison, aesthetic experience of greatness makes us yearn for the true greatness of God. Beauty and newness testify to the goodness of God in making our life on earth more pleasurable. Hutcheson is similar to Addison in saying beauty is a testimony to divine goodness. He gives particular attention to how uniformity amidst diversity is fitting to our cognitive process. They are variations of the teleological argument. The God in such theories is a benevolent Watchmaker that gives human a pleasurable faculty. In Edwards' theory, God becomes the *telos* of the universe, the apex of beauty. This set Edwards apart from the other writers. While other claim that aesthetic experience points to the goodness of God, Edwards claims that true aesthetic experience is inseparable from the perception of God. God is not merely the creator of our aesthetic experience; it is also the essence of our aesthetic experience. Instead of being a connatural to human beings, aesthetic experience in Edwards' perspective is perception of divine revelation.

By asking for the meaning of the totality of being, Edwards is driven to metaphysics. Our next chapter will be devoted to this topic. For Addison and Hutcheson, beauty is an accidental part of reality. For Edwards, beauty reveals the essence of reality. For Edwards, reality and totality is based on God. Yet, philosophically, this is not the only solution. Another solution is to propose that any knowable totality is based on the perceiving subject. It is the knowing "I" that gives meaning to the totality. This is the road taken by the great Emmanuel Kant. Like Edwards, Kant is not ready to concede aesthetic experience to merely a matter of psychology. Like Edwards, he develops aesthetic theory into a theory about the essence of totality. In his case, the totality concerns the essence of the knowing "I." After we finish our exposition of Edwards, we shall return briefly to Kant. Despite their radically different construction of total reality, their common search for grounding aesthetics in totality reveals some interesting clues to a philosophical interpretation of the nature of beauty.

We conclude this chapter by pointing out that several features of Edwards' aesthetics resembles the English aesthetics familiar to Edwards. If there are internal sense and moral sense, then spiritual sense seems a natural development. If internal sense is the idea raised in us by a physical object, then spiritual sense would similarly be the idea raised in us by a spiritual object. If the true sense of beauty comes from a right ordering of our affections, then would not true spiritual beauty come also from the right affections? If God is generally acknowledged to the source of beauty, and beauty is generally acknowledged to be related to proportions, it seems logical to suggest that God is well proportioned in some way. Of course, these look like natural development only from hindsight. It takes a theological genius like Edwards to creatively integrate the English Enlightenment with the Puritan heritage. The Enlightenment uses beauty to portray an indifferently benevolent God. Edwards joins the aesthetic experience of the Enlightenment with the Reformed concept of the glory of God, so that both redemption and condemnation are manifestations of divine beauty. In our next four chapters we shall see how Edwards develops his definition of beauty into a defense of the Reformed system of doctrine.

# 3

## Metaphysics of Beauty

FOR EDWARDS, BEAUTY IS NOT JUST A CURIOUS FACT OF HUMAN behavior. Beauty is a foundational reality that gives meaning to both the natural world and the human world. As Delattre observes, "beauty is the central clue to the nature of reality."[1] In this chapter, we shall explore how Edwards uses the concept of beauty to defend his theistic worldview against the challenges raised by the Enlightenment. We call this defence Edwards' metaphysics of beauty. It is a theory about different levels of reality and their interrelationship. The heart of their interrelationship is proportional consent, or beauty.

It has generally been recognized that Edwards is one of the greatest American philosophers.[2] Among recent scholarship, the opinion is divided on the originality of the Edwards' metaphysics. Delattre, Lee, and Matless[3] all claim that Edwards offers a revolutionary perspective on metaphysics. Whether called "depositional metaphysics" (Lee) or the "relational metaphysics of love" (Matless), these proponents claim that Edwards provides a dynamic version of reality that is particularly fruitful for the twenty-first century. On the other hand, Norman Fiering groups Edwards with "the theocentric, rationalist metaphysicians" such as Malebranche and Leibniz.[4] He emphasizes the historical continuity of Edwards with his predecessors. The novel camp claims that metaphysics is central to Edwards' thinking, while Fiering tries to shift the focus away from Edwards' metaphysics.

---

1. Delattre, *Beauty and Sensibility*, 1.

2. Flower and Murphey claim that, in the history of American philosophy, "Jonathan Edwards is the greatest figure before the Civil War." *History of Philosophy*, 142. Chapter 3 of Flower and Murphey provides probably the best summary of Edwards' metaphysics.

3. Lee, *Philosophical Theology*; Matless, *Relational Metaphysics*.

4. Fiering, "Rationalist Foundations," 93.

*Metaphysics of Beauty*

We shall claim that both perspectives are partially valid. The continuity school is correct to claim that the conclusions of Edwards' metaphysics are conventional. Edwards defends a two-tier reality (spiritual/material) that has always been part of the tradition of the church. Following the Platonic tradition of the church, he championed the priority of spiritual reality over material reality. However, Edwards employs innovative arguments, based on the ideas of Newton and Locke, to defend this worldview. His originality does not lie in a brave new metaphysics, but a new synthesis of the old Christian doctrines and the scientific perspectives of the Enlightenment.[5] Reformed theology and Enlightenment philosophy are two legs that together build the philosophical theology of Edwards.[6] We may regard Edwards as a Thomas Aquinas of the eighteenth century.[7]

While potentiality and act become are crucial concepts for Aquinas in harmonizing the Christian faith with Aristotelian science, the concepts

---

5. Fiering says that the uniqueness of Edwards lies in "his being a daring and acute philosophical speculator who shared the (perhaps naive) trust common in his time that modern philosophy—that is philosophy beginning with Descartes—could be turned to the advantage of orthodox religion" ("Rationalist Foundations," 78). Fiering is right about Edwards' uniqueness, but we would put more emphasis on Newton and Locke. To anticipate later discussion, we maintain that Fiering exaggerates the influence of Cartesianism in Edwards because he neglects the importance of sensibility in Edwards.

6. For example, Matless attempts to reduce Edwards' metaphysical thinking into the theme of "benevolent love as that which seeks no boundaries and expresses itself towards all beings and to the natural world as a whole." (*Metaphysics of Love*, 306). She ignores much of Edwards' theology (for example, the order of beings with God as the prime reality, the importance of ordering our affections according to that order) that comes from the Reformed or general Christian heritage. In Matless' analysis, Edwards' main insight is that only love matters. This Edwards is both boring and divorced from his Reformed heritage.

7. Edwards had probably never read any writings by Aquinas and the other medieval schoolmem. All the comparisons with Aquinas are our interpretations. However, Edwards is acquainted with general metaphysical notions of God of the medieval schoolmen through the writings of Reformed schoolmen (particularly Francis Turretin and Peter Mastricht). Misc. 880 (*Works* 20:121–39), for example, bears remarkable resemblance to Aquinas' theology. The title of the article is "Being of a God." Edwards begins by using *ad infinitum* arguments to demonstrate that the material universe must have a first efficient cause and a first mover, in ways similar to the famous theistic proofs in *Summa Theologica* (I.2.3). Then Edwards argues that it is almost impossible that two particles should fall just into the right distance so that the appropriate physical laws will operate (20:128–30). It follows that it is even more incredible the whole universe, with many intricate laws and millions of particles, should all work together harmoniously just by chance. In other words, Edwards uses the Newtonian conception of the universe to argue against the self-sufficiency of the universe. He uses the contemporary science to give a new twist to an old argument.

of beauty and sensibility are crucial for Edwards in his defence of the Christian faith. In particular, beauty is essential to Edwards' conception of the being in general, the being of God and the nature of morality.[8] Edwards employs the concept of beauty to harmonize traditional Christian belief with the challenges of Enlightenment. As indicated in a previous chapter, Edwards classifies beauty into two kinds: secondary beauty and primary beauty. The former applies to material objects; the second applies to spiritual objects. We shall follow this scheme and divide our discussion into the metaphysics of material objects and the metaphysics of spiritual objects. In each section, we shall begin with the questions posed by the Enlightenment to traditional Christian doctrines. Then we shall lay out the defence offered by Edwards' metaphysics of beauty.

## The Beauty of Material World

### Theistic Idealism

We shall begin our section with a review of some challenges the English Enlightenment brought to the Puritan worldview. As we have indicated in our previous chapter, empiricism is one central ingredient of the Enlightenment. What counts as evidence for our knowledge? For Locke, the most common source of knowledge is the external world. Our sensational experience reveals to us truth about the external world. In Lockean terminology, our *ideas* of the world are the evidences for reasonable knowledge. However, the Lockean paradigm immediately raises the question: how do objects in the external world become ideas in our mind?[9] My idea of a cup exists only in my mind. It is immaterial and unobservable by others. The cup, in Lockean conception, is material and it exists independent of my mind. How are the two related? First, there is the epistemological question: how does the cup generate the idea of a cup in my mind? How do I know that my idea of the cup accurately represents the physical cup? This is the challenge of scepticism, typified by Hume. Though Edwards is acquainted with Hume's writings, he seems to be unaware of the seriousness of the challenge.[10] Like Locke, he does not question the general

---

8. Cf. Delattre, *Beauty and Sensibility*, 1–3.

9. Chai, *Limits of Enlightenment*, chapter one, discusses the ambiguity of Locke on this question. For an introduction to a similar dualism (intuition and concept) in Kant and the attempt by German idealism to resolve it, see Guyer, "Absolute idealism."

10. In letter no. 212 (written in 1755), Edwards writes, "I had before read that book of essays . . . and also that book of Mr. David Hume's which you speak of. I am

reliability of our sensational knowledge. Edwards is not interested in a general theory of epistemology. For him, the important epistemological question is our cognition of spiritual truth. If our knowledge comes from sensations, and God is not a material object, how do we perceive God? We shall answer this question in the next section, on the beauty of humanity.

The second question raised by empiricism is the challenge of materialism. This can be interpreted as a metaphysical question about the reality of ideas: is my idea of cup real in the same way that the cup is real? Do abstract concepts such as love represent any reality? Is one reality more fundamental than the other? Or does a third fundamental reality undergird both types of reality? Although empiricism does not logically imply materialism, the focus on sensational knowledge naturally leads to a questioning of spiritual realities. If all our knowledge comes from senses, and our senses can only tell us material objects, perhaps all we can know is only material objects. Any claim about the significance of spiritual realities may look like empty speculations. Whether God exists or not, perhaps all rational discourse should be limited to the material world. For Edwards, such materialistic thinking is anathema to Christianity.

Beside empiricism, the second challenge of Enlightenment is the rise of Newtonian science, where the universe is described by mathematical equations. In the Aristotelian conception of science, we study objects by discerning their essence and accidents. By using the scheme of potentiality and actuality in understanding essence, medieval theologians like Aquinas build up impressive system of scientific knowledge in which God is the origin and the end of the universe. The conception of potentiality and actuality is inherently teleological. If the seed is potentially a flower, it is natural to say that the end of the seed is a flower. Beginning with the end of specific beings, Aquinas takes the next step and asks the end of beings. This final end, in which all actuality is embodied, is God. For Aquinas, the world cannot be understood apart from God. The essence of humanity cannot be understood apart from its theological virtues.

In Cartesian science, material objects have no inherent purpose. They are conceived as extension and force. Descartes himself still needs a God to guarantee that material objects are real. Once reality is established,

---

glad of an opportunity to read such corrupt books; especially when written by men of considerable genius; that I may have an idea of the notions that prevail in our nation." (*Works* 16:679). We do not what work Edwards is referring to, though he mentions *A Treatise of Human Nature* in his *Catalogue*. Edwards regards Hume as a clever and popular writer on anti-Christian themes, but not necessarily a profound philosopher. That seems to be the only reference to Hume in all of Edwards' published works.

the world of Descartes runs on its own. For Locke, who shares neither the skepticism on senses nor the confidence in innate ideas, the God of Descartes is both superfluous and unknowable. Locke may still believe in God in some sense,[11] but the world can be understood on its own without reference to God. This God may intervene once in a while in performing some miracles, but reason alone is sufficient in our search for the true and the good. Newtonian science portrays all motions as governed by mechanical laws. Motions have no *telos*; they merely follow mathematical necessities. If there is no *telos*, then there is no meaning. Without meaning, there is no intentionality. Without intentionality, God (at least a sovereign and personal God) has no place in the world. As Laplace has pointed out: we do not need the hypothesis of God.

In his defence of the traditional Christian worldview, Edwards offers an idealistic interpretation of the material world. It is idealistic in the sense that the material is dependent on the ideal. Edwards remarks, "It the more confirms me in it, that the perfect idea God has of himself is truly and properly God, that the existence of all corporeal things is only ideas."[12] For Edwards, material objects can be truly understood if only they are regarded as images of spiritual objects. "For indeed the whole outward creation, which is but the shadows of beings, is so made as to represent spiritual things."[13] While the link of *telos* has been broken by Newtonian science, Edwards offers the link of beauty. The material world is infused with secondary beauty, which is the image of spiritual beauty.

Before we examine how Edwards develops his idealism, we will briefly review how recent scholars have addressed this issue. This has been a subject of some ambiguities. Delattre ignores this question in his book. He claims that, in Edwards thought, "beauty has priority over the other categories of being, such as those summed up by scholastic philosophy under the aspects of unity, truth, and goodness."[14] However, Delattre does not delineate how this priority shapes the metaphysics of Edwards. In his analysis, the central division is between being-in-itself and being-as-perceived. While this brings out the importance of sensibility in Edwards' thought, it gives no significance to Edwards' idealism. Lee is careful in

---

11. For Locke's theology, in particular with reference to his empiricism, see Henry, *Lockean Puritan?*, chapter 3. Henry believes that Locke is likely to be a deist or even an agnostic rather than a traditional Christian.

12. Misc. 179. *Works* 13:327.

13. Misc. 362, *Works* 13:434.

14. Delattre, *Beauty and Sensibility*, 105.

delineating the objective idealism of Edwards,[15] and he is the best expositor of Edwards' philosophical theology among recent scholars. Matless is apologetic about the idealism of Edwards.[16] Perhaps she regards the term *idealism* in a primarily negative way, as denying the existence of ordinary things. But idealism does not necessarily mean a denial of the reality of the material world. "The positive meaning of 'idealism' in contrast, involves seeing the term as *adding* rather than subtracting significance, as emphasizing that, whatever we say about the status of many things that are thought to exist at a common-sense level, we also need to recognize a set of features or entities that have a higher, a more 'ideal' nature."[17] Understood in this positive sense, Edwards stands squarely within the idealist tradition that runs from Plato to Hegel.

On the other hand, Fiering regards Edwards as a (perhaps indirect) follower of Malebranche. Malebranche is led by the skepticism of Descartes to the conclusion that we really see God in all things. For Malebranche, material objects are veils for the thought of God. On this level, Edwards does bear some resemblance to Malebranche. However, Malebranche has a distinctive understanding of idea. For him, we perceive the ideas of God directly. When I perceive a round table, what I really perceive is a circle with certain color and shades. The idea in my head (the circle) is not actually some subjective mental state, but the eternal idea of God put into my mind.[18] Edwards' concept is Lockean rather than that of Malebranche. For Edwards, ideas are mental objects aroused passively by the presence of physical objects.[19] They are not eternal and infinite ideas

---

15. See his *Philosophical Theology* chapter 3 and 4.

16. "What the following analysis will strive to make clear is that if we must classify his thought as portending an 'idealism' then 'objective idealism' or 'idealistic phenomenalism' (as dubbed by Anderson), may be more helpful, but even these designations are misleading without further nuance and clarification. What this chapter will strive to show is that ideas for Edwards are 'stuff' of the really real." Matless, *Metaphysics of Love*, 209–10.

17. Ameriks, "Introduction," 8.

18. Though his best known work is *Search after Truth*, the best succinct treatment is found is the first three dialogues of his *Dialogues on Metaphysics on Religion*. See also the editor's introduction by Nicholas Jolley in Cambridge Texts in the History of Philosophy edition of the *Dialogues*.

19. Edwards' solution to dichotomy of physical objects and mental objects is occasionalism grounded on divine rule. "Our perceptions, or ideas that we passively receive by our bodies, are communicated to us immediately by God while our minds are united with our bodies; but only we in some measure know the rule. We know that upon such alterations in our bodies there follow such ideas in the mind . . . according to some rule, no doubt, only we know not what." "The Mind" 3; *Works* 6:339.

of Malebranche.[20] Secondly, Cartesianism starts with the thinking self and self-consciousness is the foundation of knowledge. For Edwards, the existence of objects and other minds is self-evident. The challenge is to comprehend their interrelations in which neither spiritual world nor the material world are rendered into phantoms. Though Malebranche's *Search after Truth* and the English idealist John Norris' *Essay towards the Theory of the Ideal or Intelligible World* were both included in the Drummer collection donated to Yale College,[21] Edwards did not refer to them in his writings. It is difficult to give a precise evaluation how much he may have been directly influenced by Malebranche (or by the Cambridge Platonists, or Berkeley).[22] Given their different concerns, we think that Malebranche and Edwards are espousing two different kinds of idealism.[23]

We begin our systematic exposition of Edwards' metaphysics of beauty. The starting point, both chronologically and logically in the development of his thought, is his conception of substance.[24] Edwards studied Gassendi and Henry Moore as a college student. He would be familiar with the debate on the nature of substance in his time, and the relation between spiritual and material substance.[25] In Newtonian science, material substance interacts with each other in mathematical precision. Newtonian science does not answer the question of the nature of substance, nor why they should have mass and other properties. Is substance identical with its properties (in other words, substance is no more than color, shape, and so on), or is there an underlying "stuff" that underlies all these properties?[26]

---

20. For a brief discussion on the various meanings of *ideas*, see Ariew and Green, "Ideas."

21. Anderson, "Editor's Intoduction," *Works* 6:20–21.

22. On the source of Edwards' idealism, see the bibliography and the brief discussion in McClymond, *Encounters with God*, 128.

23. Copan, "Philosophical Influences," argues for Malebranchean influence. The weakness of Fiering and Copan is that they emphasize the general Platonic worldview of Edwards as contrasted with a more materialistic worldview of Locke. We (unlike Miller) readily concedes Edwards' Platonic tendency, but Edwards could have received this from Turretin, Moore, or even Shaftesbury. There is nothing particularly Malebranchean or Cartesian about Edwards' idealism. On the other hand, a Lockean influence does not imply Edwards take over the whole philosophy of Locke.

24. Edwards wrote his theory of substance in 1721–22 (Schafer, "Editor's Introduction," *Works* 13:91). For further discussion of Edward's of substance, see Flower and Murphey, *American Philosophy*, 143–51; Matless, *Metaphysics of Love*, 122–44; Anderson (*Works*, 6:53–68) locates Edwards thought in the debates of his time.

25. See Anderson, "Editor's Introduction," *Works* 6:53–68 for a summary of this debate.

26. For example, Locke regards substance as an unknowable entity. "To conclude,

*Metaphysics of Beauty*

Edwards develops an idealistic answer to these questions. First, he gives an idealistic interpretation of the nature of atoms. Edwards gives this definition to atom: "That body that is absolutely plenum, or that has every part of space included within its surface impenetrable, is indivisible; and that the parts thereof can by no means [be] separated from each other, by any force how great soever."[27]

How can atoms resist all forces, no matter how great, that try to penetrate them? It follows that "it must needs be an infinite power that keeps the parts of atoms together."[28] Who can have this power except God? "[I]t is God himself, or the immediate exercise of his power, that keeps the parts of atoms or two bodies touching, as aforesaid, together."[29] Moreover, this power of resistance must work continuously as long as the atoms exist. "It follows that the constant exercise of the infinite power of God is necessary to preserve bodies in being. Hence, also an incontestable argument for the being, infinite power, and omnipotence of God: of the two latter, inasmuch as we see that the infinite power [is] actually exerted in an infinite number of places at once, even in every part of every atom of the universe."[30]

Using the same logic, Edwards concludes that solidity results from the immediate exercise of divine power. It is God who bounds two atoms together so that they cannot be separated.[31] Solidity is nothing but the binding of atoms together to form an object. Similarly, motion is also the outcome of immediate divine power. Motion is "the communication of body, solidity, or this resistance, from one part of space to another successively (that is, from one part of space to the next etc.)."[32] In other words, motion and solidity are manifestations of the same power of God. In the solidity, the resistance is stabilized in one particular space. In motion, the resistance is changing its spatial reference over time.

---

Sensation convinces us, that there are solid extended substances; and Reflection, that where are thinking one; Experience assures us of the Existence of such Beings. . . . But beyond these *ideas* [of sensations and reflection], as received from their proper Sources, our Faculties will not reach. . . . From whence it seems probable to me, that the simple *Ideas* we receive from Sensation and Reflection, are the Boundaries of our Thoughts." *Essay*, II.23.29, 312.

27. "Of Atoms," *Works* 6:208
28. ibid., 214.
29. ibid., 214.
30. ibid., 214.
31. ibid., 213.
32. ibid., 215–16.

These laws of resistance exist only as long as God is exerting his power to maintain the order. All mechanisms or physical laws do not exist by themselves. The atoms do not have an inherent power of resistance, since they are no existence independent of the power of resistance. They are willed by God moment by moment. Similar to Aquinas, Edwards believes that God is the efficient cause of the existence of all material objects. For Aquinas, this existence of material objects consists of substance and accidents. For Edwards, this existence consists of its physical laws and properties. We can understand a material object only in relationship to other objects. For example, resistance to penetration of a particular atom is comprehensible if there are other objects that try to penetrate it. Motion is comprehensible if there are objects distributed over space that try to penetrate the atom. Ultimately, these relationships must be grounded in the power of God.

With this ingenious conception of solidity and motion, Edwards provides a coherent answer to the question of the place of a personal God a mechanistic universe.[33] The mystery of the concept of substance is resolved by understanding physical laws as the working of the divine will. There is no need for a mysterious "substance" to guarantee the continuity of reality underlying changing appearances. The regularity of the changes is itself the continuity and foundation in all changes. The regularity is grounded on the constant will of God and nothing else.[34] The intentionality of the Aristotelian world is replaced by the God-instituted regularities. In Edwards' universe, God is not invoked to answer the *telos* of the world. God is invoked to explain the very existence of a mechanistic universe.[35] Edwards draws two conclusions from his construction of the physical world. First, the laws of nature are only "the stated methods of God's acting with respect to bodies, and the stated conditions of the alteration of the manner of his acting." Second, "there is no such thing as mechanism,

---

33. The theocentric nature of Edwards' idealism is emphasized in McClymond, *Encounters*, 28–30.

34. Therefore occasionalism is probably the best description of Edwards' view on causality. See Crisp, "How 'Occasional'?"

35. ". . . God's upholding created substance, or causing its existence in each successive moment, is altogether equivalent to an *immediate production out of nothing*, at each moment, because its existence at this moment is not merely in part from God, but wholly from him; and not in any part, or degree, from its antecedent existence." *Original Sin* 4.3, *Works* 3:402.

*Metaphysics of Beauty*

if that word is taken to be that whereby bodies act each upon other, purely and properly by themselves."[36]

We pause here and examine again the two interpretations of Edwards among scholars. As pointed out above, Lee has popularized the concept of a dynamic ontology in Edwards. In other words, the physical laws themselves become the substance of reality. In Matless' presentation of Edwards' metaphysics, relationship itself is what is *really* real.[37] As the discussion above indicates, the really real in Edwards are God and the power of God. On one level, we may indeed detach Edwards' dispositional metaphysics from his theocentrism. As a constructive theologian, one may take elements of Edwards' thought that are helpful and reject outdated elements. On the other hand, if our goal is to understand Edwards *per se*, then detaching his dispositional ontology from his theocentric idealism gives a distorted picture of Edwards. It may give the impression that Edwards prefers the category of becoming to the category of being. The major metaphysical division in Edwards is not being and becoming, but material and spiritual world. Dispositional ontology may sound like that the physical laws of nature are self-regulating. Thus Delattre compares Edwards to Whitehead several times in his book.[38] We claim that Edwards is closer to Aquinas than to Whitehead. The essence of matter is dynamic in the sense that it is the realization of the will of God. The will of God, for both Aquinas and Edwards, is essentially dynamic. However, God is the same yesterday, today, and tomorrow.[39]

On the other hand, Edwards' conception is also different from the Cartesianism of Malebranche. Edwards' starting point is not the thinking self, but speculations on the essence of material objects. For Edwards, the mysterious nature of substance is accessible to human knowledge. Scientific laws are not merely heuristic devices with which we construct our reality; they are the essence of material objects as created by God. Edwards' idealism is also a confident realism,[40] where the essence of the

---

36. "Of Atoms," *Works* 6:216. In Edwards time, it is common to believe that some physical laws are the immediate working of God. For example, Edwards and Whiston (from whose textbook Edwards learnt his astronomy) believe that gravity is the immediate operation of God. Ibid., 234. But Edwards is unique in asserting all physical laws are the immediate operations of God.

37. *Metaphysics of Love*, 21–23.

38. *Beauty and Sensibility*, 25, 29, 111, 130.

39. On the theological conservatism of Edwards, and the dynamic nature of both traditional and Edwards' conception of God, see Holmes, "Dispositional Ontology?"

40. Here realism means that we can have knowledge of the noumena, as contrast

material world is accessible to the human mind. Nor is the world merely a veil to God's mind. The laws of nature have their own integrity within a space-time reality. They are God's work *ad extra*, to be distinguished from the inner wisdom of God.[41]

Having laid out Edwards' idealistic understanding of material, we have to ask how is this idealism related to his concept of beauty. The short answer is that the end of the material world is to display beauty. There are two ways in which the material world fulfils its purpose: it displays the wisdom of the Creator and it serves as the image of spiritual things.

## *The World as the Theatre of God's Wisdom*

Edwards emphasizes that it is inconceivable that the material world can exist without spiritual beings. For Edwards, an idealistic understanding of the material world implies the existence of beings who can understand ideas. "[F]or we are to remember that the world exists only mentally, so that the very being of the world implies its being perceived or discovered."[42] "How impossible is it, that the world should exist from eternity without a mind."[43]

Perhaps the best way to understand Edwards is to compare the material world to mathematical theorems. In a way, mathematical theorems are objective entities. They do not perish along with the person who is thinking about the theorems. They confront the mind with an objective validity; we cannot arbitrarily decide what theorems are true. We can recognize true theorems, or we may fail to understand them. In either case, we recognize that we are recipient of truth and not the creator of truth. Mathematical theorems have meaning only in relationships. The number 1 has meaning only as a member of a set (natural numbers, real numbers etc.), operating under the rules of the set. However, it is difficult to conceive of mathematics without at least one mind who knows mathematics.

---

with only knowledge of the phenomena. Edwards' idealism is a form of realism under the terminology of Kant, as opposite to the transcendental idealism of Kant. See Allison, *Kant's Transcendental Idealism*.

41. Lee has carefully laid out the realism of Edwards, in the sense physical laws are permanent and true characteristics of the world, in *Philosophical Theology*, 56–67. Lee's own terminology, "permanence of the created world," can be misleading in suggesting the world has a permanence independent of the continuous willing of God for its existence. See Crisp, "How 'Occasional'?"

42. Misc. 247; *Works* 13:247

43. *The Mind*, 28, *Works* 6:351

*Metaphysics of Beauty*

Of course, there are particular mathematical theorems that nobody in the world today know about. However, mathematical concepts and rules in general are known by minds. If there were no mind from eternity, if this universe contains only mindless matter, does it still make sense to say that there are mathematical theorems in this universe? Is there any existence of mathematics totally independent of minds? For Edwards, the answer is no. This is a metaphysical presupposition of Edwards.

We have seen that, for Edwards, the essence of the material world is the exertion of God's power according to God-ordained rules. The laws are real in the sense that they are God's power *ad extra*, but they are inseparable from the active will of God. The relationship between the material world and God's mind is somewhat analogous to the relationship between mathematics and our mind. The mathematical theorem in our mind exists only as long as we are thinking about them. The difference is that God's creation is a working of the mind *ad extra*, while the mathematical theorem is internal to our mind.[44] The similarity is that, for both material world and mathematical theorems, intelligibility is the essence of their existence.

If intelligibility belongs to the essence of the material world, then it is natural to claim that being understood is part of the goal of the material world. Since the material world is God's will ad extra, it is also natural that the intelligibility should not be limited to God alone. If this were no intelligent being other than God, the material world would have existed in vain. What we know about the world are relations and proportions. As we have indicated in a chapter 2, secondary beauty is relations and proportions. Therefore the purpose of the material world is that its beauty should be known to intelligent beings beside God:

> 'Tis most certain that God did not create the world for nothing. 'Tis most certain that if there were not intelligent beings in the world, all the world would be without any end at all. . . . So certainly senseless matter would be altogether useless if there was no intelligent being but God, for God could neither receive good himself nor communicate good. What would this vast universe of matter, placed in such excellent order and governed by

---

44. Why can God create a world by his thinking and willing, and we cannot? Edwards does not provide a direct answer. Perhaps, for Edwards, a metaphysical answer is neither possible nor desirable. It is an incomprehensible infinite gap between Creator and creatures. The answer depends on how close we want to align Edwards with Neoplatonism. For Aquinas, the answer is that only in God is essence identical to existence. Therefore, the thinking of God (part of his essence) can generate existence.

such excellent rules, be good for, if there was no intelligence that could know anything of it?[45]

Therefore beauty is not just an accidental property of the world; it is the very essence and purpose of the world. The world is order and proportions; and order and proportions is beauty. Beauty is objective in the sense that it is there even if not perceived by human beings. But it will be meaningless. It would be like someone speaking without an audience. The words exist objectively (in the sense of vibrations of the air), but there would be no communication of meaning. The words have failed in their purpose of communication. Similarly, the order and proportions of the world are exhibitions of the wisdom of God. Its purpose is to be appreciated by spiritual beings.

The analogy of language is particularly apt in Edwards' case, because Edwards does believe that the material world is a song for spiritual things. We shall turn to this topic in the next section.

We can briefly compare Edwards with George Berkeley (1685–1753), the other leading British idealist of Edwards' time. For Berkeley, the essence of material is our perception of it: "For as to what is said of the absolute existence of unthinking things without any relation to their being perceived, that seems perfectly unintelligible. Their *esse* is *percipi*, nor is it possible they should have any existence, out of minds or thinking things which perceive them."[46]

For Edwards, there is a table first and then there is our perception of the table. For Berkeley, our perception of the table is the table itself. So why can people agree on seeing the same table? Berkeley's answer is that God has put the same perception into people thinking that they have seen the same table. It is not an external table that leads to my mental picture of a table, but God projects the mental picture directly into my mind. "From all which I conclude, *there is a mind which affects me every moment with all*

---

45. Misc. gg, *Works* 13:185. In this note, Edwards continues to argue as a corollary that human beings must be made immortal. "The world had as good have been without us, as for us to be a few minutes and then be annihilated—if we are now to own God's works to his glory, and only glorify him a few minutes, and then be annihilated, and it shall after that be all one to eternity as if we never had been, and be in vain after we are dead that we have been once; and then after the earth shall be destroyed, it shall be for the future entirely in vain that either the earth or mankind have ever been." However, the question whether ephemeral events have significance is not directly related Edwards' idealism or his concept of beauty. In any case, immortality of the human soul is not a major theme in Edwards' writings.

46. *On the Principles of Human Knowledge*, I.3, in George Berkeley, *Philosophical Works, including the Works on Vision*, 90. Emphasis is original.

*the sensible impressions I perceive."*[47] The difference between hallucinations and real things is that the former are impressions I conjure up myself, while the latter are impressions conjured up by the infinite Spirit. Therefore the latter is much more vivid and strong.

Starting from the axiom that all we can ever perceive are mental objects, Berkeley concludes that real things are also mental objects. From the need to explain the giveness of our ordinary perceptions, Berkeley concludes that there must be a Spirit who impresses those perceptions in us. Berkeley does not have a material world in his worldview. On the other hand, Edwards reaches his idealistic conclusion through musing on the nature of atoms and motions.

We take a short detour to compare this idealistic argument with the design argument of Hutcheson. Edwards' argument is a form of teleological argument, in that he argues from the purpose of the world. However, it is a question about the purpose of the existence of the material world. Why should God exert his effort to maintain a law-bound material world? It is a metaphysical quest.

For Hutcheson, the material world has an integrity of its own. Hutcheson avoids metaphysical questions such as the nature of material beings. The question of Hutcheson is why some specific laws work in those specific ways. In particular, why should uniformity amidst diversity generate pleasure in human beings? It could have been that uniformity amidst diversity would generate grief in human beings. The question is about the purpose of specific laws within the material world, not the existence of the material world as a whole. Edwards himself employ similar arguments in some of his writings. For example, he asks why spiders should always fly towards the shore in New England. His answer is that God designs spiders that way so that the vast amount of spiders can die and sink conveniently into the sea, instead of becoming a nuisance to people.[48] In Hutcheson and the "Spider" letter of Edwards, the argument is why scientific laws seem to favor human beings specifically. For Hutcheson, Edwards and many others in the seventeenth century, such favoring of human beings within the laws of nature is a sure sign of the existence of a benign Creator.

---

47. *Three Dialogues*, Second Dialogue; *Philosophical Works*, 205.
48. "Spider" letter, *Works* 6:167–68

## The Beauty of the Triune God

### *World as Images of Divine Thing*

Edwards claims that the material world is not only beautiful in its harmonious internal working, but it is also beautiful because they are externally harmonious with spiritual things. Edwards calls such harmonies between material and spiritual realities images of divine things. Edwards remarks:

> I am not ashamed to own that I believe that the whole universe, heaven and earth, air and seas, and the divine constitution and history of the holy Scriptures, be full of images of divine things, as full as a language is of words; and that the multitude of those things that I have mentioned are but a very small part of what is really intended to be signified and typified by these things: there is room for persons to be learning more and more of this language and seeing more of that which is declared in it to the end of the world without discovering all.[49]

Edwards has written about 100 pages of printed text on examples of how the natural world images the spiritual world,[50] and Edwards claims that this is but a small portion of all the existing images. As an example of Edwards creativity on this question, we quote his example of the silkworm: "The silkworm is a remarkable type of Christ, which, when it dies, yields, us that of which we make such glorious clothing. Christ became a worm for our sakes, and by his death finished that righteousness with which believers are clothed, and thereby procured that we should be clothed with robes of glory."[51] The death of the silkworm produces beautiful silk for clothes, and this typifies the death of Christ that clothes us with righteousness.

In a complete theory of typology, Edwards would need to develop criteria to distinguish true types from mere human imagination. For example, does God intend silkworm to be a type of Christ, or is it merely the product of Edwards' creative mind? Edwards himself distinguishes between true type and signification.[52] Presumably, a type is literally an im-

---

49. "Types," *Works* 11:152.

50. The "Images of Divine Things" and "Types" in *Works* 11. These notes are records of about thirty years of reflections, from 1728 to 1757. See Wallace Anderson's "Notes on the Manuscript," *Works* 11:38–46. Sang Hyun Lee gives a good introduction to Edwards theology of nature in "Edwards on God and Nature."

51. "Images" 35, *Works* 11:59.

52. "There are many things in the constitution of the world that are not properly shadows and images of divine things, that yet are significations of them; as children's being born crying is a signification of their being born to sorrow." "Images" 25, *Works*

*Metaphysics of Beauty*

age of divine things, and a signification is only metaphorically an image. Edwards does not give us any formal criteria for distinguishing between the two. For our purpose, we do not need to ask further about his method for discerning true types.

However, we do need to know the rationale for Edwards' interpretation of the nature of the material world. There are both theological and philosophical reasons for such typological reading of nature. The theological reason is obvious: Edwards is following the example of the Scripture. For example, Jesus called himself the true light (John 1:9) as well as true vine (John 15:9). For Edwards, that means that Jesus taught us that many things in nature are types of spiritual reality.[53] To vindicate his case, Edwards writes up an index of Scripture verses using natural objects as types for spiritual realities, as well as an index of Scripture verses used in his notes "Images of Divine Things."[54] In his theology and methodology, Edwards is following the Puritan tradition.[55]

The philosophical reason is more complicated. Edwards says that "as a language is full of words," so is the fecundity of divine types in the material world. In other words, nature is a form of divine speech.[56] Edwards compares the learning of reading types to the art of learning a language: "Types are a certain sort of language, as it were, in which God is wont to speak to us. And there is, as it were, a certain idiom in that language which is to be learnt the same that the idiom of any language is. viz. by good acquaintance with the language. . . . Great care should be used, and we should endeavor to be well and thoroughly acquainted, or we shall never understand [or] have a right notion of the idiom of the language."[57]

---

11:57

53. "Images" 45, *Works* 11:62.

54. *Works* 11:131–35, 141–42.

55. The Puritans regard nature and the Bible as two books of God where we can mine for images of spiritual truth. Concordances were developed to help them understand the typologies in the Bible. See Hardman Moore, "For the mind's eye only."

56. We have discussed Stephen Daniel's thesis in *Philosophy of Jonathan Edwards* in chapter 1. See also his "Postmodern Concepts of God and Edwards's Trinitarian Ontology." Beside the criticism offered there, we note also that there is no dichotomy between reason and language in Edwards. Edwards shares the Enlightenment's confidence in universal reason. In his thinking, language does hold some privileged position in contrast to ratiocination for our grasping of reality. Moreover, Edwards assumes that language's function is to refer to something extra-lingual. The material world is like a language because it refers to the spiritual world. It is quite different from Daniel's claim that meaning is totally immanent in the message.

57. "Types," *Works* 11:150–51.

In other words, God makes the world in such a way so that it will speak spiritual truths to us. As shown in the previous section, Edwards believes that the harmonious physical laws are in themselves beautiful. Here, we see that the material world is also beautiful because it speaks of spiritual beauty.

In chapter 2, we have pointed out the difficulty of the definition "uniformity amidst diversity" in explaining the beauty of sunset. For Edwards, the answer for that question is easy. It is not the orange colour of sunset *per se* that is beautiful. The reason is rather that the warmth and light of the sun remind us of God's love and holiness. For atheists, it will be like listening to a song of foreign language. They may appreciate the melody, but they do not truly understand the song. They are touched by the material beauty, but cannot sense the spiritual beauty behind it. If we ask why God designs nature to work in a certain way (for example, the source of light should usually also be the source of heat; insects who feed on garbage usually look hideous to us), the answer is that they are designed to be types of spiritual beauty. God designs the laws of nature so that they can speak to us about spiritual beauty.

Since the material world as a whole is a type of spiritual beauty, beauty becomes a bridge between the material world and the spiritual world. The Christian church has a long tradition of regarding creation in an anagogical fashion. This is usually grounded in a Neoplatonic framework of process and return. Edwards seems to have little direct acquaintance with the Neoplatonic tradition. On the other hand, the Puritans have a strong tradition in the typological reading of history and Scripture.[58] Edwards is distinguished from other Puritans by his pursuit of a philosophical basis for typology. He succeeds in providing an alternate explanation to Neoplatonism for the anagogical function of nature. The link in Edwards is not an ontological process of emanation, but the communication of meaning through language. The world is the language; spiritual beauty is the meaning.

We conclude this section by looking at one of the most striking examples of typology in Edwards—human appearance. For Edwards, physical appearance cannot itself be the source of real beauty. Unlike Shaftesbury, this is not about the contrast of form and material. The contrast is between physical being and spiritual being. A statue of identical appearance would

---

58. See Anderson's "Introduction" for a brief discussion of the history of types in the Christian church, *Works* 11:11–32. See also fn. 55. On his typological reading of history, see Zakai, Avihu, *Jonathan Edwards's Philosophy of History*.

*Metaphysics of Beauty*

not arouse our emotions the way a real person does. Edwards concludes that the reason is that the body is only an image of the real beauty. The beauty that we really love is spiritual beauty, the beauty of the soul within the body. For Edwards, this indicates that the physical world in general is also an image of the spiritual beauty of God. The long quotation below shows not only Edwards' idea but also some of his most poetic language:

> When we behold a beautiful body, a lovely proportion, a beautiful harmony of features of face, delightful airs of countenance and voice, and sweet motion and gesture, we are charmed with it; not under the notion of a corporeal, but a mental beauty. For if there could be a stature that should have exactly the same . . . we would not be so delighted with it; we should not fall entirely in love with the image, if we knew certainly that it had no perception or understanding. . . . And 'tis certainly because there is an analogy between such a countenance and such airs, and these and those excellencies of the mind—a sort of I know not what in them, that is agreeable and does consent with such mental perfections—so that we cannot think of such habitudes of mind without having an idea of them at the same time. Nor can it be only from custom, for the same dispositions and actings of mind naturally beget such kind of airs of countenance and gesture; otherwise, they never would have come into custom.
>
> He who by his immediate influence gives being every moment and by his Spirit actuates the world, because he inclines to communicate himself and his excellencies, doth doubtless communicate his excellency to bodies, as far as there is any consent or analogy . . . the beauties of nature are really emanations, or shadows, of the excellencies of the Son of God.
>
> So that when we are delighted with flowery meadows and gentle breezes of wind, we may consider that we only see the emanations of the sweet benevolence of Jesus Christ; when we behold the fragrant rose and lily, we see his love and purity.[59]

A body without a soul does not have real beauty. A beautiful face is a God-ordained symbol for a beautiful soul. In the quotation above, Edwards concludes that the same is true for the natural world. Why are we so deeply moved by sceneries of the natural world? Edwards believes that

---

59. Misc. 108, *Works* 13:278–79. Misc. 108 becomes well know through its reprint in *Jonathan Edwards: Representative Selections*, eds. Clarence H. Faust and Thomas H. Johnson (New York: American Book, 1935), 372–74. According to Schafer, the first paragraph in our quotation may be alluring to Sarah Pierpont. On Sarah's piety and Edwards' admiration for her, see George M. Marsden, *Jonathan Edwards*, 239–252.

mere material objects, whether a statue or a flower, cannot truly fill our soul with joy. We are moved by the natural world because, consciously or unconsciously, the beauty of God has touched us through the world. Unlike the Neoplatonism of the medieval age, Edwards does not rely solely on the forms residing in material objects to communicate spiritual meaning. The forms along with the affections aroused by the object together communicate the spiritual truth.

We note here Edwards intuitively recognizes the difficulty of explaining the relationship between the signs and the signified. Modern philosophy of language has rejected the solution of logical positivism (the attempt to develop a one-to-one mapping between signs and the things signified). Stephen Daniel follows the postmodern trend in claiming that meaning is totally immanent in the message. The signs merely point to other signs.

As indicated in the quotation above, "there is an analogy between such a countenance and such airs, and these and those excellencies of the mind—a sort of I know not what in them, that is agreeable and does consent with such mental perfections." In other words, the beauty of the body somehow speaks of the beauty of soul ("there is an analogy"), yet the way it communicates it is unclear to Edwards. Meaning (mental perfections) is communicated through the signs (the countenance) in a way that cannot be explained rationally. The signs do refer to something beyond the signs, yet how this referring works cannot be explained rationally.

For Edwards, we are primarily spiritual beings. Therefore only spiritual beings can truly satisfy our soul. Ultimately, nothing is beautiful except divine beauty. To participate in divine beauty is our destiny. This destiny will be the theme of our next section.

## The Beauty of Humanity—The Divine Image

From the material world we now enter into the world of spiritual beings—human beings. For Edwards, human beings possess the archetype of the beauty of the material. Their potentiality for beauty is therefore infinitely greater than material objects. "Excellency may be distributed into greatness and beauty. The former is the degree of being, the latter is being's consent to being."[60] Spiritual beings have a qualitatively higher degree of being than material beings, so their excellencies (if they consent to being) are also infinitely higher than material beings.[61] To be exact, the beauty

---

60. "The Mind" 64, *Works* 6:382

61. The diagram of Delattre in *Beauty and Sensibility,* 31, is misleading in a

*Metaphysics of Beauty*

of spiritual beings is divine. The purpose of this section is to show how Edwards substantiates this claim.

In our previous section, we have seen that material beauty, or secondary beauty, is an image of spiritual beauty. In our previous chapter we have shown that consent to being is primary beauty, or the beauty of spiritual beings. In this section we want to show that how, in Edwards' thought, primary beauty serves as an ontological link between human beings and God. We can use Aquinas as an analogy again. In Aquinas' thinking, we participate in God by fixing our mind on the eternal truth of God and fixing our will on God. Theology is no mere intellectual exercise; it is a participation in the being of God that can lead to climatic union with God. For Edwards, meditation on the being of God means appreciating the beauty of God. When we appreciate the beauty of God, we participate in the Holy Spirit; the Holy Spirit is God's infinite beauty, or "God's infinite consent to being in general."[62] For Edwards too, meditating on God is participation in God. The originality of Edwards lies in his articulating the traditional doctrine of divine perception and participation in Lockean vocabulary.

## *Sensing the Beauty of God*

Lockean empiricism poses one difficulty for the Christian worldview of Edwards: how do we perceive God and God's revelation? If knowledge about external objects comes only through sensations, and if God is external to us and immaterial, how may we arrive at any knowledge of God? The traditional Christian vocabulary of participation in being is tied to an outdated mode of Neoplatonism. In medieval science, hotness in a specific object comes from participation in hotness-in-itself (understood as the element of fire). Therefore it is natural to conceive existence of specific beings as participation in being-in-itself. We process from God, and we perceive God when we return to God through ecstasy.

---

fundamental way. The most important thematic division in Edwards is not the distinction between being as existence and being as perceived, but material beings and spiritual beings. The discussion in *Beauty and Sensibility*, 38–41 is unnecessarily confused when Delattre tries to categorize the divine Being as part of being-in-general. Edwards has little interest in being-in-general. For him, the divine Being (as necessarily existence) is the source both beauty and being of all other beings. Being-in-general or beauty-in-general are concepts alien to Edwards' thought.

62. "The Mind" 45.9, *Works* 6:364.

In the new science of the Enlightenment, there is no such thing as hotness-in-itself. Hotness is merely a form of energy. There is no such thing as whiteness-in-itself either. Whiteness is merely a form of light energy. Energy is conceived in a mathematical form as interaction between objects. If the new science cast away the quality-by-participation concept of physics, can human participation in God be understood intelligently? Is there an alternative to Neoplatonism to understand divine participation philosophically?

Moreover, Locke has insisted that there are no innate ideas in the human mind. All our knowledge comes from senses.[63] The Reformed tradition, following a long Christian tradition, has insisted that the idea of God is in some ways innate to human being. Reformed tradition, along with medieval theologians such as Aquinas, has always insisted that faith includes knowledge. In Aquinas, faith (or knowledge of the First Principle) is infused into the mind. The Reformed tradition is less specific about how God illumines our mind. If, as insisted by Locke, knowledge comes only through ideas formed through senses, how can we arrive at knowledge about God? God is obviously not a material object, and therefore God is not accessible through the senses of bodily organ. Is there a way we can talk about knowledge of God within a Lockean framework?

Faced with this Lockean challenge, one may abandon the concept of faith as knowledge or try to adjust the nature of doctrines to harmonize with the delivery of reason. The former is the route of mysticism and the latter is close to the path taken by Locke. Edwards is unique in emphasizing perception as a way of vindicating the unique revelation of Christianity.[64] Edwards' theory of spiritual perception asserts that spiritual realities are sensible to our soul in a similar way that the material realities are sensible to our bodily organs.

In an important note,[65] Edwards distinguishes between signs and ideas in our mind. Signs are symbolic constructions in our mind. For Edwards, the most important example of sign is the term *God*. When we

---

63. *Essay* I.2, 48–65. Locke does claim that the existence of a eternal, thinking God is the certain delivery of reason (*Essay* IV.10). The question at issue is whether we can have immediate knowledge of God, i.e. divine knowledge not mediated through our knowledge of material world.

64. Michael J. McClymond points this out in *Encounter with God*, vi–vii. His review of on the interpretation of Edwards' theory of spiritual perception as well as his exposition of Edwards' teaching (chapter 1) is quite helpful.

65. Misc. 782, *Works* 18:452–66. Also published in Perry Miller with an introduction in "Jonathan Edwards on the Sense of the Heart," *Harvard Theological Review* 41 (1948) 123–45.

read the word *God* or think about *God*, we do not actually have an idea (in a Lockean sense) of God. *God* is really a sign to represent a highest being, however we may understand that being. Edwards claims most general terms (e.g., *humanity, sanctification,* or *perplexity*) are signs. While a table in front of me can give me immediately the idea of a table, nothing in the real world can give me an immediate idea of perplexity. Edwards refers to Locke explicitly by calling such general things *mixed modes*.⁶⁶ "Very commonly we discourse about them in our minds, and argue and reason concerning them, without any idea at all of the things themselves in any degree."⁶⁷ Thus, we may write volumes on the beauty of God without actually having the idea of divine beauty in our mind. Even for things that we can actually form an idea, we often think symbolically anyway to speed up our thinking. For example, we do not usually evoke the idea of a table in our mind when we come across the word *table* in books. Only God can and does always think in ideas.⁶⁸

However, Edwards believes that there are objects that cannot be thought only in signs. "[P]ersons can't have actual ideas of mental things without having those very things in the mind."⁶⁹ To understand the statement "A triangle has three angles," one must necessarily invoke the idea of a triangle. But the mental object called *triangle* is exactly the idea of a triangle. Therefore, we cannot understand "a triangle" only symbolically. Similarly, when we think of our love to someone, "we either so frame things in our imagination that we have for moment a love to that thing or to something we make represent it, or we excite for a moment that love which we have and suppose it in another place, or we have only an idea of the antecedents concomitants and effects of love, and suppose something unseen, and govern our thoughts about [it] as we have learned how by experience and habit."⁷⁰

In other words, our thought of our love may either be a reliving of that loving affections, or just a recounting of some actions done presumably under the motive of love. In the first case, we truly have an idea of that love. In the latter case, that love is merely a presumed motive. Edwards claims that we cannot have an idea of that love unless that loving affection is actually in our mind.

66. Ibid., 454. Lock discusses mixed modes in *Essay* II.22, 288–95.
67. Ibid., 455.
68. Ibid., 455–56.
69. Ibid., 459.
70. Misc. 238, *Works* 13:353.

## The Beauty of the Triune God

Therefore, our knowledge of spiritual beings can be distinguished into mere speculation and sense of the heart.[71] Speculation is "all that understanding that is without any proper ideal apprehension or view, or all understanding of mental things of either faculty that is only by signs."[72] For example, if I had never tasted any apple before, then my knowledge of the sweetness of apple is speculation. After I have tasted one, I have sensible knowledge of its sweetness. Only sense can give us a concrete idea of an object. Edwards extends Locke by claiming that we have an inward sense for spiritual realities: "All knowledge of this sort [greatness, meanness, contemptibleness, value, etc.], as it of things that concern the heart, or the will and affections, so it all relates to the good or evil that the sensible knowledge of things of this nature involves; and nothing is called a sensible knowledge upon any other account, but on the account of the sense, or kind of inward tasting or feeling."[73]

Suppose that I tell you that the way American soldiers treat Iraqis in Abu Ghraib is disgusting. You have only a speculative knowledge of the disgust involved. Then you look at the photos and feel the disgust. Now your internal sense has a sensible knowledge of the disgust of the situation. Edwards claims that the same distinction applies to our knowledge of God. There is a difference between a speculative knowledge of the beauty of God as well as a sensible knowledge of it. In the latter case, our internal sense actually grasps the beauty of God as our eyes grasp the sight of a table.

In seeing the table, our sense is passive. We may imagine a table, but we cannot force our eyes to see a table. They can see a table only when they are presented with one. Edwards claims that the same situation applies to the spiritual realities. You cannot actually feel the disgust of Abu Ghraib unless you have encountered with the pictures or something similar. The same applies to divine things. In a sensible knowledge of divine things, we are passive recipients of divine revelation. "[T]his knowledge is above any flesh and blood can reveal." "They [the saints] believe the doctrines

---

71. Erdt, *Jonathan Edwards: Art and the Sense of the Heart*, 1–42, discusses the sense of the heart in Calvin, the Puritans, and Edwards. Erdt correctly points out that Edwards' spiritual sense builds on the Reformed and Puritan doctrine of the sweetness of the Lord, while reshaping the Puritan concept into an aesthetic quality with Lockean vocabularies. The meaning of Edwards' spiritual sense has generated substantial discussion, one of the best is Vetö, "Spiritual Knowledge according to Jonathan Edwards." We focus on the epistemology of spiritual sense and its role in the union of God and human beings.

72. Misc. 782, *Works* 13:459.

73. Ibid., 13:459.

of God's Word to be divine, because they see divinity in them, i.e., they see a divine, and transcendent, and most evidently distinguishing glory in them; such a glory, as if clearly seen, don't leave room to doubt of their being of God, and not of men."[74] Only a table can give us sensible knowledge of table, so only God can give us sensible knowledge of God. Once you see a table with your eyes, you do not need further proof that the table exists. So the glory of God is self-evident to those who have beheld it.

There is a second reason for the need for revelation. A person born blind cannot have any sensible knowledge of sight unless her eyes are healed. Similarly, "a sense of divine things with respect to spiritual good and evil, because these don't consist in any agreeableness or disagreeableness to human nature as such, or the mere human faculties or principles, therefore man, merely with the exercise of these faculties and his own natural strength, can do nothing towards getting such a sense of divine things; but it must be wholly and entirely a work of the Spirit of God, not merely as assisting and co-working with natural principles, but infusing something above nature."[75]

Like Aquinas, Edwards claims that human beings do not have the natural faculty to perceive God. Are human beings made that way or is it a result of the Fall? Edwards does not elaborate. As Edwards puts it, God must first put new principles into the human soul. It is "through the saving influences of the Spirit of God, there is a new inward perception or sensation of their minds, entirely different in its nature and kind, from anything that ever their minds were the subjects of before they were sanctified."[76]

However, this new inward perception is not a new faculty, but a new exercise of our natural faculties: "So this new spiritual sense is not a new faculty of understanding, but it is a new foundation laid in the nature of the soul, for a new kind of exercises of the same faculty of understanding. So that new holy disposition of heart that attends this new sense, is not a new faculty of will, but a foundation laid in the nature of the soul, for a new kind of exercises of the same faculty of will."[77]

Edwards does not elaborate on how a new exercise of the faculty is possible. In the case of the person born blind, a healing of the bodily organ is needed. It would seem strange to suggest that we have spiritual organs.

---

74. "A Divine and Supernatural Light," a sermon on Matt 16:17, preached 1733, in Works 17:405–25. The quotations are from 409 and 415 respectively. The sermon expounds on the difference between speculative and sensible knowledge of God.

75. Misc. 782, Works 13:463.

76. Religious Affections, Works 2:205.

77. Ibid., 206

How does the soul acquire new exercise? How many different kinds of exercises can the soul possibly have? How do we experimentally differentiate between a new exercise and an old exercise of the soul in a new way? Edwards does not answer these questions. However, the purpose of stressing a new kind of exercise is clear. He wants to deny the claim of the enthusiasts that ecstatic visions are bona fide evidence of regeneration. Those visions may be (or may not be) pure human imaginations.[78] Imaginations can be fabricated, but new spiritual sense cannot be fabricated. In theory the distinction is clear; in practice, it is difficult to differentiate. Since we are not studying Edwards' religious psychology, we shall not go further into these issues.

We return to the questions that we raise at the beginning of the section: how can we defend Christian revelation in a Lockean framework? The answer by Edwards is both simple and controversial: divine realities are presented to the soul through the spiritual sense the same way as a table is presented to the soul through visual sense. Since the latter kind of apprehension is self-evident knowledge, Edwards claims that the first kind of apprehension is self-evident knowledge too. It need not be justified by rational arguments.[79] Perhaps it cannot even be fully justified rationally. However, for those who have seen the glory of God, rational justification is superfluous. For those who have not seen the glory of God, no rational arguments can produce the sensible knowledge of God.

## *Sensing as Deification*

We are finally ready to bring in our major theme—beauty. For Edwards, God presents divine beauty to our soul through our spiritual sense.[80] Why does God present divine beauty? First, our souls are inevitably drawn to the greatest beauty, and God wants to draw our souls to Himself. Second, God is beauty itself. We shall return to the second theme in the next chapter. Here we want to know how human soul can participate in divine beauty. Earlier on, we have seen that Edwards distinguishes the knowledge of table from the knowledge of our affections. While our knowledge of the table is not the table itself, Edwards claims that genuine (as contrasted

---

78. Ibid., 210–13.

79. The fifth sign of genuine gracious affections in *Religious Affections* is the certainty of conviction. *Works* 2:291–311.

80. The third sign of genuine gracious affections is that they are founded on the moral excellency of divine things, as distinguished from natural excellency such as aesity. *Works* 2:253–66.

*Metaphysics of Beauty*

with symbolic) knowledge of affections consists of reliving those affections. In other words, our knowledge of the affections is exactly those affections themselves. Similarly, to truly know God is to have the love of divine excellency in our mind. We do not merely know the excellency in signs or speculatively, but we actually have that love dwelling in our soul.

The next step is to claim that loving affection towards God is the essence of the Holy Spirit. This affection is not just a product of the Holy Spirit, but it is the Holy Spirit: "Holiness is the nature of the Spirit of God, therefore he is called in Scripture the Holy Ghost. Holiness, which is as it were the beauty and sweetness of the divine nature, is as much the proper nature of the Holy Spirit, as heat is the nature of fire."[81]

Since the saints have holy affections, they literally have the Holy Spirit within their souls and partake in divine beauty: "The Spirit of God so dwells in the hearts of the saints, that he there, as a seed or spring of life, exerts and communicates himself, in this his sweet and divine nature, making the soul a partaker of God's beauty and Christ's joy, so that the saint has truly fellowship with the Father, and with his Son Jesus Christ, in thus having the communion or participation of the Holy Ghost."[82]

The Holy Spirit is holy affections. In imparting holy affections to our soul, the Spirit communicates himself and therefore we are made "partakers of divine nature."[83] We are not made into God. The Holy Spirit is God's affection for himself, and our affection remains our affections. However, if our affections are truly holy affections, then it must be by participation in the nature of the Holy Spirit.

Beside the nature of the Holy Spirit, Edwards also makes a crucial assumption about the nature of personhood. The assumption is an extension of his concept of solidity. For Edwards, the material world is essentially a set of interacting laws sustained by God. By analogy, the person is only the aggregation of the operations of the soul. At one point of his thinking, the young Edwards claims that the following: "Well might Mr. Locke say that identity of person consisted in identity of consciousness; for he might have said that identity of spirit, too, consisted in the same consciousness. A mind or spirit is nothing else but consciousness, and what is included in it. The same consciousness is to all intents and purposes the very same

---

81. *Religious Affections*, Works 2:201.
82. Ibid., 2:202.
83. 2 Pet. 1:4, quoted in ibid., 203.

spirit of substance, as much as the same particle of matter can be the same with itself at different times."[84]

If a person is "nothing else but consciousness, and what is included in it," then there is no deep ego underlying the operations of the mind. The operations taken together are the essence of a person. However, further reflections lead to his retraction of such a bold assertion. In a note in the same series written after the above notes, Edwards assert that "identity of person is what seems never yet to have been explained."[85] Edwards goes on to muse two hypothetical questions. If God annihilates me, and then God recreate another individual with identical set of memories and other mental operations, is that person the same as I? Suppose also that after my annihilation, God creates two people in different parts of the universe with identical memory as mine when I was annihilated. Should we say that now there are two I's living two separate lives? The young Edwards concludes by saying that the essence of identity or personhood cannot be answered.

On the other hand, the mature Edwards believes that "there is no such thing as any identity or oneness in created objects, existing at different times, but what depends on *God's sovereign constitution*."[86] If God constitutes a set of mental acts (memories, affections, etc.) as forming the same person, then that set of mental acts has the identity of one person. If God puts holy affections into the set of mental acts that God sovereignly constitutes as Kin, then those affections become part of the essence of me. I do not have divine beauty accidentally; divine beauty is an integral part of me.

Edwards' definition of personal identity can lead to bizarre consequences. Can God arbitrarily constitute my conscience and Britney Spears' conscience into one person? Even if the fundamental reason for identity is God's sovereign will, how do we discern for ourselves what God has constituted as one person? Edwards provides no answer to these questions.

---

84. "Mind" 11, *Works* 6:342. The reference is probably to *Essay* II.27.9–29, 335–48. Locke says, "For as far as any intelligent Being can repeat the *Idea* of any past Action with the same consciousness it had of it at first, and with the same consciousness it has of any present Action; so far it is the same *personal self*." (ibid., 336) Note the importance of memory in Locke's definition of personhood.

85. "Mind" 72, *Works* 6:385

86. *Original Sin, Works* 3, Part IV, chapter 2, 404. In his chapter, Edwards argues that Adam and all his descendants are constituted by God to be one moral person. Therefore we are all guilty of Adam's sin. To back up his argument, Edwards claims that all identities (e.g., the same atom, the same person) among creatures are arbitrary established by the laws of God.

However, we do not need to resolve these questions. Whatever a complete definition might be, it will include affections as part of the essence of personhood.[87] According to Edwards, "the word 'spirit,' most commonly in Scripture, is put for affections of the mind."[88] The spirit of a person means the affections of the mind. Therefore, when a person acquires loving affections towards God, these affections are part of her essence. Since her essence has changed, we can also say that she has a new human nature. In her new nature, she participates in the divine nature.

For Edwards, loving affections toward God are essentially part of divine nature. "The Holy Spirit is the act of God between the Father and the Son infinitely loving and delighting in each other."[89] In other words, the act of loving and delighting in the Father and the Son is the Holy Spirit. When Edwards claims in *Religious Affections* that the Holy Spirit indwells in all saints, he is not talking metaphorically. Since true love for God is by essence the Holy Spirit, saints are literally partakers of divine essence.

We can illustrate the perspective of Edwards by comparing it to our loving affections for apple. How does the love for apples become part of us? The process begins with our eating apples. By divine establishment, when the apples touch our tongues, they create a sweet favor in our soul. Then the sweet sense generates the loving affections towards it. In the case of our affections towards God, we have no natural sense that can let us taste divine beauty. Therefore, for the saints, God directly generates the loving affections to God in our soul. But then affections are not a "thing" that you can put into someone's soul. The notion of affections may be understood abstractly. However, there are no affections without their being the affections of somebody specifically. Affections are part of the essence of a person. In particular, loving affections toward God is part of the ontological essence of God. When God implants loving affections toward God in our soul, God is implanting God's own love towards the God-self. That love is the Holy Spirit.

We shall now summarize the main theme of this section: spiritual beauty is the ontological bridge between God and human beings. We have indicated that the Enlightenment worldview challenges the medieval

---

87. "And if we come even to the *personal identity* of created intelligent beings, though this be not allowed to consist wholly in that which Mr. Locke places it in, i.e., *same consciousness*; yet I think it can't be denied, that this is one thing essential to it." *Original Sin* IV.3, *Works* 3:398. For further discussion, see Helm, "A Forensic Dilemma."

88. Misc. 146, *Works* 13:299.

89. Misc. 94, *Works* 13:260.

doctrine of illumination and divine participation. By formulating an idealistic understanding of personhood in which affections stand in the center both human and divine persons, Edwards reinterprets the traditional doctrines with Lockean vocabularies. He reaffirms their credibility. Illumination is an extension of external sense to a spiritual sense, and divine participation is the implanting of divine affections into our soul. We have seen that loving affection between spiritual beings is, by definition, spiritual beauty. We partake the divine nature when we hold the divine beauty and acquire the same beauty in our soul.

As a footnote, we examine the metaphysical relation between God and human beings in Edwards. This is a perennial question for medieval mysticism. If the human person can truly participate in the divine person, does it mean that humanity and God really share the same essence? In a remarkable note, Edwards claims exactly this point: "Many have wrong conceptions of the difference between the nature of the Deity and created spirits. The difference is no contrariety, but what naturally results from his greatness and nothing else, such as created spirits come nearer to, or more imitate, the greater they are in their powers and faculties. So that if we should suppose the faculties of a created spirit to be enlarged infinitely, there would be the Deity to all intents and purposes, the same simplicity, immutability, etc."[90]

Behind this cryptic remark, Edwards seems to assume that affections and knowledge ("their powers and faculties") are the essence of spirits. Since both human beings and God are spiritual beings, their affections and knowledge differ only in quantity, not in kinds. The gap between God and all other creatures is the infinity of God.[91] The differences between God and the spirit of human beings are that God has perfect knowledge and infinite affections.

On the other hand, Edwards suggests that there is a radical break between God and human beings. That break is the aseity of God. All creatures have only dependent identity. Only God has "that absolute independent identity of the First Being, whereby 'he is the same yesterday, today, and forever.'"[92] The existence of all creatures are purely contingent. Only God has existence and identity in the God-self. "Therefore the existence of created substances, in each successive moment, must be the effect of the

---

90. Misc. 135, *Works* 13:295.

91. In this aspect, Edwards is similar to Dun Scotus. For Aquinas, simplicity is the dividing line between God and creatures.

92. *Original Sin*, *Works* 2:400.

*immediate* agency, will, and power of God."[93] Therefore God and creatures are radically different in that only God has existence within himself. All creatures are merely expression of the power of God.

How do we reconcile the two conflicting views? One is to say that the continuity is a product of the young and speculative Edwards. "Miscellanies" No. 135, our quotation above, was written in 1724, along with earlier entries of the "Mind."[94] Those early writings are full of philosophical speculations. Perhaps by the time Edwards wrote *Original Sin* in the 1750s, he had learnt to trim his speculations and emphasized the transcendence of God for apologetic purpose. The problem with this solution is that the *Religious Affections* was written in the mid-1740s, and the book represents the view of the mature Edwards. As we have seen, in that work Edwards is emphatic that we truly partake the divine nature. Edwards is probably unaware of the contradiction in his view. On the one hand, within the metaphysics of beauty, he believes that God and human beings share the same spiritual beauty. Since spiritual beauty (a kind of affection) is part of the essence of spiritual beings, Edwards is logically led to great continuity between God and human beings. On the other hand, Edwards believes in the complete sovereignty of God. That implies that only God is ultimate, and human beings cannot share the same ultimate nature of God. Perhaps Edwards can claim that aseity is actually a consequence of God's infinity. Just as the infinity mass of a black hole leads to the annihilation of matter, so the infinite scale of being in God makes God a self-generating being. Though Edwards has much to say about the beauty of God, he offers little for a metaphysical theory of the aseity of God. We shall not try to resolve what is left unresolved by Edwards.

On the other hand, Edwards devotes considerable effort in expounding the relationship between divine beauty and the Holy Spirit. This will be the topic of our next chapter.

---

93. Ibid., 401.
94. Schafer's introduction, *Works* 13:95.

# 4

# The Beautiful God

"God is God, and distinguished from all other beings, and exalted above 'em, chiefly by his divine beauty, which is infinitely diverse from all other beauty."[1] For Edwards, God is *beauty itself*—the archetype and source of all beauty. Our purpose in this chapter is to explicate the beauty of God according to Edwards. God is beautiful both in himself and as the redeemer of the world. In this chapter, we shall address the first kind of beauty. In this and the following chapters, doctrinal concern will be more prominent than the previous chapters. Consequently, we shall pay more attention to the doctrinal background of Edwards' thinking.

For Edwards, God is beautiful only because God is triune. Strictly speaking, beauty is not as attribute of the undivided divine essence. Divine beauty is a moral perfection of God, which is embodied in the triune life of God.[2] Edwards is not eager to develop a complete theory about divine essence. However, the essence of God is what makes God's beauty "infinitely diverse from all other beauty." In Edwards' thought, the triune life of God is the bridge between God and humanity, while the essence of God makes clear the infinite gap between God and humanity. Before going into the Trinity, we shall say a few words about Edwards' thinking on the divine essence.

---

1. *Religious Affections* 2.5, *Works* 2:298.
2. Therefore, it is somewhat misleading to say that "there are three stages or moments in our knowledge of God, . . . the knowledge of God's natural perfections, the knowledge of His moral perfections, and finally the knowledge of His beauty" (Delattre, *Beauty and Sensibility*, 133). Delattre suggests that first we can know that God is holy, and then we can know the beauty of God's holiness. For Edwards, if we have a sensible knowledge of God's holiness (as opposed to a notional knowledge of it), we necessarily know also the beauty of this holiness.

## Divine Essence

For Edwards, "God is a necessary being, as it is impossible but that God should exist, because there is no other way."[3] In his early philosophical speculations, Edwards claims that the statement "nothing exists" is absolutely meaningless: "The mind can never, let it stretch its conceptions ever so much, bring itself conceive of a state of perfect nothing. It puts the mind into mere convulsion and confusion to endeavor to think of such a state, and it contradicts the very nature of the soul to think that it should be."[4] From the necessity that something must exist, he argues that there exists a necessary being.[5] This necessary being guarantees that absolute nothingness is an impossibility. It encompasses all possibilities of existence.[6] God is, of course, the name for this necessary being.

We can challenge Edwards on the coherence of his theistic proof on a number of issues. Is it coherent to talk about the ground of existence as a being similar and yet in contrast to all other beings?[7] Is this necessary

---

3. *Misc.* 587, *Works* 18:122

4. *On Being*, *Works* 6:202. Flower and Murphey, *Philosophy in America*, 151, are wrong to challenge Edwards on the premise that he misunderstands the semantic content of the statement "nothing exists." Edwards does not claim that the statement "nothing exists" is self-contradictory. He does not mistakenly assume "nothing" is a subject that we can predicate attributes such as existence. His point is that the concept "absolute nothingness" is inconceivable in our mind. To use modern modal vocabulary, Edwards claim that "There is nothing at all" is not a possible world because it is not conceivable.

5. Edwards muddies the water considerably by claiming that "space is this necessary, eternal, infinite and omnipresent being. . . . I have already said as much as that space is God" (6:203). Yet Edwards goes on to clarify that "all the space there is not proper to body, all the space there is without the bounds of the creation, all the space there was before the creation, is God himself." So the space that Edwards refers to here is not merely the physical space of the universe, but some kind of "space of existence." Edwards is adopting here the concept of absolute space of Henry More. See Reid, "Jonathan Edwards on Space and God," 385–403, for details. Reid argues that later on Edwards reversed course and rejected the concept of absolute space. However, he maintained throughout his life that all reality is contained in God.

6. Edwards' concept of necessary being is different from the contemporary of necessary being as expressed in, for example, Plantinga, *Nature of Necessity*, chapter 10. For Edwards, God is necessary not only in the sense of existing in every possible worlds, but God is necessary in the sense of being the ground for the possibility of having any worlds at all. Edwards' argument is closer to the Third Way of Aquinas' Five Ways (*Summa Theologica*, I.2.3) than modern modal arguments of God. Aquinas argues from the contingency of all beings in the world to the existence of a necessary being undergirding the existence of our world.

7. Paul Tillich has raised this point prominently among theologians. See his

being just a pantheistic God, like substance in the thought of Spinoza?[8] How do we know that this ground has a mind and a will? Edwards does not attempt to demonstrate that this necessary being has the usual attributes associated with God; he merely assumes it.[9] We shall not pursue these issues further. For Edwards, these difficulties are more symptoms of our finite intelligence rather than the inherent intelligibility of the concept of necessary being: "'Tis from the exceeding imperfect notions that we have of the nature or essence of God, and because we can't think of it but we must think of it far otherwise than it is, that arises the difficulty in our mind of conceiving of God's existence without a cause."[10]

The crucial idea here is that God contains the possibility (or space) of the existence of all beings. All other beings derive their existence from God. In this sense, God includes the being of everything else. Therefore, all beauty is included within God. "Existence or entity is that into which all excellency is to be resolved."[11] Edwards is not claiming that beauty and existence are materially the same.[12] As we have shown before, beauty is most basically agreement. Nothing cannot agree with anything else. Only something existing can agree with other beings. In this sense, "being and existence is what is necessarily agreeable to being."[13] The greater the scale of being, the greater is the potentiality for agreement: "Therefore, not only may greatness be considered as a capacity of excellency, but a being, by reason of his greatness, considered alone, is the more excellent because he partakes more of being; though if he be great, if he dissents from more

---

*Systematic Theology*, 1:235–41. In contrast to Tillich, Edwards wants to emphasize the ontological continuity between the ground of being and human beings. For Edwards, God is a spiritual being similar in structure to the human mind.

8. On the Spinozian concept of God, see Donagan, "Spinoza's Theology," 343–82. Both Spinoza and Edwards try to reformulate the concept of God to incorporate Cartesian concept of nature. It is significant that both identify the essence of God as space. Though, as we have indicated in footnote 5, we should not simply identify space in Edwards as physical space.

9. Edwards does believe that God's infinity implies God's omnipresence, omniscience and immutability. Yet he also confesses that such concepts are full of logical difficulties. We cannot be sure of the attributes of God apart from divine revelation. (*Misc.* 1340, *Works* 23:371–72.) On this issue, he is closer to the Reformed schoolmen than to the medieval schoolmen. The Reformed schoolmen usually do not try to deduce divine attributes from theistic proofs.

10. *Misc.* 650

11. *The Mind* 62, 6:381.

12. By contrast, Aquinas argues the being and goodness are materially the same in *Summa Theologica* I.5.1.

13. *The Mind* 62, 6:381.

general and extensive being, or from universal being, he is the more odious for his greatness, because the dissent or contradiction to being in general is so much the greater."[14]

Only beings can be beautiful; non-beings have no capacity for beauty. Since God is the ground of all existence, God is also the ground of beauty. All beauty is a participation in divine beauty firstly because a being can be beautiful only when God calls it into existence. However, existence itself does not produce beauty. A being must also assent to universal being before it can be truly beautiful.[15]

For Edwards, universal being is another name for God.[16] This brings us to the second essential divine attribute—infinity. Divine beauty is the prototype of all other beauty because God is infinite. God is infinite in the sense that its existence includes the existence of everything else: "The unity of Godhead will necessarily follow from God's being infinite: for to be infinite is to be all, and it would be a contradiction to suppose two ALLS, because if there be two or more, one alone is not all but the sum of the put together are all."[17]

Infinity is the natural corollary to God's necessity, as understood by Edwards. Since all beings are dependent on God for their existence, nothing can exist outside God. Outside of God is only nothing or nowhere. So God must be everywhere, or infinite.[18] God is simply being in general. Since God is everywhere, Edwards deduces that there cannot be more than one God.

14. Ibid., 6:381.

15. Some of Delattre's remarks on the relation between being and beauty are confusing and misleading. For example, he says, "The beauty of any being designates its ontological weight, its distance from nonbeing or 'nothing.'" (*Beauty and Sensibility*, 45). Edwards states explicitly that ontological weight only gives a greater potential to beauty. Delattre also says that "beauty is an abiding principle of being, tending not only to sustain itself in being but also to nourish and enrich the universal system of being by bestowing being and beauty." (Ibid., 108). Delattre seems to give a self-generation power to beauty, similar to the effulgence of being in Neoplatonism. For Edwards, it is God alone who brings beings into existence out of freedom. Beauty is not a creative principle by itself.

16. Does this make Edwards pantheistic, or panentheistic? This is Charles Hodge's accusation against Edwards. See Gerstner, *Rational Biblical Theology* 2:10–15. Gerstner is correct in stressing that Edwards' eschatology is incompatible with panentheism. As we shall see, his eschatology emphasizes divine freedom in relation to human beings. Unlike panentheism, existence does not imply participation in divine life. "We may say that he is a Calvin with a metaphysical mind." (2:15)

17. *Misc. 697, Works* 18:281.

18. *On Being, Works* 6:202.

As we have discussed before, Edwards differentiates between particular and general beauty. General beauty is "that by which a thing appears beautiful when viewed most perfectly, comprehensively and universally, with regard to all its tendencies, and its connections with everything it stands related to."[19] We have also shown that beauty for spiritual beings is love. Therefore the most general beauty for spiritual beings is love for being in general. Since God is being in general, the love for God is the highest beauty for a spiritual being. In loving God, a spiritual being also loves everything. There cannot be a greater love. For medieval schoolmen such as Duns Scotus, the infinity of God is the heart of a metaphysical theory of divine essence. For Edwards, the primary importance of the infinity of God is its implication for moral or spiritual beauty.

A modern reader may raise this question: can there be really a love for being in general? Does not love require a definite object? Is God, as being in general, really an object that we can love? In a way, Edwards would readily agree with such an objection. As we have seen, Edwards insists that divine love is supernatural. We cannot grasp or love God by our natural ability. True virtue is both our necessary duty and our morally impossible duty.[20] Edwards is not troubled by this seeming inconsistency, and we shall not enter the debate on whether Edwards has provided a cogent concept of true virtue.

Edwards believes that we can love God truly only when God put this love in our soul. Only God can grasp God as an object, and only God can have divine love naturally. God understands and loves himself, and these acts of understanding and loving form the Trinity. We shall now turn to the doctrine of the Trinity of Edwards.

## The Triune God

### Background

In an often quoted phrase, Edwards asserts that "One alone, without any reference to any more, cannot be excellent; for in such a case there can be no manner of relation no way [*sic.*], and therefore, no such thing as consent."[21] Therefore, to truly appreciate the beauty of God is to participate in the triune life of God.

---

19. *Nature of True Virtue* ch. 1, *Works* 8:540.
20. See the correspondence between Gillespie and Edwards in *Works*, 2:470–513.
21. *The Mind* 1, 6:337.

Pauw[22] has given us the most detail published work on Edwards' doctrine of Trinity. Her main thesis is that Edwards' Trinitarian theology is an ambidextrous theology. According to Pauw, Edwards employs both the social model of Trinity and the psychological model of Trinity. "Edwards appeared unconcerned to render a coherent biblical portrait of God or Christ."[23] Pauw believes that Edwards is to be recommended for leaving the two models in mutual contradistinction. "There is really no alternative to Edwards's multi-lingual approach."[24]

Though Pauw believes both models are equally important in Edwards' theology, she believes that Edwards advances beyond his Reformed heritage mainly in his social model.[25] Pauw thinks that the Reformed schoolmen[26] have let the doctrine of simplicity control their Trinitarian theology. Since simplicity implies unity, the Trinitarian images of God are hampered and left undeveloped in Reformed scholasticism. Edwards, while not rejecting the doctrine of simplicity outright, put little importance on the doctrine. In fact, he is somewhat critical of the doctrine.[27] Therefore, he is able to develop a relational ontology in which God's beauty is defined in terms of relationships. In Edwards, divine excellency is exemplified not by unity, but by diversity. This allows the more profound social image of the Trinity. The editor of Edwards' *Discourse on the Trinity*, Lee, adopts Pauw's thesis.[28]

Pauw thesis is severely criticized by Studebaker.[29] First, Studebaker questions whether it is appropriate to contrast a Western oneness model of God with an Eastern threeness model. Modern theologians, including Pauw, tend to associate the psychological model with Augustine and the social model with the Cappadocian Fathers. They assert that the Augustinian model begins with and accentuates the unity of God, while the Cappadocian model begins with and accentuates the threeness of God. Studebaker questions the historical reliability of such a paradigm. He as-

22. Pauw, *The Supreme Harmony*.
23. Ibid., 184; see also her summary on pp. 50–55.
24. Ibid., 190.
25. See chapter 2, "A Redefinition of Divine Excellency" in ibid., 57–90. In a reply to a book review of her *Supreme Harmony* by Studebaker, Pauw retracts partially her claims.
26. Peter van Mastricht and Francis Turretin are the most cited examples in Pauw, *Supreme Harmony*.
27. Ibid., 72.
28. Sang Hyun Lee, "Editor's Introduction," *Works* 21:22–27.
29. Studebaker, *Social Augustinian Trinitarianism*. See especially chapter 2.

serts that the main concern of Augustine is the unity of operations rather than unity of essence. His concern is actually similar to that of the Cappadocian Fathers.[30] In particular, the analogy of three human persons is regarded by Gregory of Nyssa as a distortion of orthodox doctrine.[31] It is not clear in what sense the Cappadocian conception of the Trinity is more social than the Augustinian conception. While Pauw cites the formula of the Fourth Lateran Council as an example of the triumph of the oneness of God over the threeness of God, Studebaker points out that the same formula also contains explicit reference to the threeness of God.[32] It is beyond our concern to assess the history of the doctrine of Trinity. We share Studebaker's concern that the oneness-threeness paradigm is too often adopted uncritically.[33]

Like Pauw, we shall examine how Edwards develops the traditions that he grew up with. We shall give a brief survey of the doctrine of Trinity in Reformed scholasticism. Edwards is both faithful to the framework of scholastic theology that nurtured him, and creative in the way he develops this framework.

We begin with a correction to Pauw's reading of Reformed scholasticism. She claims that the importance of the doctrine of simplicity inhibits the development of a social image of the Trinity.[34] She also claims that, since Edwards explicitly claims that there is a triplicity in God,[35] he contradicts Turretin's claim that triplicity is opposed to the simplicity of God.[36] If we read the passage referred to by Pauw in its totality, we shall find that there is no contradiction after all: "Simplicity and triplicity are so mutually opposed that they cannot subsist at the same time (but not simplicity and Trinity because they are said in different respects): simplicity in respect to

---

30. Ibid., 91–99.

31. *On "Not Three Gods,"* 649–53.

32. Studebaker, *Social Augustinian Trinitarianism*, 97–98. Pauw, *Supreme Harmony*, 26.

33. Studebaker, *Social Augustinian Trinitarianism*, 83–87, gives a succinct summary of theology of modern social trinitarian theologians.

34. Pauw, *Supreme Harmony*, 66–68.

35. *Misc.* 94, *Works* 13:262.

36. Pauw, *Supreme Harmony*, 69–70. Studebaker does a similar re-examination in *Social Augustinian Trinitarianism*, 103–5. Our discussion differs from him in emphasizing the doctrine of simplicity is actually regarded by Reformed scholasticism as a defence of the doctrine of Trinity.

essence, but Trinity in respect to persons. In this sense, nothing hinders God (who is one in essence) from being three persons."[37]

In Turretin, triplicity refers to either three gods or three parts of Gods. In Edwards, triplicity refers to three persons in God. Turretin explicitly states that the simplicity of God is consistent with the doctrine of Trinity. Simplicity is an attribute of God's essence, while the Trinity is about God's mode of existence. In fact, Turretin claims that the Socinians deny the doctrine of simplicity in order to discredit the doctrine of Trinity.[38] Since the doctrine of simplicity asserts that there are no accidents in God, it follows that the relations between the Father, Son and Holy Spirit are no mere accidents. The Trinitarian relations together constitute the divine essence. The Trinity is not a matter of the number of Gods, because quantity cannot be part of the essence of a being. (For example, the number of people on earth plays no role in defining the essence of a human person.) The Trinity is about the essence, not the number of God.[39] Richard A. Muller summarizes the relationship between the doctrine of simplicity and Trinity in Reformed scholasticism as following: "In short, the plurality of persons in God does not contravene the divine simplicity, but can even be said to imply it. As far as the seventeenth-century orthodox are concerned, moreover, the doctrine of divine simplicity is a corollary and support of the doctrine of the Trinity: in the polemics of the day, in fact, the Vorstian and Socinian denials of simplicity were directly connected with the affirmation of an alternative, seemingly tritheistic view in Vorstius' case and with an overt antitrinitarianism in case of the Socinians."[40]

Pauw is correct to point out that neither Reformed scholasticism nor the Puritans develop a social conception of the Trinity. However, it is dubious to claim that the reason is the doctrine of simplicity. The social model is not considered and rejected for theological reasons; it is neglected because it serves no useful functions in the Reformed tradition. Edwards does have some problems with the scholastic doctrine of simplicity,[41] but this is not related to his desire to develop a social model of Trinity.

In general, Reformed scholasticism is rather circumspect in using any model to describe the immanent Trinity. Neither the Augustinian model

---

37. Turretin, *Institutes* III.7.9 (Third topic, Question 7, section 9), vol. 1:193.

38. Ibid. III.7.1, 1:191.

39. Turretin does not formulate the connection between simplicity and the divine persons. The classic statement of this viewpoint is Aquinas, *Summa Theologica* I.28.2.

40. Muller, *Divine Essence*, 282.

41. Studebaker, *Social Augustinian Trinitarianism*, 108–13.

nor the social model plays a significant role in the Reformed scholastic doctrine of Trinity. Reformed scholasticism does use different analogies (the sun and its rays is one of the most popular) to illustrate the Trinity. However, they are merely heuristic device, not to be raised to the level of doctrinal statement: "The orthodox, thus, feel that dogmatic discussion of the Trinity is mandated by revelation even though the doctrine be an impenetrable mystery and that, further, the revelation, insofar as it can be understood, must be illustrated or explicated with the tools of reason. The illustrations, however, cannot be considered any more than very limited aids to understanding: here the epistemological side of the Reformed *non capax* comes to the fore."[42]

We may take Turretin's discussion of the Trinity as typical of the teachings received by Edwards.[43] Turretin begins with clarification of terms such as essence, person, homoousia and emperichoresis.[44] The main concern for Turretin is to claim, against the Socinians and Remonstrants, that the Trinity is a fundamental doctrine necessary for salvation.[45] Then Turretin defines the doctrine of Trinity as followings: "In the one only and most simple essence of God there are three distinct persons so distinguished from each other by incommunicable properties or modes of subsisting that one cannot be the other although by an inexpressible circuminsession (*emperichōrēsin*) they always remain and exist in each other mutually."[46]

Turretin deliberately uses traditional and abstract vocabularies so that the mystery of the Trinity remains a mystery with his definition. He claims that various similitudes from the human soul or the sun are only

---

42. Muller, *The Trinity of God*, 153. See 157–67 for the reservations in Reformed scholasticism to the idea of *vestigia trinitatis* in creation.

43. On the divinity textbooks used by Puritans in the seventeenth and early eighteenth century, see Miller, *Seventeenth Century*, 96–97. Ames, Wollebius and Mastricht were all popular during this period. Edwards mentioned Turretin four times in his letters to Joseph Bellamy. In one, he recommended Turretin and particularly Mastricht to Bellamy as excellent textbook on divinity (No. 73, *Works* 16:217). In another, he sent the books of Mastricht and Turretin to Bellamy (No. 76 16:223). In the other two, he asked Bellamy to bring Turretin's book back to him so that he could consult it (No. 91, 16:266; No. 224, 16:701). Edwards also refers to Turretin in his private musings on soteriological issues (*Misc.* 292, 13:384; *Misc.* 706, 18:327). Both Mastricht and Turretin would be excellent guide to doctrinal teachings received by Edwards. We choose Turretin because it is easily accessible to modern readers.

44. Turretin, *Intitutes* III.23.1–30, 1:253–60.

45. Ibid. III.24.1–11, 1:261–65.

46. Ibid. III.25.1, 1:265.

## The Beautiful God

obscure analogies.[47] While Turretin cites copious Scripture verses to substantiate the doctrine of the Trinity,[48] he refuses to suggest any rational ground for believing the Trinity. While he does employ the traditional vocabulary of generation and procession, he emphasizes that any model cannot explain those terms:

> That this procession differs from the generation of Son cannot be denied because they are different persons who stand related to each other in origin. But the nature of this distinction cannot be explained and may more safely be unknown than inquired into.... I know that the Scholastics wish to derive this difference from the operation of the intellect (*modum intellectus*)—hence he is called the Wisdom of God; but procession by way of the will (*modum voluntatis*)—hence he is called Love and Charity. But as this is unsupported by Scripture, so it entangles rather than explains the thing.[49]

What does it mean to say that the Father, Son, and Spirit are different persons? What is a person? Turretin explains: "Thus the person may be said to differ from the essence not really (*realiter*), i.e., essentially (*essentialiter*) as thing and thing, but modally (*modaliter*) as a mode from the thing (*modus a re*)."[50]

In other words, the three persons of the Trinity are three modes of subsisting of the one divine essence. But what are modes? Could there have been four modes of subsisting in God? Turretin does not provide further answers. He emphasizes that the differences between the modes of subsisting are real and positive, but it cannot be explained.[51] The major concern of Turretin is that we should reject both Sabellianism and Tritheism.[52] Turretin is wary of using any model to explain the Trinity. He is contented to repeat the orthodox formula of "one essence in three persons."

---

47. Ibid. III.25.4, 1:266.

48. Ibid. III.25.7–13, 1:267–70; III.26.4–11, 1:273–77;

49. Ibid. III.31.3, 1:309. We can cite John Owen as another example of agnosticism concerning the meaning of procession. Owen, a Puritan divine familiar to Edwards, writes a two-volume tome on the person and wok of the Holy Spirit. Yet he claims that the manner of immanent procession is incomprehensible to saints on earth (*PNEUMATOLOGIA*, 156, pages number according to *Ultimate Christian Library* [DVD].) Edwards cites Owen's *Discourse on Holy Spirit* in *Misc.* 1047 to support the notion that the Holy Spirit is the love and the blessedness of God.

50. Ibid. III.27.3, 1:278.

51. Ibid. III.27.14–15, 1:280.

52. Ibid. III.27.9, 1:279.

There are Reformed schoolmen who adopt the Augustinian model of Trinity. William Ames, for example, claims that "the Father is, as it were, *Deus intelligens*, God understanding; the Son who is the express image of the Father is *Deus intellectus*, God understood; and the Holy Spirit, flowing and breathed from the Father through the Son, is *Deus dilectus*."[53] However, Ames does not develop this analogy into a theology of the inter-Trinitarian life or a model of our spirituality. As a minority, Keckermann and Ainsworth use the Augustinian model to defend the reasonableness of the Trinity.[54] The majority of the Reformed schoolmen rejects philosophical defense of the doctrine of Trinity.[55]

## *The Psychological Model*

We have examined the theological background to Edwards' doctrine of Trinity. It is time to turn to Edwards. We shall not examine all aspects of his doctrine.[56] Our focus is the relationship between the Trinity and beauty. Compared with Reformed scholasticism or the Puritan tradition, Edwards is very bold in developing a speculative theology of the Trinity. His breakthrough with the Puritan tradition is not in the development of a social model of Trinity. His breakthrough is in using a philosophical model to explain the immanent Trinity. Moreover, the inter-Trinitarian dynamics becomes the archetype for the spiritual life of the saints. The beauty of the Trinity also binds God and humanity together.

The young Edwards asserts that "it is within the reach of naked reason to perceive certainly that there are three distinct in God, each of which is the same [God], three that must be distinct."[57] For Edwards, the psychological model of Trinity is not merely illustrative; it is demonstrative of the

---

53. *Marrow of Theology*, 89.

54. Muller, *Trinity of God*, 163,

55. Ibid., 167.

56. Studebaker has given a detail exposition in *Social Augustinian Trinitarianism*, 186–245.

57. Misc. 94, *Works* 13:257. According to the chronology of Schafer (*Works* 13:94), Edwards was merely twenty years old when he penned this note. According to Schafer again (13:256, fn. 2), there was a fierce debate on the doctrine of Trinity at that time among Samuel Clarke, Isaac Watts and others. All the parties were eager to avoid what were regarded as speculations. Against this background, the rationalism of Edwards is even more remarkable. Edwards developed his thoughts on the immanent Trinity most carefully in *Discourse on the Trinity* (*Works* 21:109–44), written in early 1730s. Since this does not reflect significant departure from *Misc.* 94, we shall integrate *Misc.* 94 and the *Discourse* in our discussion.

reasonableness of the Trinity. In order to illustrate the logic of Edwards in explaining the generation of the Son, we shall quote Edwards at length:

> The Almighty's knowledge is not so different from ours, but that ours is the image of [it]. It is by an idea, as ours is, only his [is] infinitely perfect. If it were not by idea, it is in no respect like ours; 'tis not what we call knowledge, nor anything whereof knowledge is the resemblance; for the whole of human knowledge, both in the beginning and end of it, consists in ideas. . . . But yet it would suppose imperfection in God, to suppose that God's idea of himself is anything different from himself. . . . The immediate object of the mind's intuition is the idea always, and the soul receives nothing but ideas; but God's intuition of himself, without doubt, is immediate. But 'tis certain it cannot be, except his idea be his essence, for his idea is the immediate object of his intuition. An absolutely perfect idea of a thing is the very thing, for it wants nothing that is in the thing, substance nor nothings else.[58]

Edwards begins by asserting that God's way of knowing must be similar to ours. Our mind operates spiritually, and Edwards assumes that spiritual operations in human beings and in God do not differ qualitatively. Since human beings know an object through ideas, Edwards believes that God knows in a similar way too. The difference is not in the way of knowing, but in the clarity of the ideas. God perceives all ideas in its full clarity, while human beings often have only opaque ideas. In particular, our ideas of other spiritual beings are always mediated. I do not know immediately what you are thinking. I can only know your thinking through your speech. You describe your thinking with words, and I reconstruct your thinking in my mind through interpreting your words. For God, he knows your thinking immediately. God can literally think your thoughts while you are thinking about them. God also knows his own thought completely, and his thoughts know God completely. The idea of a table is not the same as a table, because a table is not a spiritual object. The ideas that belong to a spiritual being are the essence of those spiritual beings. In other words, a spiritual being is simply its thoughts and affections. For human beings, we do not fully understand even our own thoughts, nor are we fully aware of all our own affections. We can know ourselves through imperfect self-reflection. By contrast, God's knowledge of himself

---

58. Ibid., *Works* 13:257–58.

is immediate and complete. God's knowledge contains completely and perfectly all of God's thoughts and affections. It is in fact God again.[59]

For illustration, we may compare Edwards' approach to Aquinas. Aquinas claims that, though God knows all other things by ideas, God does not know himself through ideas.[60] For Aquinas, ideas are plans through which God creates everything else. Ideas are the essence of earthly objects, in the sense that the idea of a table in the divine mind defines whether a particular object is a table. For God, essence and existence are identical. So God's essence cannot be given an abstract definition (or in Aquinas' terminology, God does not belong to any genera). The definition of the divine nature is simply what God actually is. Therefore God is not known through ideas. Aquinas describes the Son as the thoughts that proceed from the thinking of God.[61] The focus is not on what God is thinking about, but on the thinking process. To explain why the thinking of God is itself God again, Aquinas invokes the principle of simplicity.[62] If God's acts are different from the nature of God, then there is potentiality in God. Therefore God's operation must itself be part of the divine essence. Therefore, the thinking of God is also God. The Word of God, as the thinking of God, contains the forms or ideas of all creatures. Thus the Word is a mediator ontologically between the Father and the world.[63]

Edwards does not operate with the paradigm of potentiality and act, and simplicity is not as important for his theology of divine nature. He adopts the epistemology of Locke, and he creatively projects it into the inner life of the Trinity. He extends the meaning of ideas to all mental

---

59. Is Edwards' argument logically cogent? Oliver Crisp ("Trinity and Individuation") argues that Edwards' theory suffers from the problem of "the third man." If God has an idea of himself, he can also have an idea of that idea of himself, and the process can go on forever, giving us infinite Sons of God. Yet Edwards does not claim that the Son is an idea of a certain thought about God or any particular object. The Son is God's idea of the whole thinking and willing process. Even when God has an idea of the idea of his thinking process, this idea still belongs to God's thinking process. It is not a separate thinking process, therefore not a separate Son. In Kantian idealism, the apperception of the transcendental ego is very tricky question (see Allison, *Kant's Transcendental Idealism*, ch. 13). Implicitly, Edwards claims that God can have experiential knowledge of the divine transcendental ego, something impossible for a human thinking subject. Crisp raises other important issues that we cannot go into now. I think that while Edwards' model has its problems, but it is not logically incoherent.

60. *Summa Theologica* I.15.1.r02.

61. Ibid. I.27.1.

62. Ibid. I.27.2.r02.

63. Ibid. I.34.3.

objects, not just impressions received through physical sensations.⁶⁴ Insofar as something can be grasped mentally as an object, it is grasped through ideas. For example, our affections can be known mentally through self-reflection. As discussed in a previous chapter, Edwards believes that a true idea (as contrasted with mere notions) of an affection is having that same affection in our mind again at the moment of self-reflection. With this conception of ideas, Edwards can claim that even God know himself through ideas. Insofar as God can be known concretely (not abstractly or notionally), God is also known through ideas. There is no other alternative within Edwards' epistemology. By focusing on God's self-knowledge (as opposed to God's thinking in general), Edwards constructs speculatively the Son as a divine person. Since the Son is God's self-knowledge, the Son does not serve as an ontological link between the Father and the world in the thought of Edwards.⁶⁵

If the Son is the self-knowledge of God, the Spirit is the self-love of God:⁶⁶

> Again, that image of God which God infinitely loves and has his chief delight in, is the perfect idea of God. It has always been said, that God's infinite delight consists in reflecting on himself and viewing his own perfections, or which is the same thing, in his own perfect idea of himself; so that 'tis acknowledged, that

---

64. On Edwards' extension of Lockean ideas into imaginations or non-physical impressions, see Lee, *Philosophical Theology*, 115–46.

65. Lee claims that Edwards' conception of the Trinity is dispositional and inherently dynamic. Lee believes that Edwards breaks new ground from traditional conception of Trinity in terms of static actuality (*Philosophical Theology*, 185–95). The problem with Lee's interpretation is that the traditional conception of Trinity—as exemplified by Aquinas—is dynamic by nature too. When Aquinas claims that God is pure act, by definition God is always acting. The Trinity is the internal acting (thinking and willing) of God in both Aquinas and Edwards. Lee claims that the traditional doctrine of Trinity is obscured by divine impassibility. Therefore, there is a divorce between the doctrine of Trinity and Christian life ("Editor's Introduction," Works 21:3). This is a debatable assessment. For medieval theologians like Aquinas, the doctrine of the Trinity is closely tied to the theology of the divine image in human beings. This divine image is the foundation of medieval mystical theology. As far as Edwards is concerned, there is no evidence that he wants to revise traditional understanding of divine aseity. For further critique of the bifurcation between a traditional static God and the dynamic God of Edwards, see Holmes, "Dispositional Ontology?"

66. Edwards' doctrine of Holy Spirit is discussed in details by Caldwell, *Holy Spirit*. We shall limit ourselves to issues where the concept of beauty is important. Caldwell (ibid., 52–55) agrees with Studebaker (*pace* Pauw) that Edwards works within the Augustinian model.

> God's infinite love is to, and his infinite delight in, the perfect image of himself.[67]
>
> The Holy Spirit is the act of God between the Father and the Son infinitely loving and delighting in each other. . . . This is certainly distinct from the other two; the delight and energy that is begotten in us by an idea is distinct from the idea. . . . It is distinct from each of the other two, yet it is God; for the pure and perfect act of God is God, because God is pure act. It appears that this is God, because that which acts perfectly is all act, and nothing but act.[68]

The Holy Spirit is the love between God and his perfect self-image. It is the perfect self-love of a perfect being. To put it crudely, it is the perfect narcissism.[69] For illustration, we may bring in Aquinas again. Aquinas also believes that the name of the Holy Spirit is love, and the Father and Son love one another by the Holy Spirit.[70] However, the Holy Spirit also has the name "Gift." It is the essence of love to give, as Scripture tells us that the Father has given the Son in love.[71] In eternity, the Holy Spirit is the love between the Father and the Son because only God exists eternally. However, it is significant that Aquinas does not deny that God's love for the world is also embodied by the Holy Spirit. Edwards, on the other hand, calls specifically the Holy Spirit as love for God. Holy Spirit is not the spirit of love in general. For example, he never associates brotherly love between human beings as work of the Spirit according to his nature.

Does it seem blasphemous to suggest that God is engaged in a perfect act of narcissism? Edwards believes that self-love, in a broad sense, is not evil at all. It is merely the capacity of a spiritual being to take delight in an object:

> But if he is capable of inclination, will and choice, then what he inclines to, and chooses, is grateful to him; whatever that be, whether it be his own private good, the good of his neighbors,

---

67. *Misc.* 94, *Works* 13:259.

68. Ibid. 13:260.

69. Matless and Lee, who emphasize the centrality of relationship in Edwards' thinking, fail to appreciate that it is not relationship *per se* that is beautiful in Edwards' thinking. It is always relationship in reference to God.

70. *Summa Theologica* I.37.1–2.

71. Ibid. I.28.1.r02.

> or the glory of God. And so far it is grateful or pleasing to him, so far it is a part of his pleasure, good, or happiness.[72]
>
> Self-love is a man's love of his own pleasure and happiness, and hatred of his own misery; or rather, 'tis only a capacity of enjoyment or taking delight in anything. For to say a man loves his own happiness and pleasure, is only to say that he delights in what he delights [in]; and to say that he hates his own misery, is only to say that he is grieved or afflicted in his own affliction.[73]

Insofar as a spiritual being inclines towards whatever delights him, this is self-love in the broad sense. The greater a spiritual being is, the greater is his capacity for self-love. Edwards believes that this is simply the natural constitution of spiritual beings to incline towards what is perceived as good.[74] Self-love in this broad sense is the source of all other kinds of love. Given that self-love in this sense is not bad, can self-love in a narrow sense be justified? Self-love in the narrow sense is the loving of oneself, and Edwards clearly condemns this kind of self-love in human beings.[75]

Why is the case different for God? We need to recall Edwards' definition of true virtue: "The primary object of virtuous love is Being, simply considered; or that true virtue primarily consists, not in love to any particular beings, because of their virtue or beauty, nor in gratitude, because they love us; but in a propensity and union of heart to Being simply considered; exciting 'absolute Benevolence' (if I may so call it) to Being in general."[76] As we have shown in the last section, infinity is the primary property of God in Edwards' thought. God is the ground of all beings. God is ground both in the sense of being the original source of all beings, and in the sense that God supports the existence of all beings at every moment. It is impossible for God to be selfish. "This is impossible, because he comprehends all entity, and all excellence in his own essence. The first Being, the eternal and infinite Being, is in effect, *Being in general*; and comprehends universal existence."[77] In loving the God-self, God also loves every being. Far from carrying a bad connotation, self-love is a virtue for God. If God is

---

72. *Nature of True Virtue* ch. 4, Works 8:576

73. *Misc.* 530, Works 18:73.

74. Edwards' theory of human choices is remarkably similar to Aquinas. The will always follows what the intellect perceives as the greatest good. See Studebaker, *Jonathan Edwards*, 164–84.

75. See, for example, "Charity Contrary to a Selfish Spirit," *Works*, 8:252–71.

76. *True Virtue* ch. 1, Works 8:544.

77. *End of Creation*, Works 8:461.

good, God must love himself: "From hence also it is evident that the *divine virtue*, or the virtue of the divine mind, must consist primarily in *love to himself*, or in the mutual love and friendship which subsists eternally and necessarily between the several persons in the Godhead, or that infinitely strong propensity there is in these divine persons one to another."[78]

We have seen that the beauty of spiritual beings consists in virtuous affections. Therefore, the Holy Spirit is the beauty of God. This idea is expressed in various ways. "Holy Ghost is divine beauty, love and joy."[79] "This makes the third, the personal Holy Spirit or the holiness of God, which is his infinite beauty, and this is God's infinite consent to being in general."[80] "'Tis peculiar to God that He has beauty within himself, consisting in being's consenting with his own being, or the love of himself in his own Holy Spirit; whereas the excellence of others is in loving others, in loving God, and in the communications of his Spirit."[81]

For Edwards, true spiritual beauty is the love of Being simply considered. Besides God, nothing can be Being simply considered. For all finite beings, they must love more than themselves. Therefore their beauty is judged in relation to their relationship to something outside of themselves. God is Being simply considered. For God, self-love is God's love for Being simply considered. Therefore, God has "beauty within himself." His beauty is included within himself. Moreover, the beauty of God is the archetype of all beauty. Beauty is the consent of being to being. In God, the infinite Being consents to the infinite Being. Any consent of particular being to any particular being is included in the consent of the Infinite to the Infinite. Since love for particular objects can be beautiful only if it is pursued in accordance to love for Being simply considered, all spiritual beauty must implicitly be the love of God. The Holy Spirit is the perfect love from God to God. When God communicates the Holy Spirit to spiritual beings, God communicates beauty too. One cannot truly receive the Spirit without at the same time receiving spiritual beauty.

Does that mean that particular objects or the love of particular objects cannot be beautiful? The answer is that, in Edwards' thinking, the beauty of a particular object cannot be understood apart from the context of the totality of being. As we have indicated, a knife may be beautiful to look at. It will turn into an ugly thing if it is used for killing. However, the

78. *True Virtue* ch. 2, Works 8:557.
79. *Discourse on the Trinity*, Works 21:144.
80. *Mind* 45.9, Works 6:364.
81. *Mind* 45.12, Works 6:365

knife may be beautiful if the killing is somehow mandated by God (e.g., Abraham's knife for the slaughter of Isaac).

A similar case applies to our affections. Edwards emphasizes that "a Christian spirit is not contrary to all self-love."[82] This self-love becomes corrupt only when he loves himself too much when compared with others, or when he places too much of his happiness on things confined to himself. We should love things according to their ontological weight. We should love people more than things. Since God has formally all the ontological weight, we should love God above all things.

## *The Social Model*

So far, we have emphasized that the Trinity is a self-reflective movement. This obviously runs counter to a social model of the Trinity. We admit that there are other passages from Edwards that suggest a more interpersonal form of love within the Trinity:

> No reasonable creature can be happy, we find, without society and communion, not only because he finds something in others that is not in himself, but because he delights to communicate himself to another. . . . So that we may conclude, that Jehovah's happiness consists in communion, as well as the creature's.[83]

From the above passage, we see that Edwards considers the Son as "another" to God the Father. Strictly speaking, God's love for the God-self is not narcissism, because what God loves is the idea of himself, not himself directly. Similarly, God is loved by his own idea. Moreover, since everything is virtually in God, God also loves everything in loving himself. God also loves all the saints through Christ the Head of the church.[84] However, the "another" in Edwards' Trinity should be distinguished from the concept of "others" usually championed by social trinitarianism. The Son does not have a separate intellect and will from the Father. The Son and Father are totally transparent to one another. Within the immanent Trinity, any dialogue (in the sense of revealing to and learning from one another) between the Father and the Son is neither necessary nor possible. As we shall see, the case is somewhat different when Edwards comes to the economic Trinity.

Lee has a different interpretation of the Trinitarian model of Edwards:

---

82. "Charity Contrary to a Selfish Spirit," *Works* 8:254.
83. *Misc.* 96, *Works* 13:264.
84. "Sermon Fifteen: Heaven is a World of Love," *Charity*, *Works* 8:373.

# The Beauty of the Triune God

With his dispositional argument for the real distinctions, however, Edwards has transformed the psychological analogy into a perspective that clearly emphasizes the three-ness of the Trinitarian persons. His use of the psychological analogy ends up reinforcing the social analogy, or at least makes the two analogies compatible.[85]

How is the psychological model transformed into the social model? First, Lee cites the following textual evidence: "They are equal in honor besides the honor which is common to 'em all, viz. that they are all God; each has his peculiar honor in the society or family."[86]

Secondly, Lee claims that Edwards has a different understanding of the divine essence:

> For Edwards, there is no substance lying behind God's self-repeating and self-communicating activities. Direct existence, reflexive knowing, and reflexive loving do not belong to the Divine Being but rather are, and constitute, the Divine Being. The divine disposition is the general law that governs their pattern. This divine disposition is an abiding reality apart from its exercises.[87]

Thirdly, Lee claims that the Father, Son and Holy Spirit have their own separate will and mind. He quotes the following passage from Edwards:

> There is understanding and will in the Father, as the Son and the Holy Ghost are in him and proceed from [him]. There is understanding and will in the Son, as he is understanding and as the Holy Ghost is in him and proceeds from him. There is understanding and will in the Holy Ghost, as he is the divine will and as the Son is in him.[88]

Lee claims that the above passage shows that Edwards has moved from a unitary conception of the Trinity to a perichoretic formulation of the Trinity.

How strong is the case of Lee? While Edwards uses words such as "family" or "society," we have to interpret these words within the context of his theology. Within his immanent Trinity, this is a family of the

---

85. "Editor's Introduction," *Works*, 21:19.

86. *Discourse on the Trinity*, *Works* 21:135; cited in "Editor's Introduction," *Works*, 21:20.

87. "Editor's Introduction," *Works* 21:20.

88. *Discourse on the Trinity*, *Works* 21:134; cited in "Editor's Introduction," *Works*, 21:27.

different aspects of the same subject. The bond of the Trinitarian family is not mutual love among the three independent persons. Edwards emphatically points out that, in Scripture, "we never once read either of the Father or the Son loving the Holy Spirit, and the Spirit loving either of them."[89] The reason is that the Spirit is the love between the Father and the Son. Similarly, the Son does not know the Father like the way we know another person; the Son is simply God's self-knowledge. The bond of the Trinitarian family is the one subjectivity of the Father.

Our argument is actually confirmed by the passage quoted by Lee in his third argument. In that passage, Edwards argues that the Son has will because the Spirit is in him. The Spirit has understanding because the Son is in him. In other words, there is no separate will of the Son independent of the will of Father, which is the Spirit. Similarly, right after the quoted passage, Edwards says that it should not be "looked upon as a strange and unreasonable figment that the persons should be said to have an understanding or love by another person's being in 'em."[90] Edwards claims that this is warranted by Scripture, because Scripture claims that the Father has wisdom by the Son's being in him. Edwards does claim that "all the three are persons, for they all have understanding and will."[91] However, they all have the same understanding and will; the three persons form the same subject.

As for Lee's second argument, a full answer will take us too far from our concern. Nonetheless, we believe that Lee's picture needs to be corrected. First, the traditional concept of God does not say that thinking and loving belong to the divine substance. Aquinas clearly states that the triune relations are the essence of God:

> Thus it is manifest that relation really existing in God is really the same as His essence and only differs in its mode of intelligibility; as in relation is meant that regard to its opposite which is not expressed in the name of essence. Thus it is clear that in God relation and essence do not differ from each other, but are one and the same.[92]

Even in Aquinas, there is no substance lying behind the thinking and loving of God. To use the terminology of Lee, Aquinas also believes that the divine act of thinking and loving constitutes the divine substance. This is the implication of simplicity. As we have indicated above, Edwards

89. *Treatise on Grace, Works* 21:186.
90. *Discourse on the Trinity, Works* 21:134.
91. Ibid., 134.
92. *Summa Theologica* I.28.2, p.371.

does depart from Aquinas by emphasizing that thinking and loving are self-reflexive. That would hardly argue for a social analogy of the Trinity. The crucial claim of Lee is that "divine disposition is an abiding reality apart from its exercises." In other words, the divine essence is constituted by divine disposition, but divine disposition is not exhausted by divine acts. This dispositional God is not pure act, but pure disposition. The consequence is that God's being can be enlarged by further acts without changing its essence. Lee claims that creation is an act that enlarges God's being.[93] As a crude analogy, we may define a running machine as a machine that has the disposition to run fast. It is not identical with all the races it has run yet. It can always enlarge its life by another race. Similarly, Lee claims that God has the disposition to communicate. This disposition is not exhausted by the immanent Trinity. The creation is the further act coming from the divine disposition to communicate. Thus the creation enlarges the being of God.

We have textual evidence that runs against Lee's claim. In order to answer the question why the Holy Spirit is God again, Edwards claims that "the pure and perfect act of God is God, because God is pure act."[94] This self-love is God again because the act of God is also God. God is "nothing but act."[95] The text argues against a distinction between dispositions and their exercise within God. This would also go again Edwards' thought to say the Holy Spirit is merely a disposition to act. The Spirit is the act of love.

It is indeed true that Edwards claims that God is by nature communicative. In an often quoted passage, Edwards says that "a disposition in God, as an original property of his nature, to an emanation of his own infinite fullness, was what excited him to create the world; and so that the emanation itself was aimed at by him as a last end of creation."[96] What does divine disposition mean? Edwards gives the analogy of the root of a tree. It is the natural disposition of the root to diffuse life and sap.[97] This

93. See also *Philosophical Theology*, 184. We shall return to this issue in the context of heaven in chapter 6.

94. *Misc.* 94, *Works* 13:260.

95. Ibid., *Works* 13:260. Though Edwards does not invoke the concept of simplicity, his reasoning is similar to the medieval concept of simplicity. His misgivings about the doctrine of simplicity (*Works* 21:132) come from a misunderstanding of divine simplicity. Divine simplicity does not claim that God's immutability is equivalent to God. Rather, it claims that God's immutability and other attributes all necessarily belong to the essence of God. For a modern defense of divine simplicity, see Ross, *Philosophical Theology*, 52–63.

96. *End of Creation* 1.2, *Works* 8:435.

97. Ibid., *Works* 8:435.

would suggest that creation is not a voluntary choice of God. The root does not consciously choose to support the fruits. An involuntary creation would run against Edwards' Reformed heritage. A more appropriate interpretation would take disposition as action that befits the character of God. In other words, such action is delightful to God. Edwards claims that "if God both esteem and delight in his own perfections and virtues, he can't but value and delight in the expressions and genuine effects of them."[98] When Edwards claims that there is a disposition in God to emanate his own full *ad extra*, he probably means that it is delightful to God to communicate his fullness *ad extra*.

What is the fullness that God delights in communicating? First, it is the exercise of God's infinite power, wisdom, and goodness. The second is the knowledge of God's glory. The third is the delight or love of divine glory.[99] Though Edwards does not say it explicitly, the first fullness corresponds to the Father, who is the source of all acts. The second fullness corresponds to the Son, who is God's self-knowledge. The third corresponds to the Holy Spirit, who is the God's self-love. It is the inter-Trinitarian life that is communicated *ad extra*.

## *Creation and the Trinity*

Finally, we return briefly to Edwards' theology of creation and spiritual theology in order to show some implications of his Trinitarian theology.[100] Edwards believes that the goal of creation is the emanation of the intra-Trinitarian life. Since this life is the life of personal subjectivity, its emanation would imply creatures with personality. In order for the Son's life to be duplicated, there must be knowledge in creation. Therefore it is natural for Edwards to argue that the goal of the material world is to be known by immortal souls. The significance of the material world is that it shows the wisdom of the Father. The Son can appreciate the Father's perfections directly; human beings appreciate the Father's perfections indirectly through creation. The theology of the Son as self-knowledge corresponds to the theology of creation as a messenger for divine perfections. Similarly, the Holy Spirit as the self-love of God corresponds to the theology that the

---

98. *End of Creation* 1.3, *Works* 8:437.

99. *End of Creation* 1.2, *Works* 8:428–32.

100. See McClymond, *Encounters with God*, ch. 4 for a critical evaluation of Edwards' creation theology.

Holy Spirit is the divine love in the saints. God's self-love is duplicated in the saints' love for God.

We should note that this extension of intra-Trinitarian life is not automatically associated with creation and existence. If the social model were the prominent model of Trinity in Edwards, it might suggest (e.g., Matless) that relationship *per se* is the emanation of divine life. Insofar as anything exists in this world, it must necessarily have relationship with things around it. This makes Edwards' theology similar to the panentheism of Neoplatonism. The psychological model implies that participation in divine life is based on a certain model of spiritual life. One must consciously know and love God in order to replicate the intra-Trinitarian life. The extension of intra-Trinitarian life is actually a two-stage process. First, material and spiritual beings are created. Second, some spiritual beings receive the gift to know and love God. As we shall see, Edwards emphasizes the second stage is a free act of God. The emphasis on divine nature in the creation account is balanced with the emphasis on divine will in the redemption account.

In conclusion, beauty serves as the binding principle of the whole system. We recall again that beauty, for Edwards, is fundamentally consenting. For spiritual being, this consenting consists in love, or embracing with the will. The scale of beauty is measured by ontological weight of the object of love and the intensity of the love. Since God is Being simply considered, and God loves the God-self with perfect love, God is beauty essentially. All other beings are beautiful to the extent that they love God, because their love for God (or divine love) is their consent for Being simply considered. Therefore, they are beautiful to the extent that they participate in the nature of the Holy Spirit, which is divine love. God, in turn, loves the saints with an everlasting love. In loving the saints, God loves the divine love, the emanation of the Holy Spirit, that is within the saints. God's love of saints is an extension of the intra-Trinitarian life, because God loves his own beauty in loving the saints. Logically, spiritual beings that do not love God would have no beauty in them. They have no share in the intra-Trinitarian life of God. If they in turn would receive no love from God, this would be beautiful in the Edwardsian sense. A being that does not participate in the Holy Spirit, which is divine love, will also receive nothing of God's love for others. If there is an equality of love between God and the saints, there is an equality of enmity between God and the reprobates. According to this logic, God and the saints would appreciate the beauty of eternal damnation. This is, in brief, Edwards' argument for the beauty of hell. Before we examine this in detail, we shall first turn to the beauty of the economic Trinity.

# 5

# The Beautiful Christ

HAVING EXAMINED THE BEAUTY OF THE IMMANENT TRINITY IN THE theology of Edwards, we are now in a position to examine the role of beauty in the economic Trinity. While Edwards is unique among both Puritans and Reformed scholasticism in emphasizing the beauty of the triune life, he stands within his tradition in heaping praises of beauty on Jesus. Though staying within the mainstream of the Reformed understanding of Christology, Edwards also has his idiosyncratic perspectives. Most of these come from Edwards' zeal to provide a rational defense of traditional doctrines. Where his Reformed predecessors are content to accept as revealed mysteries, Edwards strives to make them reasonable beliefs. Pushing those doctrines to their logical ends, Edwards demonstrates some of the strength and the weaknesses of his tradition. We shall not offer a complete overview of his Christology or his soteriology.[1] Our goal is to show how Edwards develops his theory of beauty in the work of the economic Trinity. In what sense are the Redeemer and the redemptive plan of God beautiful? We shall go about in a roundabout way. We shall begin by examining Edwards' theology of the covenant of redemption. This will provide us with important insight into Edwards' understanding on the beauty of Christ. It also serves as a footnote to the question whether there is a social model of the Trinity in Edwards.

## Covenant of Redemption

### Background

The covenant is a central doctrine in the Reformed tradition. Our concern here is with the relationship between the covenant and the intra-Trinitarian

[1]. See Bush, *Jesus Christ*, for Edward's Christology; Morimoto, *Catholic Vision*, for his soteriology.

life. Edwards is unique in this tradition in justifying the need for a covenant of redemption upon the dynamics of intra-Trinitarian life. We want to examine briefly the covenant of redemption in Reformed scholasticism and Puritan theology to provide a background for Edwards' treatment on this issue.

Most Reformed schoolmen give ample attention to the covenant of grace. Turretin, for example, devotes a whole topic to the covenant of grace in his *Institute of Elenctic Theology*.[2] Turretin defines the covenant of grace as "a gratuitous pact entered into in Christ between God offended and man offending. In it God promises remission of sins and salvation to man gratuitously on account of Christ; man, however, relying upon the same grace promises faith and obedience."[3] While going into a detail exposition of the history of the covenant of grace in its twofold economy (Old and New Testament), Turretin does not mention the covenant of redemption at all. His main concern is to defend the continuity of the Old and New Testament against the opinion of the Socinians and Remonstrants.[4]

Other Reformed schoolmen postulate a pre-temporal pact between the Father and the Son.[5] Witsius writes: "In Gal. 3:17 Paul tells of a certain διαθήκην προκεκυρωμένην ὑπὸ τοῦ θεοῦ εἰς Χριστόν, a pact or testament ratified beforehand by God to Christ. The contracting parties are indicated, on the one hand God, on the other Christ, and the convention ratified between the two."[6]

The schoolmen emphasize that the pact is a testament, in that God has promised unilaterally a heavenly inheritance for the saints. If it is a covenant between God and people, the people may fail (as Adam did). Since the pact is between God and Christ, it cannot fail. Our inheritance is assured.

For the schoolmen, the covenant of grace "is at once a covenant and a testament, more properly a testament."[7] Wyttenbach writes: "The covenant

---

2. *Institutes* XII.1–12, 2:169–270. In the English text, the length of this section on the covenant is similar to the section on the twelfth topic, on the person and state of Christ.

3. Ibid. XII.2.5, 2:175.

4. Ibid. XII.5.2–3, 2:192–93.

5. Cocceius and the federal theologians develop the doctrine covenant of redemption explicitly in the seventeenth century, but it had significant roots in earlier orthodox Reformed meditation on the eternal decrees of God and its economical working *ad extra*. See Muller, *Trinity of God*, 263–67.

6. Cited in Heppe, *Reformed Dogmatics*, 374.

7. Ibid., 375.

of grace is nothing but the execution of the eternal testament of grace. In the eternal testament the Father asked the Son to make a placation in time etc.,—Hence it follows that this covenant is in itself a testament and only a covenant in its execution."[8]

What is the content of this pact? Heidegger explains: "The covenant of God the Father with the Son is a mutual agreement, by which God the Father exacted from the Son perfect obedience to the law unto death which he must face on behalf of chosen seed to be given him; and promised him, if he gave the obedience, the seed in question as his own perquisite and inheritance; and in return the Son, in promising this obedience to God the Father and producing it in the literal act., demanded of Him in turn the right to demand this seed for himself as an inheritance and perquisite."[9] In coming into this pact, the Father and Son act freely and equally. The Father cannot simply command the Son to enter into the covenant. Mastricht says: "The Reformed recognize both that God most freely demanded the Son should take up the province of mediator, and that the Son had undertaken it with equal freedom, in that each acted on rational design and assent. . . . They likewise acknowledge that as divine persons both Father and Son were *sui iuris* and to such an extent, that considered in Himself and in His nature the Father could not have demanded it, and to this extent too the Son might not have accepted what was demanded."[10]

With the Reformed schoolmen, we are concerned with two questions. First, why do some schoolmen emphasize the Father-Son pact, while others choose to ignore it? The main reason is that some want to emphasize the unilateral dimension of the covenant of grace, while others want to emphasize its bilateral dimension. The bilateral dimension means that saints are called to obedience when they enter into covenant of grace. The danger here is that obedience may sound like a condition to be fulfilled by human effort. The unilateral dimension emphasizes that our salvation is initiated and completed by divine power alone. Only in the divine promise can we be assured of our ultimate salvation. The danger here is that people may sound like mere puppets in this scheme. As we shall see, Edwards' inclination is to stress the all-sufficiency of divine power. The covenant of redemption is a natural component of his theology.

The second question is why the emphasis on the freedom of the Father and the Son in entering into the pact. Unfortunately, Heppe gives us

8. Ibid., 375.
9. Ibid., 376.
10. Ibid., 379.

*The Beautiful Christ*

no clue on this question. Our guess is that this is to safe-guard the gratuitousness of the Incarnation. Calvin debated with Osiander about whether the Son would be incarnated in the absence of sin.[11] Osiander believes that Christ, as the Second Adam, would have come to even a sinless humanity in order to complete the divine image in human beings. The Incarnation is therefore implied in creation. By emphasizing the freedom of the Father and the Son, the schoolmen deny any suggestion that the Incarnation is implied in creation. It is out of sheer mercy that the Son and Father entered into a separate covenant to redeem fallen humanity. As we shall see, Edwards will make Christ voluntary entry into the covenant of redemption a major theological theme. Edwards goes beyond the Schoolmen in making the voluntary humiliation of the Son a central aspect of the beauty of Christ.

The covenant of grace is also a major theme to the Puritans.[12] As in the Reformed scholastic tradition, the covenant of redemption is a not central issue among the Puritans. The Westminster Confession gives this reason for the need of a covenant: "The distance between God and the creature is so great, that although reasonable creatures do owe obedience unto Him as their Creator, yet they could never have any fruition of Him as their blessedness and reward, but by some voluntary condescension on God's part, which He hath been pleased to express by way of covenant."[13] It continues to articulate the meaning of the covenant of works and the covenant of grace. God enters into the covenant of grace: "wherein He freely offereth unto sinners life and salvation by Jesus Christ; requiring of them faith in Him, that they may be saved and promising to give unto all those that are ordained unto eternal life His Holy Spirit, to make them willing, and able to believe."[14]

The Confession understands the covenant as an instrument through which God condescends to relate humanity in a partnership. In particular, the covenant of grace is the means through which sinners can enter into partnership with God. Since the Father and Son are in partnership from eternity, there would be no need for a covenant between them. Indeed, the Confession says nothing about a covenant of redemption.

According to von Rohr, the theological motivation for developing explicitly a covenant of redemption among the Puritans is to ground the

11. *Institutes* II.12.5–7.
12. See von Rohr, *Covenant of Grace*, for an excellent general treatment.
13. Westminster Confession of Faith (WCF) VII.1.
14. WCF VII.3.

covenant of grace firmly on Christology. A second motif is that "in the intra-Trinitarian covenanting there was the inclusion of those who were to be its ultimate beneficiaries."[15] In the covenant between the Father and the Son, the elect is the reward that the Father promised to the Son for the Son's agreement to carry out the work of redemption. Thus the covenant of redemption provides a Christological foundation for predestination and limited atonement. However, the covenant of redemption has the potentiality to render the covenant of grace superfluous. If God has already made a covenant with Christ to save the elect, why does God need to make another covenant with the elect (the covenant of grace)? Nevertheless, except for the Antinomian wing, most Puritans insist on dwelling extensively on the covenant of grace.[16] For them, the covenant of grace brings out clearly the mutuality in our process of salvation. God has unilaterally offered the gospel, but we need to embrace it personally.

Among the Puritans, Owen is the Trinitarian theologian *par excellence*.[17] In his various writings, he emphasizes that the redemption must be understood in a Trinitarian framework. He believes that "the agent in, and chief author of, this great work of our redemption is the whole blessed Trinity."[18] Owen explicitly adopts the importance of a covenant of redemption between the Father and the Son:

> The third act of this sending [his Son as redeemer] is his entering into covenant and compact with his Son concerning the work to be undertaken, and the issue or event thereof; of which there be two parts:—First, His promise to protect and assist him in the accomplishment and perfect fulfilling of the whole business and dispensation about which he was employed, or which he was to undertake.[19]
>
> Secondly, [His promise] of success, or a good issue out of all his sufferings, and a happy accomplishment and attainment of the end of his great undertaking.[20]

In this covenant, the Son promises to the task of "willingly undergoing the office [of Mediator], wherein by dispensation the Father had and

15. Von Ruhr, *Covenant of Grace*, 44.

16. Ibid., 44.

17. See Trueman, *Claims of Truth*, for a general exposition of the Trinitarian structure of his theology.

18. *Death of Death*, Works 10:212 (*Ultimate Christian Library*).

19. Ibid., I.3, 10:219.

20. Ibid., I.3, 10:221.

exercised a kind of superiority, which the Son, though 'in the form of God,' humbled himself unto, Philippians 2:6–8."[21] The Son promises to subject himself to the eternal decree of God. In return, the Father offers the Son "a promise of applying the benefits purchased by this Savior so designed to them that should believe on him, to be given in fullness of time."[22]

For Owen, the covenant of redemption is one way to emphasize the intimate relationship between Christ's work and the salvation of the elect. Unlike the Arminians, which have two separate decrees for Christ's mediation and the predestination of the elect, Owen includes the sending of Christ as mediator and the elect of the saints in the single event of the covenant of redemption. In the same event that the Son promises to be mediator, the Son is also promised the elect as a reward. The issues of predestination and limited atonement are formulated as a distinctively Christological problem.[23] Since the work of Incarnation, satisfaction, and intercession are included in one covenant of redemption, the accomplishment and application of the redemption of Christ are tied together. There is no need for separate decrees for Christ's mediation and the application of Christ's benefits.

## Edwards

Edwards pushes Owen's reasoning to its logical conclusion.[24] Following the Reformed tradition, he believes that there is a covenant of works between God and Adam.[25] Building on Mastricht, he emphasizes the unilateral dimension of grace by denying that there is a covenant of grace between the Father and the elect.[26] If there is a covenant of grace, and faith

21. Ibid., I.3, 10:214.
22. Ibid., I.3, 10:216
23. Here I follow the analysis of Trueman, *Claims of Truth*, 134–39.
24. Edwards never cites Owen's *Death of Death*. He does refer to Owen's commentary on the book of Hebrews several times in his *Miscellanies* (No. 1282, No. 1352, the "Table"), though not specifically on the question of covenant. Owen discusses the covenant of redemption in the first volume of his commentary. Edwards should at least be familiar with Owen's teaching of the covenant of redemption.
25. See, for example, *Misc.* 1215, *Works* 23:147.
26. Since Edwards rejects the covenant of grace, there is a debate on whether Edwards is really a covenant theologian (See Bush, *Jesus Christ*, 101). Weir believes that the heart of federal theology is the consecutive administration of the covenant of work and covenant of grace (*Origins of the Federal Theology*, 3–5). In this technical sense, Edwards is not a federal theologian. On the other hand, he is a covenant theologian in the sense of employing the concept of covenant as a crucial mean to organize his

is a condition to enter this covenant, then it is structurally similar to the covenant of works. In both covenant of works and covenant of grace, God promises blessings on condition that human beings perform certain acts. "The second covenant is as much a covenant of works as the first."[27] To emphasize the graceful nature of salvation, the young Edwards believes that the covenant of works and the covenant of redemption are the two only covenants. "It seems to me to be true, that as the first covenant was made with the first Adam, so the second covenant was made with the second Adam; as the first covenant was made with the seed of the first Adam no otherwise than it was made with them in him, so the second covenant is not made with the seed of the second Adam any otherwise than as it was made with them in him."[28]

In the covenant of redemption, Christ is the only one that performs the condition of the covenant. Faith is not so much a condition for us to enter a covenant of grace, as it is one of the benefits accrued by Christ for the elect. Christ's work of redemption and its application to us become totally united in one covenant.

Edwards later postulates a second covenant to highlight the active participation of the elect. The two covenants are "the covenant that God makes with Christ and with his church or believers in him, and the covenant between Christ and his church or between Christ and men."[29] The first is the covenant of redemption. The second is a marriage covenant between Christ and his people. For Edwards, this scheme allows both the passivity and the agency of human beings to be understood correctly: "So that those things that are promises in one of these covenants, are conditions in another. Thus regeneration and closing with Christ, is one of the promises of the covenant of the Father with Christ, but is the condition in the covenant of Christ with his people. So, on the other hand, the incarnation, death and sufferings of Christ, are promises in Christ's covenant with his people, but they are conditions of the covenant of the Father with his Son."[30]

Edwards provides an original and interesting solution to the perennial Reformed theological question: how does one balance the unilateral

---

theology. Unfortunately, Weir does not address the origin of the concept of covenant of redemption among Reformed thinkers.

27. *Misc.* zz.2, *Works* 13:197
28. *Works* 13:198.
29. *Misc.* 617, *Works* 18:148.
30. *Works* 18:149.

*The Beautiful Christ*

offer of grace and bilateral relationship between God and his people? Since our concern is the aesthetic theory of Edwards, we shall not pursue this topic further.[31] The importance of this discussion for us is that Edwards has put the covenant of redemption into the center of the work of redemption. The majority Puritan view, as represented by the Westminster Confession of Faith, uses the covenant of grace as the central concept in the work of redemption. In order to understand the beauty of the Redeemer, we need to understand the nature of the covenant of redemption in Edwards' theology.

Besides focusing on the covenant of redemption, Edwards is unique among the Puritans in pushing for a theology of intra-Trinitarian covenant. Edwards asks a question ignored by his predecessors: what is so unique about the work of redemption that it requires an intra-Trinitarian covenant? The orthodox tradition of the church has for a long time believes that creation is also the work of the whole Trinity, yet there is no covenant of creation. What is the difference between creation and redemption? Why does the latter alone require a covenant?

To answer the question, Edwards makes the crucial distinction between the economic work of Trinity in general and the work of redemption in particular. The economy of the Trinity in general refers to all their actings towards creatures. Aspects of the general economy of the Trinity can be demonstrated from "pretty plain reasons."[32] The work of redemption, on the other hand, can only be known through revelation.

What may reason tell us about the economic Trinity? First, there is subordination within the Trinity, "so that the Father in that affair acts as Head of the Trinity, and Son under him, and the Holy Spirit under them both."[33] Second, "the persons of the Trinity are not inferior one to another in glory and excellency of nature."[34] Third, "the other persons' acting under the Father don't arise from any natural subjection."[35] Fourth, and crucially,

> Though a subordination of the persons of the Trinity in their actings be not from any proper natural subjection one to another, and so must be conceived of as in some respect established

---

31. See Bush, *Jesus Christ*, 102–8, for further discussion on the covenant theology of Edwards.

32. *Misc.* 1062, *Works* 20:430. This long (20:430–43) and important *Miscellanies* is examined in Bush, *Jesus Christ*, 98–102. Bush only addresses this note from the perspective of the history of redemption.

33. *Works* 20:430.

34. Ibid. 20:430.

35. Ibid. 20:430–31.

> by mutual free agreement, whereby the persons of the Trinity of their own will have as it were formed themselves into a society for carrying on the great design of glorifying the Deity and communicating its fullness, in which is established a certain economy and order of acting; yet this agreement establishing this economy is not to be looked upon as merely arbitrary, founded on nothing but the mere pleasure of the members of this society.... 'Tis fit that to the order of their subsisting: that as the Father is first in the order of two persons are from the Father in their subsistence, and as to their subsistence naturally originated from him and dependent on him ... so he should be the fountain in all the acts of the Deity.... Decency requires it.[36]

Here Edwards launches into an explicit social model of the Trinity. There is a "mutual free agreement" between the persons of the Trinity to form "themselves into a society" for carrying out the economic work of the Trinity. Why does Edwards need such a model at this point? The reason, as stated by Edwards, is that the immanent model fails to explain how there can be subjection within the Trinity. In the immanent model, as discussed in our last chapter, the persons of the Trinity are equal in nature and excellency. They are elements within a single subjectivity. It does not make sense to talk about one element of subjectivity being under the authority of another element of the same subjectivity. Therefore Edwards extends his model by talking about a free agreement between the persons. While the structure of the immanent Trinity reflects the essence of the Godhead, the structure of the economic Trinity is a product of the free choice of the persons of the Trinity.[37]

Though the economic Trinity is a decision of free will, Edwards emphasizes that this is a reasonable decision. First, the work of the economic Trinity is "glorifying the Deity and communicating its fullness." The immanent Trinity necessarily glorifies itself by loving itself. The economic Trinity extends this divine love into beings other than God. As we have

---

36. Ibid. 20:431.

37. Does it make sense to say that elements of one's own subjectivity can enter into a mutual free agreement? "It is a question whether there is not a significant tension between Edwards's (Amesian) version of Trinitarianism and his (Olevianian) version of Federalism. It is not clear that the triunity constituted of God, God's (Lockean) self-reflexive idea, and God's perfect self-love can readily be conceived as a 'society of persons' capable of negotiating and concluding a covenant. Is it possible to speak meaningfully of a perichoretic relationship among God, God's Idea, and God's Love?" (Bush, *Jesus Christ*, 112). Edwards, like all great theologians, has his moments of inconsistency.

shown in a previous chapter, creatures glorify God by knowing and loving the beauty of God. The glorifying of God through creatures is the end of creation. The goal of the economic Trinity is harmonious with the inner life of the immanent Trinity: "For God's determining to glorify and communicate himself must be conceived of as flowing from God's nature; or we must look upon God, from the infinite fullness and goodness of his nature, as naturally disposed to cause the beams of his glory to shine forth, and his goodness to flow forth."[38]

Second, the way of subjection in the economic Trinity is also harmonious with the inner life of the immanent Trinity. Since the Father is the source of the immanent Trinity, "decency" requires that any subjection should be on the part of the Son and the Spirit. God is the head of the Trinity, so it is reasonable that the Son and the Spirit are under the direction of the Father. Going beyond Edwards, we may say that the economic Trinity is a beautiful extension of the immanent Trinity because it agrees with the inner dynamics of the immanent Trinity. For such an extension, only a mutual agreement is needed.

The work of redemption is a different case. While God is naturally inclined to magnify divine glory, God is not naturally inclined to save sinners. "Therefore this particular invention of wisdom, of God's glorifying and communicating himself by the redemption of a certain number of fallen inhabitants of this globe of earth, is a thing diverse from God's natural inclination to glorify and communicate himself in general, and superadded to it or subservient to it."[39]

Redemption means saving sinners from their just condemnation. This is just one particular way of glorifying God. While it is difficult to imagine God extending his beauty beyond the Godhead without creation of creatures distinct from God, we can easily imagine the God of Edwards glorifying Himself without redeeming sinners. For example, God could have annihilated all creatures in this sinful world and create a new world. That God does choose to save sinners in this world is an arbitrary decision of the Trinity. It is one of the many means in which God could have followed the natural inclination to extend divine glory. "We must distinguish between the covenant of redemption, that is an establishment of wisdom wonderfully contriving a particular method for the most conveniently obtaining a great end, and that establishment that is founded in fitness and decency and the natural order of the eternal and necessary subsistence of

---

38. Ibid. 20:432.
39. Ibid. 20:432.

the persons of the Trinity."[40] The latter establishment, the ordering of the economic Trinity for extending God's glory beyond the Godhead, is prior and fundamental to the former establishment, the covenant of redemption.

Not only is the goal of redemption an arbitrary decision, the kind of subjection that Christ has to go through in the work of redemption is also arbitrary. Decency does not require Christ to go through the humiliation of incarnation. The incarnation is "the Son undertaking and engaging to put himself into a new kind of subjection to Father, far below that of his oeconomical station, even the subjection of a proper servant to the Father and one under his law—in the manner that creatures, that are infinitely below God and absolutely dependent for their being on the mere will of God, are subject to his preceptive will and absolute legislative authority—engaging to become a creature, and so put himself in the proper circumstances of a servant."[41]

In the incarnation, the Son goes beyond the subjection proper to his status as the Son. Proper subjection merely requires the Son to obey the Father as one of similar honor. Christ undergoes the subjection of a creature. For Edwards, there cannot be a lower subjection. A creature is completely dependent on the Father for every moment of its existence. The creator owes nothing to the creature, but the creature owes everything to the creator. This kind of asymmetrical relationship is radically different from the equal status of persons within the immanent Trinity. According to decency, the Father cannot ask the Son for such a kind of subjection. It requires something stronger to validate such humiliation:

> The Father, merely by his economical prerogative, can direct and prescribe to the other persons of the Trinity in all things not below their economical character. But all those things that imply something below the infinite majesty and glory of divine persons, and which they can't do without as it were laying aside the divine glory, and stooping infinitely below the height of that glory, those things are below their oeconomical divine character, and therefore the Father can't prescribe to other persons anything of this nature, without a new establishment by free covenant empowering him so to do.[42]

In the covenant of redemption, the Son voluntarily gives the Father the authority to send him into the world in the form of a creature. In

40. Ibid. 20:432.
41. Ibid. 20:437
42. Ibid. 20:436.

exchange for such voluntary humiliation, the Son acquires an authority that is different from the order in the immanent Trinity:

> That the place and station that the Son attains to by this establishment is entirely distinct from that which he stands by the economy of the Trinity, insomuch that by the covenant of redemption the son of God is, for a season, advanced into the economical seat of another person, viz. the Father, in being by this covenant established as the Lord and Judge of the world in the Father's stead, and as vicegerent, and as ruling in the Father's throne, the throne that belongs to him in his economical station. For by the economy of the Trinity it is the Father's province to act as the Lawgiver and Judge and Disposer of the world.[43]

In the covenant of redemption, the Son promises the Father to be sent as servant; in return, the Father promises to institute the Son as Lord and Judge of the world. Neither the status of the servant nor the status of the Lord is equivalent to the status of the Son within the immanent or economic Trinity. Therefore, there must be a free and new covenant established in which the Father and Son both agree to such subversions of roles. Creation does not require an intra-Trinitarian covenant because there are no subversions of roles in the work of creation. A covenant within the Trinity is necessary only when the roles of the Triune persons go against the order within the economic Trinity.

For the same reason, there is no covenant of redemption between the Father and the Holy Spirit. In the work of redemption, the Spirit is indeed subject to a new kind of subjection: "That whereas by the economy of the Trinity the Spirit acts under the Son as God or a divine person, he now acts in like manner under the same person in two natures united, or as God-man, and in his two natures the husband and vital head of the church."[44]

In other words, the person to whom the Spirit submits is transformed. Whereas previously the Son is only divine, now he is a God-man. However, the manner of subjection is not changed:

> The Spirit's subjection to the Son as God-man (though the human nature in its union with the divine be a sharer with the divine in this honor and authority) implies no abasement of the Spirit, i.e., is no lower sort of subjection, than that which the Holy Spirit is in to the Son by the economy of the Trinity.... The Holy Spirit is not thus subject to the Son by any abasement he

---

43. Ibid. 20:435.
44. Ibid. 20:440.

submits to, by any special covenant, but by the gift of the Father, exercising his prerogative as Head of the Trinity, as he is by his economical character.[45]

In the work of redemption, the Spirit submits to the God-man as one divine person submitting to another divine person. There is no difference from the submission within the economic Trinity. Though the Spirit submits to the God-man now, he does not submit to the human nature of the Son intrinsically. The human nature of the Son becomes sharer of the honor of the divine nature. The Spirit submits to the human nature in the Son only inasmuch that the human nature is united to the divine nature. The Spirit suffers no abasement in the work of redemption, neither is he exalted beyond his economic status in this work. Therefore there is no covenant of redemption between the Father and the Spirit. The Father is free to assign the role of the Spirit in the work of redemption by exercising his prerogative as Head of the Trinity.

For Edwards, the concept of abasement also helps to explain why Christ's obedience is meritorious for us. It is meritorious because it goes beyond what is proper to the economic role of the Son:

> Hence it comes to pass that that obedience that Christ performs to the Father even as Mediator, and in the work of our redemption, before his humiliation and now in his exalted state in heaven, is no part of that obedience that merits for sinners. For 'tis only that obedience which the Son voluntarily and freely subjected himself to from love to sinners, and engaged to perform for them in the covenant of redemption and that otherwise would not have belonged to him, that merits for sinners; and that is only that obedience that implies an humiliation below his proper divine glory.[46]

The Incarnation is a humiliation below the Son's proper divine glory. It is precisely this willingness to go beyond the proper order that allows the Son to earn merits for sinners.[47] These merits are sufficient to cover all

---

45. Ibid. 20:441.
46. Ibid. 20:438.

47. The talk about merit makes Edwards close to the Catholic concept of salvation. Unfortunately, Morimoto (*Catholic Vision of Salvation*) concentrates the question of virtues within the saints and ignores the question of Christ's merits for us. Reformed tradition has understood Christ's active and passive obedience as righteousness earned by the human nature of Christ. Here Edwards suggests that the Son (as the divine Son) needs to earn merits before the Father in order to purchase salvation for us. This comes closer to the Anselmian transaction theory than the Reformed imputation

the debts of the sinners. Saving sinners is not a natural inclination of the Triune God; therefore the achievement of that goal requires the Son to commit unnatural abasement. On the other hand, the Spirit's subjection to the God-man is not below the proper divine glory; so the obedience of the Spirit is not meritorious for us.[48]

Despite the emphasis on unnatural abasement in the covenant of redemption, Edwards also believes that subjection of the Son: "[It] is not contrary to their economical order, but in several respects agreeable to it, though it be new kind. . . . That the Father should be servant to the Son would be contrary to the economy and natural order of the persons of the Trinity."[49]

Moreover, in the covenant of redemption, the Father acts in the natural role of the first mover and Head.[50] It is the Father who initiated the covenant and decided to send the Son. Though the work of redemption may be extraordinary, the establishment of the covenant is itself in harmony with the order in the immanent Trinity.

What is the significance of this distinction between the general work of the economic Trinity and the covenant of redemption in particular?[51] We suggest that, at the beginning of our discussion, Edwards tries to give reasons for a covenant of redemption. While his predecessors are satisfied with acknowledging that there is a covenant of redemption at the foundation of the covenant of grace, Edwards presses the question further by inquiring why a covenant of redemption is needed at all. Could the Triune God have saved sinners without first establishing a covenant of redemption? In answering the question, Edwards goes into the question about the natural inclinations of God. For Edwards, order and beauty are central to

---

theory. It would be worthwhile to explore further the atonement theology of Edwards and Catholic theories of atonement.

48. Ibid. 20:441.

49. Ibid. 20:437.

50. Ibid. 20:435.

51. Bush recognizes that this distinction is important to Edwards, but Bush is unaware of the significance of this distinction. Bush thinks that Edwards may be motivated mostly by polemical reason. "It is probable, however, or at any rate typical for him, that Edwards gave such attention to the question because someone had argued the contrary" (*Jesus Christ*, 100). Bush cannot point out any author that had argued the contrary. I do not know of any either. The general theme of Bush's dissertation is that Edwards' Christology such be understood within the almost Neoplatonic framework of the *End of Creation*. The failure to recognize the difference between the work of creation and the work of redemption in Edwards' theology is a serious gap of his dissertation.

the acts of God. God is the essence of beauty, and his acts should reflect his essence. Edwards finds a way to explain creation as an extension of God's beauty. However, in the act of redemption, he finds divine acts that do not readily fit into his conception of God. The forgiveness of sinners and the Incarnation involve an abasement of God that is not congruent with the natural inclinations of God. For Edwards, that is the reason for the covenant of redemption.

For our purpose, the importance of this discussion is that Edwards has blocked the possibility of reading the Incarnation back into the life of the immanent Trinity. The work of the economic Trinity in creation reflects a natural inclination of the immanent Trinity. The covenant of redemption, on the other hand, is an *ad hoc* covenant that establishes both the goal (justifying sinners) and the means (the Incarnation and subsequent exaltation of the Son) of the work of redemption. This covenant does not express the natural inclinations of the immanent Trinity. Given that Edwards regards the life of the immanent Trinity as the essence of beauty, this would suggest that the saving of sinners and the Incarnation are not inherently beautiful acts. Edwards never explicitly denies that these acts are beautiful, but that would be the logical conclusion of his reasoning. Redemption is glorious in the sense that God is glorified through the divine love of the saints; but the method of redemption is not, strictly speaking, a manifestation of God's beauty. Edwards is indeed insistent that the saints recognize the beauty of the Redeemer. In what sense can the Redeemer be beautiful? That is the theme of our next section.

## Excellency of Christ

### Edwards

In August 1736, Edwards preached an important sermon *The Excellency of Christ*.[52] We shall base our exposition on this sermon, supplemented by various *Miscellanies*.[53] The text of the sermon is from Revelation 5:5-6: "And one of the elders saith unto me, Weep not: behold, the Lion of the

---

52. *Works* 19:560-94. The sermon is No. 406 among Edwards' dated sermon (see *Works* 19:805). Both Bush (*Jesus Christ*, 184-96) and Mitchell (*Experience of Beauty*, 33-41) provide an exposition of the whole sermon. In Bush, this forms one section of a whole chapter on the beauty of Christ (*Jesus Christ*, 182-212). Bush has provided the most detail exploration of this theme yet. Nonetheless, Bush does not address the issue whether the process of incarnation itself can be beautiful.

53. *Misc.* 791, on the example of Christ, is especially important.

tribe of Judah, the Root of David, hath prevailed to open the book, and to loose the seven seals thereof. And I beheld, and, lo, in the midst of the throne and of the four beasts, and in the midst of the elders, stood a Lamb as it had been slain."

As is common with Edwards, the verse serves more as a pretext for the content of the sermon. Edwards seizes on the contrast between the Lion and the Lamb in the verse, and the theme of the sermon is that "there is an admirable conjunction of diverse excellencies in Jesus Christ."[54] The sermon is a meditation on several contrasting excellencies in Jesus.

First, Edwards claims that "there is a conjunction of such excellencies in Christ, as, in our manner of conceiving, are very diverse one from another."[55] There are two cases of such conjunction. The first one is that "there do meet of infinite highness & condescension."[56] Christ, as God, has infinite highness. Yet he condescends to become a person of the lower rank. He takes notice of beggars and children. The second case is that "there meet in Jesus Christ, infinite justice & infinite grace. As Christ is a divine person he is infinitely holy just, infinitely hating sin, and disposed to execute condign punishment for sin."[57] Yet he suffers the tormenting of people and the wrath of God in order to bring us salvation.

Second, Edwards claims that "there do meet in the person of Christ, such really diverse excellencies, as otherwise would have seemed to us utterly incompatible in the same subject; such as are conjoined in no other person whatever, either divine, human or angelical." Edwards gives seven instances of such conjunction. First, there is the conjunction of infinite glory and lowest humility. No creatures can have the divine glory of Christ. Then Edwards explains why Christ is the only divine person who can have humility: "For though the divine nature be infinitely abhorrent to pride, yet humility is not properly predicable of God the Father, and the Holy Ghost, that exist only in the divine nature; because it is a proper excellency only of a created nature; for it consists radically in a sense of a comparative lowness and littleness before God, or the great distance between God and the subject of this virtue; but it would be a contradiction to suppose any such thing in God."[58]

---

54. *Works* 19:565.
55. Ibid. 19:565
56. Ibid. 19:565.
57. Ibid. 19:567.
58. Ibid. 19:568.

We shall return to this crucial passage later. Our task now is to complete the summary of his sermon. The second case is that in Christ there meet "infinite majesty, and transcendent meekness." Again, Edwards emphasizes that meekness is a virtue "proper only to the creature."[59] The third instance is that there is "the deepest reverence towards God, and equality with God."[60] The fourth case is that there is in Christ "infinite worthiness of good, and the greatest patience under sufferings of evil." Indeed, he is "worthy of the infinite love of the Father" and "infinitely worthy of all possible esteem, love and service from all men."[61] The fifth instance is that in Christ are conjoined "an exceeding spirit of obedience, with supreme dominion over heaven and earth."[62] The sixth case is the conjoining of "absolute sovereignty and perfect resignation."[63] The last example is the meeting together of "self-sufficiency, and an entire trust and reliance on God."[64] As a divine person, Jesus lacks nothing. Yet he entirely trusted in God while he walked on earth.

Third, the Son has manifested a diversity of excellencies towards human beings through the Incarnation:

> Such diverse excellencies are exercised in him towards men, that otherwise would have seemed impossible to be exercised towards the same object; as particularly these three, justice, mercy and truth.... He manifested an infinite regard to the attribute of God's justice, and that when he had a mind to save sinners, he was willing to undergo such extreme sufferings, rather than that their salvation should be to the injury of the honor of that attribute.... Though he be the just judge of a sinful world, yet he is also the Savior of the world.... So the immutable truth of God ... for there never was any other so great a trial of the unalterableness of the truth of God, in those threatenings, as when sin came to be imputed to his own Son.[65]

In these three excellencies, Edwards highlights both the active and passive roles of Christ in our salvation. Christ manifests justice and truth by willingly suffering the wrath of God. In his human nature, Christ

---

59. Ibid. 19:568.
60. Ibid. 19:569.
61. Ibid. 19:570.
62. Ibid. 19:570.
63. Ibid. 19:571.
64. Ibid. 19:571.
65. Ibid. 19:572.

suffered death and condemnation. Christ manifests mercy by taking the initiative to save the world. It is the prerogative of the divine Son to initiate such kind of work.

Edwards continues to expound how these excellencies are exhibited in Christ's life. These excellencies are exhibited in his Incarnation, virtuous acts and miraculous acts in his public ministry, but most clearly in his last week of life.[66] His meek submission to the abuse of people and the wrath of God is the climax manifestation of his excellencies. These excellencies apply to the Christ who is now sitting at the right hand of the Father:

> Though Christ be now at the right hand of God, exalted as King of Heaven, and Lord of the Universe; yet he still is in the human nature, he still excels in humility. Though the man Christ Jesus be the highest of all creatures in heaven, yet he as much excels them all in humility, as he doth in glory and dignity; for none sees so much of the distance between God and him, as he does.[67]
>
> Even now Christ is carrying his human nature. So he treats saints with condescension and meekness; he remains to be their friends and brethrens. Lastly, these excellencies are manifested in the eschaton. Christ will be a lion to his enemy and a lamb to his saints.[68]

The sermon concludes with a series of applications of the foregoing discussions. The incomparable excellencies of Christ are meant to draw us to him, so that we may choose him to be our savior: "If Christ accepts of you, you need not fear but that you will be safe; for he is a strong lion for your defense: and if you come, you need not fear but that you shall be accepted; for he is like lamb to all that come to him, and receives them with infinite grace and tenderness."[69]

Similarly, his glorious divine nature and humble human nature should draw us to choose Christ to be our Lord, and our lover.[70] He concludes by claiming that the excellencies of Christ are especially tailored to the human mind: "Christ has no more excellency in his person, since his incarnation, than he had before; for divine excellency is infinite, and can't

---

66. Ibid. 19:576–80. Cf. "The time of Christ's last suffering, beginning with the night wherein he was betrayed, till he expired on the cross, was in almost all respects more [excellent] than all the rest of his life." *Misc.* 791, *Works* 18:488.

67. Ibid. 19:581.

68. Ibid. 19:582.

69. Ibid. 19:584.

70. Ibid. 19:588.

be added to: yet his human excellencies are additional manifestations of his glory and excellency to us, and are additional recommendations of him to our esteem and love, who are finite comprehension."[71] Since Christ has the infinite glory of God dressed in the perfection of a human person, we have every possible reason to adore and love him.

As Bush observed, Edwards is working with a "Christological maximalism," where every possible importance is to be ascribed to Christ.[72] Edwards wants to maximize the attractiveness of Christ for pastoral reasons. He conveniently grosses over the agony of Gethsemane or some of the harsh announcements of Christ. For Edwards, the man Jesus is the epitome of creaturely virtue. As God is essentially the infinite being, human beings are essentially finite and dependent beings. As dependent beings, the highest virtue for human beings is to acknowledge their complete dependence and to submit unconditionally to God.[73] Christ manifests perfectly such absolute dependence. "It is fit that he that is the most excellent of all creatures, that is nearest and that is to be set highest by him in eternal honor and happiness, should be the greatest instance of obedience."[74] Due to this perfection in the manifestation of humility, Christ is worthy to become the king of all kings. Even in heaven, Christ is still aware of the infinite distance between the Father and his human nature. His perfect humility persists in eternity. His humility is the perfect example for all the saints and the most excellent person ever.[75] The excellency of human beings lies in their perfect submission to God.[76]

---

71. Ibid. 19:590.

72. Bush, *Jesus Christ*, 180.

73. From Edwards' first published work, a sermon preached in 1730 called *God Glorified in Man's Dependence* (*Works* 17:196–216), this emphasis on the greatness of God and our need for obedience permeates the whole corpus of Edwards' works. As another example, in the first sermon of *Charity and its Fruits*, Edwards emphasizes that divine love flows from a sense of the greatness of God. This love "will dispose to all acts of obedience to God." (*Works* 8:134).

74. *Misc.* 664b, *Works* 18:203.

75. Moreover, Christ's humility is an example to angels too. "CHRIST'S HUMILATION many ways laid a foundation for the humiliation of all elect creatures. . . . It tends to humble the ELECT ANGELS, and to set 'em forever at an immense distance from any thought that anything that God can require 'em can be too great an abasement" (*Misc.* 941, *Works* 20:199). Thus Christ is a counter-example of Lucifer for the angels.

76. While acknowledging and expounding the role of Christ as an moral example, Bush also notes that Christ does not play a very significant role in the ethics of Edwards (*Jesus Christ*, 197). He cites Fiering, *Edwards' Moral Thought*, as an indication that one can write an important monograph on Edwards' moral thought without referring to Christ at all. A better definition of ethics is needed here. Fiering's work is a study of the

Edwards magnifies the humility by stressing the divine origin of the person of Christ: "To be sensible of the greatness of the trial of those virtues in Christ that were exercised under his sufferings, two things must be considered: (1) the infinite height and dignity of his person and state, and (2) the degree of suffering and humiliation that he was subject to."[77]

In *The Excellency of Christ*, the repeated conjunctions of so-called incompatible excellencies are meant to make these two points sensible to the audience. On the one hand, Christ has the infinite glory of the divine nature. On the other hand, Christ has the glory of humility proper to his human nature to its highest degree. For Edwards, the humility of Christ is made all the more remarkable by his status as the Son of God. The application section exhorts us to trust in his divine power as well as his human humbleness. The first guarantees that he can help us; the second guarantees that he will not refuse to help us.

## *Edwards and Barth on the Beautiful Christ*

How does Edwards' understanding of the excellencies of Christ relate to his general theory of beauty? In particular, what is the relationship between the beauty of the incarnate Son and the Trinity? When the question is posed this way, we find that there is a strict dichotomy of human and divine beauty in Edwards' exposition. This dichotomy is crucial to Edwards' conception of the beauty of Christ. As we have indicated, the main human virtue exhibited by Christ is his humility. However, as indicated above, Edwards also believes that humility is a virtue only proper to creatures. Humility means humble submission to someone. There is no one to which God should or would submit to. The divine Son, properly speaking, cannot be humble. In the section on the covenant of redemption, we have seen that the Incarnation does involve a kind of humility for the Son. He has to humble himself to the status of a creature. We also indicate that this is foreign to the intra-Trinitarian life of God; thus this is not a natural extension of the beauty of God. When Edwards limits the virtue of humility

---

moral philosophy of Edwards, which means (in the vocabulary of Edwards' time) the theory of the human psyche. Edwards indeed develops his anthropology quite separated from his Christology. On the other hand, if we understand Christian ethics as the study of the moral principles for actions for the saints, then Christ's example is an indispensable element. We can affirm this by studying how the moral ideal of *Charity and its Fruits*, Edwards' most comprehensive work on Christian ethics, is mirrored in Edwards' depiction of the virtues of Christ. This is an area for future work.

77. *Misc.* 791, *Works* 18:489.

to the human nature, he is consistent with his exposition on the covenant of redemption. The human beauty of the Redeemer is demonstrated in the man Jesus being humble to God and people. The divine Son cannot and should not be humble to people.

What is the divine glory in Christ? Most of the time, it is veiled in humility.[78] Yet it shines forth when the shepherds come to adore the infant Jesus, when the teenage Jesus disputes with the doctors in the temple, when Jesus is transformed at Mount Tabor.[79] The Cross is the supreme manifestation of humility. Yet after the Resurrection, Christ's divine glory shines forth brilliantly in the heavenly council, as recorded in the fifth chapter of the book of Revelation.[80] In other words, the divine glory of Christ is manifested only when he no longer acts as a humble servant, but as judge and king. The divine glory and human glory are manifested in different moments in Christ's life, as divine virtue is incompatible with creaturely virtue. For Edwards, it is virtuous for God to judge and rule; it is indecent for God to be weak and humble. It is virtuous for human beings to be meek and humble; it is a manifestation of pride for human beings to exalt themselves as judge and king.

What is the theological importance of this separation of divine and human glory? The importance is that, like his discussion on the covenant of redemption, Edwards has essentially blocked any attempt to interpret the glory of God through the gospel story. Edwards indicates that the Incarnation and Crucifixion do not add anything to the glory of God. Indeed, they are not even natural manifestations of divine beauty. Rather, they are divine glory veiled in human humility with the purpose of drawing our heart to God. While the weak may be dazzled and frightened by naked divine glory, they may be attracted and encouraged by the gentle glory of the incarnate Son. The Incarnation does not reveal another dimension of divine beauty. It is God manifesting himself in human glory. The life of Christ makes proper human glory sensible to us in ways impossible without the Incarnation. For Edwards, sensing our proper glory will draw

---

78. "Now such is the nature of all creatures, that the seeing of this [Christ being made a curse before God and men] would have tended to have diminished that humble adoration of Christ's infinite highness and glory and awful majesty. It would have tended to take off the awe of their mind, and to have made the object to appear more cheap, and less adorable" (*Misc.* 944, 20:202). According to Edwards, this implies that God revealed to angels during the time of Incarnation the great eschatological misery of those who reject Christ. Only then will the angels maintain a proper respect for Christ.

79. *Excellency of Christ*, Works 19:574–75.

80. Ibid., 19:576.

us to our Redeemer. We are naturally drawn to someone who epitomizes our situation as mere creatures.

According to Edwards' aesthetic theory, the beauty of spiritual beings is proportional love according to the scale of being. The metaphysical gap between God and creatures means that there is a radical difference between divine beauty and creaturely beauty. The beauty of God is his infinite love for the God-self. The Incarnation is definitely not a manifestation of God's self-love. The Incarnation is a mystery that lies beyond the explanation of Edwards' aesthetic theory. Christ manifests divine glory only to the extent that he asserts the authority and power of the Creator. On the other hand, the beauty of human beings lies in loving God unreservedly. Christ is the supreme example of such absolute dependence on God. Though the two kinds of excellencies are placed together the one God-man, they remain separate without mixing. Edwards' theory of aesthetics will not allow such mixing.

To further understand the significance of Edwards' aesthetic theory, we may contrast it with Barth's understanding of divine beauty. Barth defines divine beauty as follows: "If we can and must say that God is beautiful, to say this is to say how He enlightens and convinces and persuades us. . . . Or rather, He has it as a fact and a power in such a way that He acts as the One who gives pleasure, creates desire and rewards with enjoyment. . . . God loves us as the One who is worthy of love as God."[81]

For Barth, to say that God is beautiful is to say that God's revelation is totally pleasant and enjoyable. God's proclamation is not only majesty, but also lovely. Yet Barth refuses to give a formal definition of such loveliness. A formal definition of divine beauty will lead us into aestheticism.[82] We can only perceive this beauty when God's revelation speaks to us and creates joy in us. For Barth, the triunity of God is one example of divine beauty. Why is triunity beautiful? "It is radiant, and what it radiates is joy. It attracts and therefore it conquers. It is, therefore, beautiful."[83] In other words, the triunity of God is beautiful not because it corresponds to some preconceived idea of beauty, but because it has the capacity to kindle joy in our heart.

Barth also believes our Redeemer is beautiful, but in ways radically different from Edwards. For Barth, the condescension of God in the act of Incarnation is precisely the manifestation of divine glory: "God could not

---

81. *Church Dogmatics* II.1, 650–51.

82. Ibid., 652, 656.

83. Ibid., 661.

be more glorious as God than in this inconceivable humiliation of Himself to man and the no less inconceivable exaltation of man to Himself. He is glorious in this very differentiation, this renunciation of Himself. And this, His supreme work towards what is outside Him, is the reflection and image we see Him as He is in Himself."[84] For Edwards, the Incarnation is an *ad hoc* act of the Trinity that requires a special intra-Trinitarian covenant as its foundation. For Barth, the Incarnation is a reflection of what "He is in himself."

What does the Incarnation tell us about the essence of God? According to Barth, "He is One, and yet not imprisoned or bound to be merely one. He is identical with Himself, and yet free to be another as well; simple and yet manifold; at peace with Himself, yet also alive."[85] The essence of God is that while always remaining God, God is free to become another and bring the other into the Godhead. This is the beauty of God revealed in Christ. For Barth, there are no separate moments in which divine and human glory are alternatively displayed. The whole life of Christ is the story of the divine condescension and the exaltation of humanity. This capacity for the communion with the other is the beauty of God.

To elaborate his point, Barth claims that the glory of Solomon's temple is not real beauty: "in Solomon's glory as such we are not really dealing with beauty but rather with its preconditions: riches, brilliance, magnificence, inexhaustible possessions and the lavish development of material means for it."[86]

For Barth, Solomon represents cold magnificence. It is the beauty of Athens, the splendor of this world. In contrast, the beauty of Jerusalem is "the divinely human beauty of its God in the form of its Messiah." For Barth, it is either the beautiful forms of this world or the personal beauty of God. If true beauty is the person and revelation of God, and God is radically different from any objects of this world, then true beauty is radically different from the beauty of this world. We cannot come to understand divine beauty if we start from the meaning of beauty in the secular world.

There are many questions we can pose to Barth. If divine beauty is so radically different from other kinds of beauty, does it mean anything to call God beautiful? Or, putting it the other way, does it not make beauty of this world irrelevant or even demonic to the saints? With his emphasis on beauty as communion between God and another, does it not make God's

---

84. Ibid., 663.
85. Ibid., 663.
86. Ibid., 664

## The Beautiful Christ

beauty correlative to something external to God? In other words, can God be beautiful without human beings? More crucial to Barth's project, is his interpretation of the Incarnation just another conceptual interpretation? Has not Barth just substituted one formal definition of beauty (communion between the divine and the human) for other definitions? Why should the Incarnation serve as the exclusive standard for understanding divine beauty?[87] However, Barth is not our concern here. We shall return to some of these questions in our concluding chapter. We bring in Barth here merely to demonstrate an alternative theological aesthetics with a radically different methodology. For Barth, divine beauty is an event that cannot be given any definition. Barth wants the story of Jesus to be the controlling factor in understanding divine beauty. The meaning of the Christ-event is the manifestation of divine beauty

Edwards starts with a general theory of aesthetics and applies it to discover the excellencies of Christ. In particular, his concept of spiritual beauty finds a perfect example in Jesus. The strength of Edwards' approach is that we can readily relate divine beauty to other kinds of beauty. Edwards clearly demonstrates how God can be the source and norm of all beauty. On the other hand, Edwards also indicates how God is beautiful in himself without reference to any external things. The danger of this approach is that every general theory must be selective. Significantly, Edwards does not give an explanation for the Son entering into a covenant of redemption. In his writings, Edwards often reminds us that Christ's love for his brothers and sisters motivates him to bear his sufferings. Yet, this already assumes that Christ regards human beings as his brothers and sisters. Why should the divine Son regard sinners as his brothers and sisters in the first place? This issue will become more prominent when the question of hell is brought into discussion. Edwards applies all aspects of his theological aesthetics in the defense of the doctrine of hell. This will be the topic for our next chapter.

---

87. "We not only may but must say also that even in His glorification through creation God wills to be and actually is God and glorious, that it is not too small a thing of His glorification through creation. But we must keep strictly to Jesus Christ. It is indeed only of Him that we can speak when we dare to say such extravagant things about ourselves and the rest of creation." Ibid., 668.

# 6

# Eschatological Beauty

FOR EDWARDS, THE ESCHATON IS THE FINAL AND SUPREME MANIFESTAtion of divine glory: "And when the Creator takes the world in hand the second time, it will be as a Creator, not only bringing to pass some external change of the order and situation of the more gross parts, but will cause a most inward change in the nature of things, and bring all in that respect into a much more perfect state (it being their last and eternal state), more fit to show forth the glory of his perfections."[1]

Since the eschaton is the eternal state, Edwards deduces that it must also be the perfect state. God will have finished perfecting his creation by that time. Therefore the eschaton is the end or *telos* of creation and providence. The eschaton is the fulfillment of the work of redemption, and the work of redemption is the greatest work of God:

> We see that all revolutions in the world are to subserve to this grand design, so that the Work of Redemption is, as it were, the sum of God's works of providence. This shows us how much greater the Work of Redemption is than the work of creation, for I have several times observed before that the work of providence is greater than the work of creation because 'tis the end of it, as the use of house is the end of the building of an house.... And so all the decrees of God do some way or other belong to that eternal covenant of redemption that was between the Father and the Son before the foundation of the world; every decree of God is some way or other reducible to that covenant.[2]

Edwards' vision is purpose-driven. The God of Edwards does everything according to his final purpose. The end guides the beginning and the middle. Creation is the beginning; providence is the middle; and

---

1. *Misc.* 929, *Works* 20:172
2. *History of Redemption*, 29th sermon, *Works* 9:513.

## Eschatological Beauty

fulfillment of the work of redemption in the eschaton is the end. Since redemption is the last end temporally, it must also logically be the ultimate end. Since the work of redemption is founded upon the covenant of redemption, Edwards can claim that "every decree of God is some way or other reducible to that covenant." For Edwards, every decree of God is ultimately directed towards the final end. We may question whether the temporal end must necessarily also be the logical end of all of God's work. We may think that alternatively, that all works of God are glorious in and of themselves. It may be questionable that all of God's decrees should be or can be explained by the eschaton. However, the importance of eschatological beauty in Edwards' thought is unquestionable.

What is the final end of the work of redemption? It is the arrival of heaven and hell: "The glorious issue of this whole affair, this has been discoursed this day in this sermon in the perfect and eternal destruction [of the wicked], and in that consummate glory [of the saints]."[3] For Edwards, the redeeming of the elect to heaven and the casting of the enemies of the elect to hell are two parts in the one work of redemption. The church will "enter the harbor and landed in the highest heavens, in complete and everlasting glory," with "all the church's enemies fixed in endless misery."[4] The promise of the Father to the Son in the covenant of redemption includes both the joy of heaven and the triumph over the Son's enemies.[5] For Edwards, both heaven and hell are the glorious promises of the Father in the covenant of redemption.

This chapter will explore the glories of heaven and hell. There are different questions that the doctrines of heaven and hell address; we shall concentrate on the question of the beauty or glories of heaven and hell. We shall argue that the glories of heaven and hell basically, though not exclusively, reflect two different kinds of glories. These two kinds of glories actually permeate much of Edwards' theology, giving it unresolved tensions as well as remarkable richness. Edwardsian scholars in the past have overlooked this diversity and tension. We shall begin on a more hopeful note—the beauty of heaven. Then we shall discuss the beauty of hell. Finally, we address the question of theological consistency between the two kinds of glory.

---

3. Ibid. 9:512. Words in bracket are added by the editor (John Wilson) to the manuscript.

4. Ibid. 9:508.

5. Ibid. 9:509.

## Beauty of Heaven

### *Background*

The Reformed scholastic traditions do not spend a lot of time speculating on the beauty of heaven. They all agree that heaven must be a most blessed place, but they usually do not speculate on the nature of that joy. They also agree that the souls of the saints immediately go to heaven after death. Regarding the intermediate state (the stage between our death and our final bodily resurrection), the Westminster Confession of Faith categorically rejects the theory of soul-sleep. It says that: "The bodies of men, after death, return to dust, and see corruption: but their souls, which neither die nor sleep, having an immortal subsistence, immediately return to God who gave them: the souls of the righteous, being made perfect in holiness, are received into the highest heavens, where they behold the face of God, in light and glory, waiting for the full redemption of their bodies."[6] Regarding the final glory, the Confession has only this short statement: "At the last day, such as are found alive shall not die, but be changed: and all the dead shall be raised up, with the self-same bodies, and none other (although with different qualities), which shall be united again to their souls for ever."[7]

The focus of the confession is on the fact of bodily resurrection, rather than the nature of the joy in heaven. The phrase "self-same bodies" emphasizes the continuity between our bodies in this world and our eschatological body. The focus of the confession is in harmony with Calvin. His chapter on the final resurrection in the *Institutes*[8] defends the belief of bodily resurrection against the pagan idea of immorality. For Calvin, we need to meditate on the glory of heaven so that we shall not be overcome by trials and temptations in this world. He said little about the nature of heavenly glory.

The Continental Reformed scholastic tradition gives a similar story. It rejects the theory of soul-sleep.[9] It does not enter into extensive discussion about the nature of the glory of heaven. It does believe that bodily resurrection and bodily glory are part of the picture. "There will be added the clarification of their bodies, supreme beauty and majesty, by which

---

6. *WCF* 32.1.
7. *WCF* 32.2.
8. *Institutes of Christian Religion*, Bk. 3, ch. 25.
9. Heppe, *Reformed Dogmatics*, 696.

*Eschatological Beauty*

they will be made like to Christ's glorious body."[10] Our heavenly beauty will be Christocentric: "Life eternal is the glorious state in which, after the coming resurrection of the dead, the elect, united most fully to Christ their Head, are to know God in heaven along with the angels, to enjoy His presence and to celebrate it eternally, to obtain the highest good acquired for us by Christ, to be conformed in body and the soul to His image, so far as he is man."[11]

Besides the image of Christ, the greatest beauty in heaven is the vision of God: "The form of eternal life consists in (1) the clearest vision of God, which is the intuitive awareness of God; and the *mental* [vision] if God's spiritual essence is in view, the *ocular* [vision] in God incarnate such as the angels have."[12] Therefore, we shall see the beauty of God both with our bodily eyes and with our mind. There are both spiritual and bodily sensibilities in heaven, and they will both rejoice in the beauty of the vision of God.

As for the Puritans, they build their picture of heaven around Christology. "In Puritan theology the *extra calvinisticum* serves as the foundation for heaven's christological focus."[13] In a nutshell, it means that the divinity of the Son is not circumvented by the humanity of the man Jesus. The infinite life of the Godhead is beyond the comprehension of the human spirit. We cannot approach God directly; we must approach God through the mediation of Christ. In heaven, saints will behold the glory of God only through the glory of Christ.

Among the Puritans, Owen provides some of the most detail theological speculations about the glory of heaven. In his work *Meditations and Discourses on the Glory of Christ*, Owen speculates on the difference between the glory of Christ enjoyed by saints on earth and that enjoyed by saints in heaven. The key Scripture verse is 2 Cor 5:7: "We walk by faith, not by sight." For Owen, this spells out the difference between our joy on earth and our joy in heaven. While on earth, we can only behold Christ's glory by faith through the gospel. Christ's glory in itself is always perfect. However, the means we use to behold it is imperfect. "This is our faith, which, as it is in us, being weak and imperfect, we comprehend the representation that is made unto us of the glory of Christ as men do the

10. Ibid., 707–8.
11. Ibid., 706–7.
12. Ibid., 707.
13. Trueman, "Heaven and Hell," 77.

sense of a dark saying, a riddle, a parable."[14] The limitation lies within our capacity. We have no capacity to comprehend Christ's glory directly. Even if Christ were to stand before us in his full glory, we would not be able to apprehend the glory.[15]

By contrast, "in the vision which we shall have above, the whole glory of Christ will be at once and always represented unto us; and we shall be enabled in one act of the light of glory to comprehend it."[16] First, we shall behold the substance of Christ's glory. "There are three things to be considered concerning the glory of Christ, three degrees in its manifestation,—the shadow, the perfect image, and the substance itself."[17] The Old Testament is the shadow, the gospel is the perfect image, and heaven is the substance. Second, our faculties will be perfected to view Christ's glory. Our mind will be cleansed from all sins and weakness. In particular, we shall learn spiritual truth in ways exceeding the capacity of the bodily faculties.[18] Moreover, "in heaven there shall be a superadded light of glory, which shall make the mind itself 'shine as the firmament,' Daniel 12:3."[19] Just as the natural light of the mind cannot comprehend the gospel, so the gospel light that makes us Christian is not sufficient to comprehend Christ's glory directly. A new kind of light of grace will supplement the natural light and the gospel to enable saints in heaven to behold Christ's glory face-to-face. Lastly, our bodily faculties will be perfected so that we can see the glorious Christ with our eyes. For Owen, the glorious Jesus that Stephen beheld at his martyrdom (Acts 6) is the prototype of what we shall see with our eyes in heaven.

Besides the different instruments (faith and vision), Owen also differentiates the effect of Christ's glory on earthly saints and on heavenly saints. In heaven, the glory of Christ will transform us into the perfect image of Christ. On earth, the image of Christ in us is never perfect.[20] In heaven, the glory of Christ will also give us perfect rest and blessedness.[21]

In summary, both the Puritans and the Reformed schoolmen look upon heavenly glory mainly as a consolation for our earthly trials and a

---

14. *Glory of Christ*, 1:485.
15. Ibid., 489.
16. Ibid., 526.
17. Ibid., 498.
18. Ibid., 491.
19. Ibid., 492.
20. Ibid., 526.
21. Ibid., 530.

motivation to persevere in holiness. They do not usually speculate on the nature of heavenly glory. When they do enter into such speculations, they portray a Christocentric glory. The glory of heaven is the glory of Christ made manifest in a way that is impossible for earthly saints to comprehend. The tradition is insistent that the saints' physical body will be resurrected at the eschaton. The body will be beautiful in that it is incorruptible and it will have superadded ability to behold divine glory.

## *Christ and the Saints*

Turning our attention to Edwards, we find that his speculations move mostly within the Puritan and Reformed tradition. On points of detail about heavenly joy, he goes beyond his tradition. Most of Edwards' musing about heaven are scattered in various *Miscellanies*. For our exposition, we adopt the framework of *True Saints, When Absent from the Body, are Present with the Lord*.[22] This is a funeral sermon, and its theme is the blessedness of the saints who have passed from this world into the presence of the Lord. Strictly speaking, the theme is not the glory of the eschatological heaven. However, there is much continuity between the glory of the intermediate state and the eschatological heaven. This sermon represents the most systematic exposition of the glory of heaven among Edwards' writings. We shall quote mostly from *Miscellanies* to illustrate various important concepts.

Edwards lists five kinds of glory enjoyed by separated souls.[23] The first is that they dwell "in the same blessed abode with the glorified human nature of Christ."[24] Edwards does not explicitly discuss the relationship between the heaven of the intermediate state and the eschatological heaven. We do know that Edwards believes in a physical heaven analogous to our physical world. Edwards occasionally speculates about the physics of heaven.[25] The glory of the saints is incomplete without bodily glory.

---

22. *Works* (BT) 2:26–36. Edwards preached the sermon at the funeral service of David Brainerd in October, 1747.

23. A term employed by Edwards to describe the soul in the intermediate state, after the death of the physical body but before the bodily resurrection at eschaton.

24. *Works* 2:27.

25. In *Misc.* 154 (*Works* 13:303), Edwards argues that the resurrection of Jesus requires the reassembly of every atom that has ever belonged to the body of Jesus. The accomplishment of such daunting logistics obviously proves the divinity of Christ. Edwards is not timid in laying out heavenly physics! By implication, our bodily resurrection would require some kind of reassembly of scattered atoms. Edwards never

In the eschatological heaven, the resurrected bodies of the saints will be beautiful in look and in manners.[26] Its appearance shall reflect the beauty of the souls. Our bodies will be the heavenly suns, filling the heaven with light.[27] Our bodies will experience exquisite bodily pleasures that amplify our spiritual pleasure.[28] While on earth, our bodily pleasures may be harmful to our spirit (e.g., fornication). In heaven, our body and soul will be in perfect harmony, so that bodily pleasures will complement spiritual pleasures perfectly.[29] Edwards is insistent that the spiritual beauty of saints is superior to their bodily beauty.[30] However, his speculations center on how the heavenly body helps us to experience the beauty of heaven. Edwards is insistent that the body exhibits and enjoys the beauty of heaven, along with the mind.

Why is Edwards so interested in the bodily aspect of heavenly beauty? First, the Puritan tradition has always emphasized the fact of bodily resurrection. Second, the young Jonathan Edwards is fascinated with speculations about natural sciences. The speculations about the nature of the heavenly body are extension of his early scientific speculations. Third, and theologically most important, it is motivated by his Christology. Edwards emphasizes that we dwell in the abode of the *human* nature of Christ. If Christ's body is in heaven, then his body is part of the glory of Christ. If Christ's body is part of heavenly glory, then our body must also be part of heavenly glory too. Even in heaven, when we are not confined to surviving and communicating through the body, the body adds a further dimension of beauty to the beauty of the mind. The creativity of Edwards lies in relating the spiritual dimension to bodily dimension through the concepts of harmony and representation. In heaven, as in earth, the body is an outward representation of spiritual beauty. In heaven, the representation and substance (the mind) will be in perfect harmony.

---

considers what would happen if the same atom belongs to two or more saints. In *Misc.* 182 (*Works* 13:328–29), Edwards argues that even the color and sound in heaven are beautiful than those on earth. In *Misc.* 263 (13:369–70), Edwards states that in heaven we will be able to discern variation in sound much better, and so will our eyes be much more sensible to light.

26. *Misc.* 149, *Works* 13:301.
27. *Misc.* 263, *Works* 13:369–70.
28. *Misc.* 233, *Works* 13:351.
29. *Misc.* 95, *Works* 13:263.
30. *Misc.* 149, *Works* 13:301.

## Eschatological Beauty

The second glory of the heavenly saints is that they "go to be with Christ, to dwell in the immediate, full, and constant view of him."[31] While on earth, saints can only behold the glory of Christ in a dark glass. In heaven, they will "see the glory of his divine nature, consisting in all the glory of the Godhead, the beauty of all his perfections; his great majesty, almighty power, his infinite wisdom, holiness, and grace, and they see the beauty of his glorified human nature, and the glory which the Father hath given him, as God-man and Mediator."[32]

When we depart from this world, we do not need the material world as the medium for beholding Christ's glory. We shall see divine glory immediately. We may use human communication as an analogy. In this world, we can communicate only through language or other forms of symbols. Our communication is always through a medium. I can never be sure that my understanding of your words is identical to your own understanding. Therefore, my understanding of your thoughts and feelings are always incomplete and subject to misunderstanding. If your thoughts and feelings can actually enter my mind directly, then I shall understand you in a much better way. Edwards speculates that, in heaven, "there will [be] immediate views of minds, one of another and of the supreme mind, more immediate, clear and sensible than our views of bodily things with bodily eyes . . . a clear and sensible apprehension of what is in [another] mind should be raised in our minds constantly, according to such and such laws."[33]

Just like a person on earth can see the rainbow according to some physical laws, so saints in heaven can see the mind of one another according to some heavenly laws. We will have the faculty to receive sensible knowledge of the thoughts and feelings of another person. We will truly understand each other. Moreover, we will have sensible knowledge of spiritual beauty in a way impossible for people on earth. We can see, in a sensible way, the harmony between my love for you and your love for me. The harmony of minds shall give us a beauty more excellent and pleasurable than any harmonies in music.[34]

Likewise we shall have a much better view of the beauty of Christ. On the one hand, our bodily organs shall be perfected. Our joy from the external senses will be great indeed: "It will be in a sight of Christ's external

---

31. *Works* 2:28.
32. Ibid. 2:28.
33. *Misc.* 182, *Works* 13:329.
34. *Misc.* 153, *Works* 13:303.

glory. And it will be so ordered in its degree and circumstances, as to be wholly and absolutely subservient to a spiritual light of that spiritual glory, of which this will be semblance and external representation."[35]

However, the spiritual beauty of Christ will outshine his external glory. The saints will have a sensible knowledge of the spiritual beauty of Christ—the supreme mind. We shall see both the beauty of his divine nature and human nature. Edwards will elaborate the implications of such intimate knowledge in the next three points.

The third glory is that "the souls of true saints, when absent from the body, go to be with Jesus Christ, as they are brought into a most perfect conformity to, and union with him."[36] As we have indicated, Edwards comes from traditions where the beauty of heaven is Christocentric. For Edwards also, union with Christ is the heart of the glory of heaven. One may say that heaven is possible only because of Christ: "The external heaven surrounds Christ not merely as an house surrounds an inhabitant . . . but rather as plants and flowers are before the sun, that have their life and beauty and being from that luminary, or as the sun may be encompassed round with reflections of his brightness, as the cloud of glory in Mt. Sinai surrounded Christ there."[37]

Christ does not merely happen to dwell in heaven; Christ sustains the very life and beauty of heaven. We can compare it to the relation between God and the world. God does not dwell in the world; God sustains the very existence of the world. Since Christ is the life-giving power in heaven, we can go to heaven only if we participate in the life of Christ. Edwards believes that, had Adam not sinned, he still could not go to heaven without Christ: "Adam, our first head, was a native of this world; he was of the earth, earthly. And if he had stood he would have obtained eternal happiness here in his own country for himself [and] all his earthly posterity. But Christ, our second head, is one that properly belongs to heaven, and the happiness he obtains by his obedience for himself and his spiritual posterity is eternal blessedness in his country, even heaven."[38]

Christ, by becoming our head, brings us a higher glory than what is possible under the covenant of works. In fact, with this Christocentric glory bestowed on us, we have a higher glory than even the angels:

---

35. *Misc.* 721, *Works* 18:351.
36. *Absent from the Body*, *Works* (BT) 2:28.
37. *Misc.* 1122, *Works* 20:494–95.
38. *Misc.* 809, *Works* 18:513.

## Eschatological Beauty

> In the gradation of ends among the creatures, man is the highest step; the next immediate step is to God. Man was not created for any other creature, but it cannot be said so of the angels; for they are created for this end, to minister to the creatures. . . . I answer, that the angels will indeed evermore excel the saints in strength and wisdom, for their office requires [them] to be the universal ministers of God in the universe, but not in grace and sweet holiness and love to God; which excellencies are the highest, and the end of the order of power and wisdom: and only for the exercise of these it is that man is made, and these are the highest end of creatures in general. Therefore the children of God and the spouse of Christ, is more nearly related and more closely united to God than the angels; for whom God has done more than ever [he has] for angels, and who in may respects shall be advance above them in glory, and shall be objects of the dearer love of God.[39]

Saints have a higher glory than angels for two different reasons. First, angels are made to serve us; we are not made to serve angels. Angels are made to serve Christ and all who belong to him. Second, though the angels are superior in their nature (power and wisdom), we are closer to God in a loving relationship. God's love to Christ and Christ's love to God is stronger than that between God and angels. Since saints are united to Christ, the loving relationship between Christ and God also applies to them. Since spiritual beauty lies not in nature but in affections, saints in heaven are more beautiful than angels.

The union between Christ and saints is a union of hearts and affections: "The *relative* union is both begun and perfected at once, when the soul first being quickened by him closes with Christ by faith. The *real* union, consisting in the vital union and that of hearts and affections, is begun in this world, and perfected in the next."[40] This perfect union of hearts and affection will purge the saints of any deformities and sins: "[I]t is impossible the least degree of sin and spiritual deformity should remain with such a view of the spiritual beauty and glory of Christ, as the saints enjoy in heaven, when they see that Sun of righteousness without a cloud."[41]

Edwards is more emphatic than his predecessors in locating the union exactly in affections. This readily follows from the dispositional metaphysics of Edwards. By his understanding of human nature, union

---

39. *Misc.* 103, *Works* 13:271
40. *Absent from the Body, Works* (BT) 2:28.
41. Ibid. 2:28

of affections is the real union of persons. Owen, for example, lays more emphasis on superadded grace in heaven. Owen does not venture to give a metaphysics of that grace. While Edwards has a most interesting metaphysics underlying his discussion about union with Christ, his doctrinal teachings on this point are mostly conservative.

The fourth glory of saints in heaven is that "they enjoy a glorious and immediate intercourse and converse with him."[42] Edwards indicates by this that Christ is our closest friend in heaven. "For he is thus exalted, not only for himself, but for them; he is instated in this glory of head over all things for their sakes, that they might be exalted and glorified."[43] This friendship is one of the purposes of the Incarnation: "Christ took on him man's nature for this end, that he might be under advantage for a more familiar conversation than the infinite distance of the divine nature would allow of; and such a communion and familiar conversation is suitable to the relation that Christ stands in to believers, as their representative, their brother, and the husband of the church."[44]

Since Christ was incarnated, we can have a more intimate relationship with him. It is not merely the relationship of creator and creatures, but also the relationship of brothers and friends. Since we are brothers with Christ, we shall have the same kind of glory as his: "Christ will conform his people to himself: he'll give them his glory, the glory of his person; their souls shall be made like his soul, their bodies like to his glorious body; they shall partake with him in his riches, as co-heirs in his pleasures."[45]

We shall have minds and bodies like Christ. This is similar to the concept of deification in the Easter Orthodox tradition. Of course, there is no evidence that Edwards is even acquainted with that tradition. Edwards is building on the Reformed and Puritan tradition of union with Christ, with distinctive emphasis on glorification of both body and mind. Since beauty is the agreement of being to being, this duplication of glory between Christ and the saints brings another dimension of beauty to heaven. Part of the beauty of heaven is the matching of the glory between Christ and the saints.

---

42. Ibid. 2:28.
43. Ibid. 2:29.
44. *Misc.* 571, *Works* 18:108.
45. *Works* 18:108.

## The Trinity and the Saints

The fifth glory is that "they are received to a glorious fellowship with Christ in his blessedness."[46] What is this blessedness? Edwards list three aspects.

First, we share the blessedness of intra-Trinitarian life: "The saints, by virtue of their union with Christ, and being his members, do in some sort partake of his child-like relation to the Father; and so are heirs with him of his happiness in the enjoyment of his Father."[47] "The saints being united to Christ, shall have a more glorious union with and enjoyment of the Father[,] . . . for being members of God's own natural Son, they are partakers of his relation to the Father, or of his sonship."[48]

As Christ is the Son of God, the saints also become the children of God through union with Christ. This gives the saints a higher glory than the angels.[49] As we have shown in a previous chapter, intra-Trinitarian relationship is beauty itself. The saints participating in the intra-Trinitarian life discover the enlargement of beauty, or the enlargement of glory of God. In heaven, God will love the saints with a love similar to God's love to his Son. God will love them as part of the family of God: "Being members of the son, they are partakers of the Father's love to the Son and his complacence in him. . . . In this family or household, God [is] the Father, Jesus Christ is his own natural and eternally begotten Son. The saints, they also are children in the family; the church is the daughter of God, being the spouse of his son. They all have communion in the same spirit, the Holy Ghost."[50]

Since we are members of God's Trinitarian family, God loves us with the love he has for Christ—complacent love: "He hath a real delight in the excellency and loveliness of the creature, in his own image in the creature, as that is a manifestation, or expression, or shining forth of his own loveliness. God has a real delight in his own loveliness, and he also has a real delight in the shining forth or glorifying of it."[51]

As the Father loves the Son as his own image, so God loves his saints as his own image. "God's love to the saints is real and proper love."[52] Since

---

46. *Absent from the Body, Works* (BT) 2:29.
47. Ibid. 2:29.
48. *Misc.* 571, *Works* 18:109.
49. *Absent from the Body, Works* (BT) 2:30.
50. *Misc.* 571, *Works* 18:109–10.
51. *Misc.* 679, *Works* 18:238.
52. *Works* 18:239.

love is the beauty of spiritual beings, we can say that there is an increase of the glory of God in the heavenly companionship of saints. God has expanded the reach of his love. Edwards does not hesitate to say that there is a real relation between the Creator and creatures.[53] The love of creatures to God and the love of God to creatures is part of the beauty of God. The beauty of heaven is simultaneously an outflow and an enlargement of the beauty of God. Edwards makes the bold move of incorporating the love of saints into the divine beauty.

Yet Edwards also insists that this is not a real increment to the being of God:

> There is no proper addition to the happiness of God because 'tis that which he eternally and unalterably had. God, when he beholds his own glory shining forth in his image in the creature, and when he beholds creature made happy from the exercises of his goodness, because these and all things are from eternity equally present with God this delight in God can't properly be said to be received from the creature, because it consists only in a delight in giving to the creature. . . . But yet in one sense it can be truly said that God has the more delight for the loveliness and happiness of the creature, viz. as God would be less happy if he were less good, or if it were possible for him to be hindered in exercising his own goodness, or to be hindered in exercising his own goodness, or to be hindered from glorifying himself.[54]

In these enigmatic remarks, Edwards tries to assert simultaneously that there is an increase in the delight of God and there is no increase in the glory of God ("no proper addition to the happiness of God"). Why is there an increase of delight in God? If spiritual beings did not actually exist, God cannot love them as actual beings. Were God to be hindered in the work of creation, he would have less opportunity to exercise his delight. Compared with the scenario where (by some incomprehensible reasons) God was hindered from exercising his goodness by creating the world, the actuality of creation is an increase of God's delight. The increase in delight is not a temporal change (God is happier now than he was before the temporal existence of the world), but it is an increase over a counter-factual situation.

---

53. Aquinas insists that there is no real relation between the Creator and creatures. See, for example, *Summa Theologica* I.13.7.

54. *Misc.* 679, *Works* 18:238.

## Eschatological Beauty

Why is there no proper addition to the happiness of God through the creation of the world? If the world is truly an extension of the intra-Trinitarian life, why is the world not an enlargement of God? Edwards offers two reasons: "these and all things are from eternity equally present with God" and "it consists only in a delight in giving to the creature." The second reason is easier to understand, but is a weaker reason. Since we live and move and have our beings in God, our love to God cannot be said to be something outside God. There is nothing outside God that can give God a love that God does not already possess within him. So God's delight in creature is only a delight of giving, not a delight of receiving something new. However, even if it is only a delight of giving, is there not an increase in God's being in the sense that he can now exercise his power and love in a new way? Where previously there were no creatures to receive God's love, now God has objects to receive his generosity. Is not an expansion of God's field of activity an enlargement of God?[55]

Edwards' answer is that "these and all things are from eternity equally present with God." What does it mean to say that everything is eternally present with God? What does it mean to say that Socrates is present with God in the year 3,000 B.C.? Does Edwards mean that, similar to Aquinas, the idea of Socrates is present with God in eternity? Given the different interpretations of this idea in Aquinas and Edwards, this is probably the wrong answer. For Edwards, the idea of Socrates in God is constitutive of the being of Socrates.[56] Here we have to be speculative. Given the importance of the infinity of God in Edwards' thought, we believe that things are all equally present with God with respect to their ontological weight. Socrates might not actually exist in 3,000 B.C., but God already knew at that time (and from eternity) that Socrates would come into existence. That knowledge and determination on the part of God is the ontological weight of Socrates. When Socrates actually came into existence, he did not actually add any ontological weight to the totality of beings. He is already included in God. In the same way, the ontological weight of God's love for

---

55. This is essentially Lee's conception of Edwards' enlargement theory. I disagree with Sang Hyun Lee that Edwards conceptualizes creation as an enlargement of the being of God (*Philosophical Theology*, 196–210). Lee does not cite any text from Edwards that directly talks about the self-enlargement of God through creation, nor can I find any such text. Edwards does talk about an increase of delight through creation, but that is not the same as an increase in the being of God. The infinity of God plays no significant role in Lee's interpretation of Edwards. Lee cites *Misc.* 679 in support of his thesis (ibid., 202), but I interpret it differently from Lee. As a corollary, I disagree with Lee that Edwards gives a "bold reconception of the very nature of God." (ibid., 170)

56. See the discussion of Edwards' idealism in a chapter 3.

Socrates and Socrates love for God (assuming that he truly loved God) are already included in God from eternity. Its actual happening in time is not a proper addition to the happiness of God.

The engrafting of the saints into divine beauty begins on earth, and reaches its fulfillment in the eschatological heaven. In the chapter on spiritual beauty, we have already shown how all true saints participate in the intra-Trinitarian life of God even while they are on earth. In heaven, this process is brought into completion. The divine glory shall reach its eternal climax.

Second, the saints share the fellowship dominion that Christ exercises over his kingdom: "As the glorified spouse of this great King reigns with and in him, in his dominion over the universe, so more especially does she partake with him in the joy and glory of his reign in his kingdom of grace; which is more peculiarly the kingdom wherein she is more especially interested."[57]

Since the saints are members of Christ's kingdom, they share in the glory of the victory of Christ's kingdom. This implies the saints in the intermediate state are aware of affairs on earth. The saints in heaven watch the drama of the church on earth with greater joy than earthly saints. Christ reveals to them the meaning of every act in the drama: "Thus Moses with great joy saw the promises of God fulfilled in bringing the children of Israel into Canaan, with far greater satisfaction than he would have seen it on earth; because he much better could see the glorious ends God proposed by it, and his wonderful wisdom in that work."[58]

Edwards argues in various *Miscellanies* that the saints in intermediate state know and rejoice in the progress of the gospel on earth.[59] Edwards emphasizes that the saints in heaven and the saints on earth are one family. Saints in heaven will regards saints on earth as their friends and family members. We shall also recognize our earthly Christian friends in heaven.[60]

## The Humble Saints

At this point, we shall bring in a dimension of heavenly glory that is not explicitly mentioned in *Absent from Body*. We have seen in the last chapter

---

57. *Absent from the Body*, Works (BT) 2:30.
58. *Misc.* 421, Works 13:478
59. *Misc.* 372, 529, 555.
60. *Misc.* 639, Works 13:171–72.

## Eschatological Beauty

that there are two kinds of glory in Christ. The divine glory of Christ lies in its dominion over nature and Satan. We have seen that saints have fellowship with this glory of dominion. On the other hand, the human glory of Christ is his humility. Christ the man is most humble before God the Father, even in heaven. Edwards believes that saints in heaven will participate in this kind of glory too. This is important because there is a gradation of glory among saints in heaven. If saints are not perfectly humble, this will lead to jealousy. The gradation of glory is according to the capacity for glory of the saints, and this capacity is determined by God arbitrarily:

> The saints are like so many vessels of different sizes cast into a sea of happiness, where every vessel is full: this is eternal life, for a man forever to have his capacity filled. But after all, 'tis left to God's own sovereign pleasure, 'tis this prerogative, to determine the largeness of the vessel; and he may determine how he pleases (Eph. 4:7). Christ's death and righteousness meddled not with this, but left in God's prerogative to determine according to his pleasure[;] . . . nevertheless for what Christ has done, he may either dispense without condition or upon condition, and upon what condition he pleases to fix.[61]

Our union with Christ implies that we shall all be filled to our capacity in heavenly joy. The saints in heaven truly participate in the joy that God enjoys himself (as part of the intra-Trinitarian life). The difference is the quantity. While the joy of God for the God-self is infinite, the saints can have only finite joy. God shall assign to each saint his capacity for joy according to the divine prerogative. We are not sure why Edwards insists on this particular prerogative. Does our heavenly capacity bear no relationship to our earthly faithfulness? Perhaps Edwards thinks that this prerogative accentuates the distance between God and the saints.

The difference in the capacity of joy means that humility is essential to the complete joy of saints in heaven. With perfect humility, the joy of the saints is not tainted by jealousy. For those that have less capacity (we shall call them the *lower ones*), their love for those with more capacity (we shall call them the *higher ones*) will make them rejoice in for others: "For most certainly there is a pure, ardent, even inconceivably vehement mutual love between the glorified saints; and this love is in proportion to the perfection and amiableness of the object loved. Therefore, seeing their love to them is proportionable to the amiableness, it must necessarily cause

---

61. *Misc.* 367, Works 13:437.

delight when they see their happiness proportionable to their amiableness and so to their [own] love to them."[62]

In other words, the saints in heaven will love one another in intensity in exact proportion to the loveliness of the other saints. Those higher ones, because of their greater joy, will have more loveliness. Heavenly joy is nothing but the love for God, and love for God is the essence of spiritual beauty. Therefore, those with more joy will have greater spiritual beauty or loveliness. The lesser ones will love the higher ones more intensely than they love themselves. Therefore, they will only rejoice in the fact that the higher ones have more joy than themselves.

On the other hand, the higher ones will have simultaneously more humility when they behold more clearly the perfection of God: "as they see further into the divine perfections than others, so they shall penetrate further into the vast and infinite distance that is between them and God, and their delight of annihilating themselves, that God may be all, shall be greater."[63]

The phrase "their delight of annihilating themselves" is striking. For Edwards, the saints in heaven are intensely aware of the difference in beauty between God and creatures. This makes them quite aware that they are *nothing* when compared with God. The higher ones see deeper into the beauty of God; therefore they see deeper into their nothingness. The larger capacity actually implies that they are more humble than the lower ones can ever be. The higher ones and the lower ones all dwell together in perfect love for one another and in perfect contentment with their allotted joy.

We shall amplify the role of humility in heaven by making a small digression into the role of angels. Edwards occasionally speculates on angelology.[64] His most distinctive thesis is on the trial for angels. Like human beings, angels are confirmed in their election by trial. The trial is based on "the creature's principle of affection of its own dignity and honor."[65] God use this affection as a test for the angels: "God may give the angels a command which obedience to would really be no degradation to them, that yet might be of such a nature that nothing but a great and

---

62. *Misc.* 5, *Works* 13:201

63. *Works* 13:202.

64. The *Table* lists nineteen *Miscellanies* under the heading of angels, most of them short notes. *Works* 13:129.

65. *Misc.* 664b.§6, *Works* 18:206.

## Eschatological Beauty

transcendent regard to God, and honor to him, and high exercise of it at that time, would make 'em think it not a degradation."[66]

The first test is God's decision that angels should minister to human beings, who are inferior to angels in their intellect and power.[67] God revealed to the angels that one among the humankind will be their head and king. Lucifer the archangel refused to accept such degradation. He led the fallen angels in rebellion, and they were cast into darkness.[68] God let Lucifer fell in order to teach a lesson of humiliation to the elect angels and the elect people: "God in his providence was pleased thus to show the emptiness and vanity of the creature by suffering the insufficiency of the highest and most glorious of all creatures, the head and crown of the whole creation, to appear by his sudden fall from his glorious height into the lowest depth of hatefulness, deformity and misery."[69] "This show that even the elect angels have their eternal life in a way of HUMILIATION and also dependence on sovereign grace, as well as elect men, though not the same sort of humiliation and dependence in all respects."[70]

Having learned a first lesson of humility in the fall of Lucifer, their ultimate test is to behold the Son in the form of the lowly Jesus.[71] Will the angels despise their Lord in this miserable form?

> They saw him in the human nature—its mean, defaced, broken, infirm, ruined state—in the form of sinful flesh. And not only so, . . . but they saw him in much lower and meaner circumstances than the generality of those in that nature, in beggarly circumstances of mean birth. . . . And not only so, but they saw [him] under his last and greatest humiliation, standing as a malefactor, mocked and scourged and spit upon, and at last put to a most ignominious and accursed death, and continuing under the power of death for a time.[72]

The angels who do not despise to serve such a wretched Lord are confirmed in their holiness and humility. They were judged and rewarded at Christ's ascension, but their full reward comes only after the Day of

---

66. *Works* 18:206.
67. *Misc.* 103, *Works* 13:271.
68. *Misc.* 320, *Works* 13:401–2.
69. *Misc.* 936, *Works* 20:192.
70. *Works* 20:193.
71. Edwards believes that angels did not know about the mystery of the Incarnation until it actually happened in time. See *Misc.* 554 & 1098.
72. *Misc.* 664b.§8, *Works* 18:208.

Judgment. In that date, the angels are judged along with the saints. In that day, God will be exalted and all creatures will love him with perfect humility.[73]

We shall conclude the exposition of Edwards' sermon by pointing out the third dimension of the fifth aspect of heavenly glory: "The departed souls of saints have fellowship with Christ, in his blessed and eternal employment of glorifying the Father. The happiness of heaven consists not only in contemplation, and a mere employment, but consists very much in action. And particularly in actively serving and glorifying God."[74]

The glory in heaven is not static. It consists in everlasting and active praises from the saints. Moreover, they shall praise God with ever increasing knowledge of his excellency:

> That the glorified spirits shall grow in holiness and happiness to eternity, I argue from this foundation, that their number of ideas shall increase to eternity. . . . For as they increase in the knowledge of God and of the works of God, the more they will see of his excellency; and the more they see of his excellency, *cæteris paribus*, the more will they love him; and the more they love God, the more delight and happiness, *cæteris paribus*, will they have in him.[75]

> There are many reasons to think that what God has in view, in an increasing communication of himself throughout eternity, is an increasing knowledge of God, love to him, and joy in him. . . . For it will forever come nearer and nearer to that strictness and perfection of union which there is between the Father and the Son.[76]

Even in heaven, the saints will be growing in their true knowledge (i.e., by the number of ideas) of God's mercy. As their knowledge increases, so will their love and praises for God increase. As their love for and delight in God are forever increasing, their beauty will be forever increasing. It will get closer and closer to, but never reaching, the perfect union between the Father and the Son. Saints in heaven are contemplative in

---

73. "Because God's design was to show the emptiness of the creature and its exceeding insufficiency, therefore God suffered both angels and men quickly to fall, and the old creation quickly go to ruin." *Misc.* 936, *Works* 20:194.

74. *Absent from the Body*, *Works* (BT), 2:31.

75. *Misc.* 105, *Works* 13:105.

76. *End of Creation* III, *Works* 8:443.

*Eschatological Beauty*

their knowledge of God and active in their praise of God. The beauty of heaven is dynamic and increasing all the time.

## *Summary*

Let us do some recapitulation. Edwards believes that the eschatological glory of the saints has five aspects. First, the saints will dwell with Christ in the heavenly abode. Second, they have a constant view of the beauty of Christ. Third, they have a most perfect union and conformity with Christ. Fourth, they have intimate discourse with Christ. Fifth, they have fellowship with the blessedness of Christ. Under the fifth aspect of glory, there are three subdivisions. First, saints share in the blessedness of the fellowship between the Father and the Son. Second, they share in the dominion of Christ as king of the universe. We point out that saints also share in the humility of Christ as the perfect creature. We go into a digression about angels to show that even angels are followers of Christ in humility. Third, the saints will be increasing forever the ideas of divine glory in their mind.

If we have to use one word to summarize Edwards' picture of heavenly glory, it would be *Christocentric*. This is true in three different senses. On the simplest sense, every creature is heaven only because of the grace of Christ.[77] Saints and angels become the inhabitants of Christ if and only if they are engrafted into the life of Christ. Heaven is the body of Christ.

The second aspect is the intra-Trinitarian life of the Son of God. The glory of the saints in heaven is a participation in the love between the Father and the Son. The beauty of the saints is an emanation of the beauty of the Triune God. Saints possesses the same divine beauty of the Son, even if their finite beauty can never compare with the Son's infinite beauty.

The third aspect is that saints reflect the glory of the incarnate Son. Christ, in his incarnated form, is an embodied being. Likewise, saints in heaven are embodied beings. Their bodily beauty is part of the beauty of heaven. The incarnated Christ possesses both divine and human glory. His human glory is his perfect humility. Likewise, the saints in heaven are beautiful in their perfect humility. Christ is more aware of the Father's perfection, so his humility is deeper than any saints or angels. Nonetheless,

---

77. *Sola gratia* and *sola Christus* for the salvation of saints are central themes in Reformed tradition. Reformed scholasticism commonly teaches that angels need to be tested before their confirmation for glory (Heppe, *Reformed Dogmatics*, 207–8). Edwards seems to be idiosyncratic in emphasizing that the elect angels are completely dependent on Christ for their salvation (*Misc.* 937, *Works* 20:195–97).

all saints and angels in heaven are perfectly humble to the extent made possible by their knowledge of God.

In associating the beauty of heaven with the beauty of Christ, Edwards stands within the mainstream of the Reformed and Puritan traditions. Compared with his predecessors, Edwards has developed a richer theology of the glory of Christ. Consequently, Edwards can also give a richer theology of the glory of heaven. In particular, Edwards seems to stand alone in his tradition in emphasizing that saints in heaven exhibit both the divine and the human glory of Christ. In the area of divine glory, Edwards goes beyond the tradition in joining divine and human glory in the intra-Trinitarian dynamics. Owen, as we have discussed above, believes that saints in heaven will conform perfectly to the holiness of Christ. However, Owen does not equate the Holy Spirit unequivocally as the holiness of God. As a consequence, he does not speculate on the relation between the glory of heavenly saints and the glory of the Trinity. Edwards follows the Puritan tradition in stressing that saints conform perfectly in the holiness of Christ. He goes beyond the tradition in associating this holiness with the intra-Trinitarian life of God. In the human aspect, Edwards put humility as essential part of the beauty of saints and angels in heaven. In contrast to their humility, the greatness of God is magnified. This greatness of God is also the glory of God. However, this glory is different from the glory of the Trinitarian life of God. As we turn to the doctrine of hell, we find that this is the controlling concept of divine glory in Edwards' theology.

## Beauty of Hell

"Edward was the most famous fire and brimstone preacher in the eighteenth century, and possibly the most famous in the entire history of Western civilization."[78] His sermon *Sinners in the Hand of the Angry God*[79] is probably the most well known and reprinted among the writings of Edwards. Edwards used to be perceived as a hellfire preacher, though the overall significance of hell in Edwards' thought has been distorted by the bias of the editors of his writings.[80] Some modern writers have gone to the

---

78. Fiering, *Edwards's Moral Thought*, 203.

79. *Works* 22:404–18.

80. According to Fiering (*Edwards's Moral Thought*, 204), less than 2 percent of Edwards' surviving sermon manuscript pertains to the afterlife of the damned. Yet 15 percent of the published sermons (before the launch of the Yale edition) belong to the imprecatory type.

*Eschatological Beauty*

other extreme to minimize the importance of hell in Edwards' thought.[81] We believe that his doctrine of hell is an integral part of the theology of Edwards. For our purpose, his polemics on hell helps us to understand better his understanding of the glory of God.

## *Background*

Reformed scholasticism believes that the damned will actively suffer in hell. It distinguishes between the negative punishment of abandonment by God (*poena damni*) and the positive punishment of sensual suffering (*poena sensus*). The active suffering can be described in graphic terms. "The positive evils are manifold, being adumbrated by pains and tortures, by racks etc. and other things of the kind, which usually import evils of every sort, as much to soul as to body."[82] The main controversy at that time was the annihilationism of Socinianism. Thus the emphasis of the schoolmen is on the culpability of the damned and the eternity of hell. The sufferings of the damned will be proportional to the depth of their guilt. The schoolmen use forensic languages to defend their teaching on hell; it seems that they do not use aesthetic categories in their defense.

Among the Puritans, Trueman discerns a certain asymmetry of their teachings on heaven and hell: "heaven has a christological reference, while hell has none."[83] Hell is marked by the absence of God. On the other hand, the Puritans also emphasize the positive punishments of God in hell. This is sometimes described in graphic terms:

> Fire is that which of all things is the most insufferable, and insupportable. Wherefore, by fire, is shewed the grievous state of the ungodly, after Judgement. Who can eat fire? Yet this must the wicked do. Again, not only fire, but everlasting fire.[84]

> Is it not a terrible thing to a wretched soul, when it shall lie roaring perpetually in the flames of hell, and the God of mercy himself shall laugh at them; when they shall cry out for mercy, yea, for one drop of water, and God shall mock them instead of relieving them; when none in heaven or earth can help them but God, and he shall rejoice over them in their calamity.[85]

81. See Fiering (ibid., 200–201) and Stephen Holmes, *God of Grace*, 246.
82. Heppe, *Reformed Dogmatics*, 710.
83. Trueman, "Heaven and Hell," 80.
84. John Bunyans, *Works* III, 286–87, cited in Holmes, *God of Grace*, 206.
85. Richard Baxter, *Works* 22, 419, cited in Holmes, *God of Grace*, 205.

Trueman points out another asymmetry between heaven and hell in Puritan writings: "while heaven is discussed using the language of the visual, hell is discussed using the language of the physical suffering of the flesh."[86] Heaven is described mainly in terms of the vision of God and Christ in order to avoid any suggestion of lust in heaven. Hell is described in physical terms to increase the sense of dread. This difference in language reflects the Bible's own language, as well as medieval vocabulary of heaven and hell.

In preaching hellfire, the Puritans are mainly concerned to convert sinners. They describe the terror of hell in graphic language in order to shake people out of their indifference. Baxter describes his own mission as following: "I am a messenger of the saddest tidings to thee, that ever yet thy ears did hear.... This sentence I am commanded to pass on thee, from the word: take it as thou wilt, and escape it if thou canst."[87]

Trueman points out that a secondary concern of the Puritans is social discipline. They believe that the fear of hell is necessary for the restraint of lawlessness in the society.[88] Beyond the Puritans, the belief of hell is widely perceived by people of the seventeen century as a necessary deterrent of evil.

On the other hand are writers who find the doctrine of eternal punishment unacceptable. "By the fourth decade of the 18th century the doctrine of eternal torment for the damned was being challenged openly, though seldom."[89] The Socinians believe the eventual annihilation of the wicked. Locke, Newton, and Samuel Clarke also believe that the punishment of the wicked is temporary. They believe that eternal torment is not compatible with a loving God. William Whiston is one of the few writers who openly write in opposition to eternal torment. Whiston proposes that the wicked will be offered a chance while waiting for the Last Judgment. The unrepentant ones will be judged and tormented for a period of time after the Last Judgment, and then they will be annihilated. These writers

---

86. Trueman, "Heaven and Hell," 80.

87. Baxter, *Works* 22:361–62, cited in Holmes, *God of Grace*, 204.

88. Trueman, "Heaven and Hell," 82.

89. Walker, *Decline of Hell*, 1. We depend on Walker for our survey of the various views against hell. Fiering (*Edwards' Moral Thought*, 225–38) provides excellent summary of the debate between Edwards and his opponents (including William Whiston, Shaftesbury, Tillotson, and Samuel Richardson). They are widely read at Edwards' time and they provide important arguments against eternal punishment. It is far more difficult to know if Edwards is writing in response to a specific author. See also Chris Morgan, *Jonathan Edwards & Hell*, 101–12.

do not reject the doctrine of hell completely. It is the eternity of torment that arouses their opposition. Shaftesbury has a more radical approach in denying the reasonableness of any kind of hell. For Shaftesbury, a person is virtuous only if she commits good for its own sake. If she does good out of fear of punishment, then she is not truly virtuous. Virtue, as a form of beauty, must be disinterested.

To respond to these criticisms, one can show that somehow eternal torment is harmonious with the beauty or glory of God. If one can show that hell is of itself beautiful to the saints and God, then one takes away the strength of those opposing arguments that argue for hell's incompatibility with divine mercy. Even if we reject hell as a deterrent for evil, we may embrace hell as a manifestation of divine glory. Edwards carries this line of defense further than any other Puritans.

## *The Glory of Damnation*

Like other Puritans, Edwards' preaching on hell has the pastoral function of urging people to accept Christ immediately. This is the purpose of his famous sermon *Sinners in the Hand of an Angry God*. He concludes the sermon with these words: "The wrath of almighty God is now undoubtedly hanging over a great part of this congregation: let everyone fly out of Sodom. Haste and escape for your lives, look not behind you, escape to the mountain, lest you be consumed [Gen 19:17]."[90]

Edwards assumes that many in his congregation were in fact in danger of falling into the hands of the angry God; the sermon is an urgent plea to escape from this wretched fate. This pastoral purpose helps us to understand why Edwards preaches much more on hell than on heaven. The sermons on heaven are meant to be a comfort to Christians facing the problem of death. The sermons on hell are meant to be a call for hypocrites in the congregation to repent. For Edwards, the latter was a much more pressing problem.[91] Most of Edwards' teachings on heaven are theological speculations recorded in the *Miscellanies*. They tend to be more abstract and theological. The hell sermons are meant to scare people out of their

---

90. *Works* 22:418.

91. This concern for hypocrisy gradually led Edwards to oppose Stoddardeanism (open admission to the Lord's Supper), and consequently his dismissal from Northampton. For the laity, church membership is political and familial affairs, as well as spiritual affairs. Edwards was afraid that easy access to sacrament would encourage complacency among the people. See David D. Hall, "Introduction" in *Ecclesiastical Writings*, *Works* 12:51–62.

complacency. Their language is much more graphic and vivid than the musings in the *Miscellanies*. It may be questionable for modern people whether hellfire preaching is conducive to conversion. Nonetheless, the impact of these hellfire sermons on Edwards' contemporaneous audience is indisputable.[92] We shall not evaluate the pastoral merits or liabilities of such preaching.

Moreover, Edwards intends to defend the belief in eternal punishment against theological attacks on this doctrine in the seventeenth century. Edwards' substantive arguments for an eternal hell are regarded as definitive by at least one contemporary theologian.[93] We shall not repeat the effort of Fiering and Morgan by entering into the details of this debate. We shall concentrate on a third question: in what sense can we say that hell is a manifestation of the glory of God?[94]

In a nutshell, hell manifests the glory of God's infinitude. Hell makes it clear that God is everything and everything else is nothing. To Edwards, a sensible knowledge of this truth is the manifestation of God's glory. Hell manifests this majestic glory to both the damned and the saints. We shall begin with the experience of the damned.

Although Edwards does not go into extremes in describing the horror of hell,[95] he insists that the extreme horror of hell is itself a manifestation of God's glory: "As God's favor is infinitely desirable, so 'tis a part of his infinite awful majesty that his displeasure is infinitely dreadful. . . . If God's majesty were not infinite, and his displeasure were not infinitely dreadful, he would be less glorious."[96] "God's wrath, which they shall experience, will doubtless be at least in the compounded proportion of that

---

92. George Marsden, *Jonathan Edwards*, 220-24, describes the impact of the sermon *Sinners in the Hand of an Angry God*.

93. Chris Morgan remarks, "In essence, Edwards' theological approach *annihilates* the theological arguments of the annihilationists in contemporary evangelicalism" (*Jonathan Edwards & Hell*, 137). Morgan expounds Edwards' theology of hell (ibid., 113-27) and uses it to refute annihilationist teachings within contemporary British and American evangelicalism. However, Morgan's brief exposition of Edwards' theology hardly does justice to the sophistications of Edwards.

94. Among contemporary Edwardian scholarship, Holmes, *God of Grace*, ch. 6, is the most relevant for our discussion. Edwards focuses his discussion the danger of hell and the glory of hell. There is little concern in Edwards for the social function of hell. In general, Edwards says little about the social function of religion in his apologetics (McClymond, *Encounters with God*, 105).

95. "When Edwards' sermons on the subject are read alongside the descriptions [of hell by Baxter and Bunyan] quoted earlier, what is striking is actually his reticence in graphic description of hell." Holmes, *God of Grace*, 211.

96. *Misc.* 288, *Works* 13:381.

manifestation of majesty and or abhorrence of their sins, which they shall then see.... God's wrath will be according to the manifestation or glory of God's power, at the day of judgment."[97]

The infinite horror of hell is the reverse image of the infinite bliss of heaven. Both are the manifestation of the God's infinite power. To be in heaven is to be engrafted into infinite joy of God's internal life. To be in hell is to have God's infinite being turned against the damned. To make things worse, the sense of God's majesty will make them absolutely abhor themselves. There will be no heroic stand before God. Even their will shall be crushed, so that they have to swallow their sufferings in shame. For Edwards, the manifestation of displeasure must be consummate with the power of the displeased. If God's wrath has not infinitely terrible, crushing both body and mind, then God is not infinite.

If God is the sole source of life, then the wrath of God must be eternal death. The opposite of eternal life is not annihilation; it is eternal death. For Edwards, eternal death means something worse than annihilation: "Without doubt the misery of the least of sinners that are damned is as terrible or more terrible than no existence, and such that those that endure it would choose rather to cease to be, and be in a state of eternal nonexistence."[98]

Hell will be so horrible that the damned will prefer eternal non-existence to existence in hell. The reality of absolute death is "*utterly to undo the subject of it*.... The soul will be, as it were, utterly crushed; and the wrath will be intolerable."[99] In heaven, the glory of the Lord will bring the saints to such humility that they delight in their annihilation. In hell, the wrath of God will be so powerful that the damned will wish for their annihilation. In either case, God's infinity is experienced by the creatures as a desire for nothingness. God's glory is manifested in both heaven and hell.

Edwards believes that the main source of sufferings in heaven will be the infinite wrath of God itself. Of course, there will be hellfire and the fire will hurt intensively.[100] However, hellfire pales in comparison to the wrath

---

97. *Misc.* 545, *Works* 18:90.

98. *Misc.* 418, *Works* 13:477

99. *Wrath upon the Wicked to the Uttermost, Works* (BT) 2:123.

100. In parallel to the joy in heaven, Edwards emphasizes that the agony in hell will be both spiritual and sensible. "As the faculties of the souls of both saints and sinners will be greatly enlarged, and to no other end but to be capable of enjoying more happiness and receiving more misery, so, since the bodies of each are to be raised to the same ends, viz. in their manner to be the subjects of happiness and misery, there is no reason to suppose any other than the faculties of the body in each will be greatly

of God: "The spiritual misery of [the] damned will very much consist in the sense of the immense hatred and displeasure of God. I speak not of feeling or fearing the effects of God's displeasure, but of the apprehension of that displeasure simply considered. Such is the nature of the soul, that simple apprehension of the hatred of another is unpleasant to it."[101]

Edwards believes that the unpleasantness of the apprehension of hatred increases according to the four following criteria: the hater is close to us physically; the hater is a great being; the liveliness of that hatred to our sense; the paucity of good available to compensate for the hatred. In hell, there is no good left to comfort the damned.[102] In hell, God will be maximally present. The damned will be devastated by the immense presence of God: "They shall then see that he is, doubtless in a more full and clear manner, and with vastly more perfect apprehension, than we now see one another to be, or than we see the sun to be; and also shall see how great a being God is, and shall have the most quick and strong apprehensions of his greatness . . . shall see that he is the great all, and all without him are nothing."[103]

Implicit in this account is the belief that hell is the reverse image of heavenly joy. Beauty, according to Edwards, is agreement of being to beings. Beauty, according to Edwards again, is enjoyable. In hell, the damned experience is infinite antagonism (the opposite of agreement) of the primal Being to their beings. "How dreadful is it to be under the wrath of the First Being, the Being of beings, the great Creator and mighty possessor of heaven and earth!"[104] Extending the terminology of Edwards, we may say that the damned experience maximal ugliness in hell. If beauty is enjoyable, then this ugliness must also be insufferable agony.[105]

---

enlarged, i.e. its sense, to be the inlets of more happiness or misery" (*Misc.* 921. *Works* 20:167). To the damned, "God enlarges their capableness of receiving misery or being made miserable, but he don't make 'em strong to bear misery" (*Misc.* 656, *Works* 18:197). Edwards speculates on the physical nature of the eschatological conflagration and how the hell fire affects the damned (*Misc.* 863, 901, 906, 924, 929–31, 1097), but discussion of this theme will be a digression from our focus on the glory of hell.

101. *Misc.* 592, *Works* 18:125.

102. In *Misc.* 427 (*Works* 13:480), Edwards argues that our souls are created with a great need for the good. Merely the complete absence of good is insufferable agony.

103. *Misc.* 592, *Works* 18:127.

104. *Natural Men in a Dreadful Condition*, in Kistler, *Wrath of Almighty God*, 13–14. *Wrath of Almighty God* is a collection of the Edwards' sermons on the theme of hell.

105. "Again, the ill will and hatred of any being, though the meanest absolutely and in itself considered—is ungrateful and contrary to the disposition of nature, whether we in the least fear any injury as the effect of it or no. (And this will appear by what has

## Eschatological Beauty

Does that turn God into a *deus ex machina*?[106] Even if the wrath of infinite being is automatically infinitely terrible, does God necessarily have to let his wrath run his full course? Does it not seem incredible that God should make any creature so miserable? Edwards answers that God has chosen not to give any second thought to the welfare of the damned, letting his wrath automatically fall fully on the damned: "For God will have no respect or consideration at all of the welfare of those that are damned, nor any concern lest they should suffer too much—they are the godly only, that God afflicts in measure (Is. 27:8, Jer. 30:11)—but only justice should take place. . . . The creature will be utterly lost and thrown away of God."[107]

Following the Reformed tradition, Edwards divides people strictly into the saints and the damned. The division is based on God's free and eternal foreordination. While on earth, both enjoy the blessings of God. In eternity, God will have no regard whatsoever to the damned. They will be punished according to strict justice. Two questions arise from this answer: is this bifurcation really just? Does this bifurcation enhance the glory of God?

We shall briefly examine the question of justice, since it shows again the importance of aesthetic categories for Edwards. As a first answer, "it was the enormity of sin that justified hell."[108] The severity of sin justifies the severity of hell. Even trivial sin is utterly horrible because we are sinning against the infinite God: "Sin is a thing of a dreadful nature, and that because it is against an infinitely great and infinitely holy God. . . . Sin rises up as an enemy against the Most High. . . . This will be very clear if we consider the difference between God and the creature, and how all

---

been said under the head of excellency and love in our Discourse on the Mind)" (*Misc.* 232, *Works* 13:348–49). Edwards argues in the same note that, therefore, the just anger of the mighty God must be terrible suffering to the damned.

106. "Thus, the salvation of a few may be exceptional, but in Edwards's eyes it was not arbitrary, and the meaning of both election and reprobation was to be understood in terms of the inherent relationship of congruity between sin and punishment and between holiness and reward even more than in terms of God's self-glorification. A lawful God could have it no other way." Fiering, *Edwards's Moral Thought*, 212–13. Here Fiering confuses reprobation with damnation. Once God has decided to cast away the damned, then damnation in hell is indeed the lawful and inherent consequence. However, the real question is why God chooses to cast away some and save others. Why is a bifurcation needed at all? As I shall argue, Edwards insists on the arbitrariness of the division as a manifestation of his glory.

107. *Misc.* 545, *Works* 18:91.

108. Fiering, *Edwards's Moral Thought*, 260.

creatures, compared with Him, are as the small dust of the balance, are as nothing, less than nothing, and vanity."[109]

In other words, all sins are enmity against God. The greater is the person against whom we rebel, the greater is the hideousness of our rebellion. Since God is infinitely great, our sins are infinitely guilty. If we think the above argument is unconvincing, Edwards argues that it comes from our insensitivity towards sin: "When I read some instances of the monstrous and amazing cruelty of some popish persecutors, I have such a sense of the horridness of what they did, that the extremity of hell torments don't seem too much for them."[110]

Someone may object that petty sins are not really so horrible. Edwards believes that the insensibility to the horridness of sin is itself the consequence of our wicked nature. In other words, if we are not sensible of the horridness of our own sins, we are so much guiltier for it.[111] The fairness of hell can be fully justified only by sensible knowledge, by applying the aesthetic category of horridness.

However, this answer is inadequate. Given Edwards' brand of Calvinism, God is ultimately responsible for all events on earth. Even sin is part of the will of God.[112] It is God who ordains that the damned are born with a sinful nature. Edwards still has to explain why God creates reprobates at all. As Holmes put it: "Can it ever be just for God to create human beings for no purpose other than to glorify Himself by damning them, as, according to Edwards, He does?"[113] Edwards put it more elegantly: "Doubtless they [the damned] will spend their eternity in blaspheming. . . Why did God give me a being, when he knew I must perish forever? Why did he decree my damnation, and decree my sin in order [to] it? Why was I born with a corrupt nature, and under a necessity of sinning?"[114]

---

109. *Natural Men in a Dreadful Condition*, in *Wrath of Almighty God*, 8. In *Misc.* 713 (*Works* 18:343–44), Edwards argues that "the sin of the creature against God is ill-deserving in proportion to the distance there is between God and the creature." But "'tis the reverse with respect to the worthiness of the respect of the creature to God." While our sin is infinitely guilty, our obedience to God is practically worthless to God. So we can never balance our sins with our merits. Some may question how sins can have degrees of severity and yet all are infinitely guilty. Edwards gives the analogy of cylinders of infinite length. They all have infinite volume, yet one can be larger than another in diameter.

110. *Misc.* 527, *Works* 13:70.

111. *Works* 13:71.

112. Holmes, *God of Grace*, 223–33, gives a good account of this issue.

113. Ibid., 232.

114. *Misc.* 470, *Works* 13:511.

## Eschatological Beauty

The answer given by Edwards is again a matter of sensible knowledge:

> Though wicked men, after they have been guilty of so much sin, do deserve it; though it must be acknowledged that there is a proportion between their sin and their punishment, yet why would he make men that he knew would be so wicked, and would deserve and must suffer such things? . . . It is much to be suspected that, notwithstanding the plausibleness of such an objection, the very principal reason of such thoughts arising in the mind is a want of a sense of the horrible evil of sin. This disposes us to pity the damned wretch, and that disposes to look back and reflect upon the Author of his being and orderer of his misery, because we han't sense enough of the evil of sin to stir up indignation enough in us against it, to balance the horror that arises from a sense of the dreadfulness of his suffering. This makes us pity the sufferer, and this raises objections against God. For I don't observe that, when I read the history of Antiochus Epiphanes and his sorrowful end, and so of other such cruel persecutors, the horribleness of whose practices I have a sense of, any such thought arises.[115]

Edwards recognize that he cannot give a rational answer to the question of justice.[116] Yet he suggests that the problem actually lies with the questioner. Why do we demand rational answers to the creation of reprobates? Edwards suggests that our motivation is pity.[117] When we pity the damned, we begin to question the right of the Creator. Edwards believes that pity is the wrong response to the damnation of sinners. When we think of monstrous sinners such as Hitler, we do not feel any pity for them. Edwards claims that this shows that, when we have a sufficient sense of the monstrosity of sin, we will not feel any pity for the damned. Our sensibility of the ugliness of sin will convince us where rational argument fails:

> There are but two ways of the soul's being convinced and silenced and stilled with respect to such things as these, either (1) by explaining of them to his understanding, untying the knots and unfolding the mysteries, so as to make the reason and justice of the things comprehensible by his reason: as probably

---

115. *Misc.* 866, *Works* 20:107

116. Thus both Holmes (*God of Grace*, 232–33) and Fiering (*Edwards's Moral Thought*, 213, 260) rightly reject Edwards' defense as inadequate. Yet they do not recognize that Edwards' final defense is based on aesthetic argument.

117. Edwards claims that pity is not a true virtue in *Nature of True Virtue* ch. 6 (*Works* 8:605–8). Fiering (*Edwards's Moral Thought*, 247–60) discusses the debate between Edwards and his opponents on the relevance of pity to the question of hell.

the wicked will be convinced when they come to be judged; they will have their understandings so enlarged that they will be able to comprehend these things, and their Judge will set clear light before them, to convince them of the justice of their condemnation. And (2) the other way is by giving of the soul a sense of the glorious, holy and excellent nature of God. That gives it true humility and assures it that God must right and just in all things, and even in those things that it cannot comprehend.[118]

We have to wait till the eschaton, when our understandings are enlarged, before we can have a full rational understanding of God's justice in condemning sinners to hell. What we can have on earth is a sufficient sense of the glory of God that convinces us of the justice of God. The question of justice is ultimately answered by Edwards as a matter of aesthetic experience. If we have a sufficient sense of God's infinitude and our nothingness, then the question will melt away.[119]

## *The Glory of Reprobation*

We now turn to the question of the glory. In what sense does the bifurcation of people into the elect and the damned increases the glory of God? If God were to bring everyone to heaven, would there be any loss to the glory of God?

In his sermon *The Wicked Useful in their Destruction Only*,[120] Edwards distinguishes two ways in which people are useful in bringing glory to God. Some bring glory to God by actively bringing forth fruit to God. Others can be useful passively, in being destroyed; "just as a barren tree, which is no way useful standing in the vineyard, may be good fuel."[121] There are different ways in which the destruction of the wicked is useful for the glory of God: they are useful for the glory of God's justice; they

---

118. *Misc.* 470, *Works* 13:511–12.

119. Fiering (*Edwards's Moral Thought*, 224) puts it somewhat sarcastically, "God's goodness and beauty were self-evident in many things in this world, and one did not have to be a Christian to see them and love them. . . . The test of faith for Edwards was whether a person could love difficult parts of God's creation and thus take delight in the beauty and order of the whole, including hell and damnation. It was a true test because no act of willpower, no conscious effort, could bring about the requisite change in the soul." Actually Edwards claims that even a sensible knowledge of the goodness of God is beyond human willpower. Moreover, as we shall argue below, Edwards claims that an adequate knowledge of God's goodness entails embracing God's terribleness.

120. *Works* (BT) 2:125–29.

121. Ibid. 2:127.

## Eschatological Beauty

are useful to display the majesty of God;[122] and they are useful to give the saints a greater sense of their happiness. We have discussed the first two uses before. We shall discuss the third use below. Here we want to point out that Edwards believes both the saints and the damned are equally useful for God's glory. The saints are useful as willing agents; the damned are useful as a passive objects.[123] However, both manifest the glory of God. In what sense is a bifurcation of people into the elect and the damned a manifestation of God's glory? A first answer is that it shows the richness and the strictness of God's glory. It is displayed both through willing agents and unwilling agents. No agents can refuse to further the glory of God.

A second and ingenious answer of Edwards is the claim that saints in heaven need to see the greatness of God in order to fully appreciate the true glory of God: "The terribleness of God is part of his glory; and that a sense of it should be kept up in the minds of creatures is needful in order to their right and just apprehensions of his greatness and gloriousness. . . . That awful and reverential dread of God's majesty that arises from such a sense, is needful in order to the proper respect of the creature to God, and the more complete happiness in a sense of his love."[124]

According to Edwards, this sense of awful glory has always been part of God's redemptive work. The flood of Noah is the image of the terror of hell.[125] The thunder at Sinai is a shadow of the terribleness of God: "God made his terribleness to appear, when he descended on Mount Sinai; and so he gives us an idea of it in thunder, not in any real works of terribleness executed upon any, but only by the appearances and sounds gives a shadow of it . . . but we can't think that God will think it sufficient, to manifest this part of his glory to the immortal spirits he has made, to all eternity, only in such shadows or noises and appearances."[126]

The Israelites became aware of God's glory of terribleness through the thunder of Sinai. However, Edwards argues, such shadows will not suffice for eternity. Shadows will lose their meaning if the reality behind them

---

122. "A sense of the majesty of an earthly prince is supported very much by a sense of its being a dreadful thing to affront him." (ibid. 2:127) Therefore God's majesty is manifested in the dreadful punishment on the damned.

123. "Although a wicked man may, by being serviceable to good men, do what will be advantage to them to their bring forth fruit to God; yet that serviceableness is not what he *aims* at. . . . He is not useful *as a man*, or as a rational creature, because he is not so designedly. He is useful as things without life may be." Ibid. 2:126.

124. *Misc.* 407, *Works* 13:469.

125. *Misc.* 985, *Works* 20:309.

126. *Misc.* 407, *Works* 13:469; cf. *Misc.* 505, *Works* 18:52.

never comes true. If God wants the saints on earth to know the shadows of terribleness, surely God wants the saints on earth to know the reality. Hell is the reality of his terribleness.

The awful glory of God is displayed in the world of nature and ordinary history too: "There are innumerable calamities that come to pass in this world through the permission and ordination of Divine Providence . . . which, if they were only proposed in theory as matters of faith, would be opposed as exceedingly inconsistent with the moral perfections of God . . . such as the innumerable calamities that have happened to poor, innocent children, through the merciless cruelty of barbarous enemies, their being gradually roasted to death, shrieking and crying for their fathers and mothers."[127]

In its original context, the message quoted above is an answer to those who claim that hell is too cruel for God. Edwards objects strongly to freethinkers of his days who believe only in the compassion of God. For Edwards, God is also a majestic God. There is no reason to believe that God cannot let human beings suffer. For us, the importance of the passage lies in its implication for the glory of nature and other providential works of God. In chapter 3, we have shown that the beauty of nature is a poem of God. There we emphasize that the harmony and power of life in nature is an image of God and of Christ. However, nature also has its cruel side. For Edwards, the cruelty of nature is also a manifestation of the glory of God. It is the manifestation of his terribleness. If we truly experience the glory of the infinitude of God, we also experience our nothingness. Our welfare depends on the sheer pleasure of the almighty God, who is not obliged to bless us. We come to appreciate this glory of God's transcendence through the sufferings in this world. We come to appreciate it fully in heaven through the sufferings of the damned.

Not only is this glory of terribleness anticipated in redemptive history and ordinary providence, but redemptive history also positively demands a final manifestation of such glory. As we have said in the previous chapter, Edwards divides the glory of Christ into his divine and human glory. His human glory is his humiliation. God cannot be humble. For Edwards, even the appearance of humility is detrimental to the glory of God. In the Incarnation, the Son appears to be weak and humble. This distracts the angels from appreciating the full divine glory of the Son:

> Now such is the nature of all creatures, that the seeing of this would have tended to have diminished that humble adoration of

127. *Concerning Endless Punishment*, in *Wrath of Almighty God*, 335.

Christ's infinite highness and glory and awful majesty. It would have tended to take off the awe from their mind, and to have made the object to appear more cheap, and less adorable. It was needful, therefore, that together with such manifestations of the grace and condescension and love of Christ that were so amazing, so beyond all that could ever have entered into the hearts of angels, there should be at the same time proportionable manifestations of the awfulness of his majesty and the terribleness of his wrath, and how infinitely dreadful a thing it is to slight him. This is represented in the infinitely aggravated punishment of gospel sinners, those that neglect so great salvation and despise so glorious a person.[128]

The Incarnation tends to degrade the terrifying aspect of the divine glory of Christ. Even though the angels may know notionally that the man Jesus is divine, they have no sensible knowledge of that glory. As we have seen, the Son manifests humility even in heaven. To counteract any tendency for angels to despise such humility, Edwards believes that it is important that the Son should also manifest his terrible wrath. The human glory of humility must be balanced by the divine glory of awfulness.

Not only does the terror of hell manifests the glory of hell, but the very arbitrariness of the bifurcation of the saints and the damned is the manifestation of divine glory: "For he is not seen to be the sovereign rule of the universe, or God over all, any otherwise than he is seen to be arbitrary."[129] Edwards believes that the arbitrary will of God is prior and fundamental to any laws of nature: "Of the two kinds of operation, viz. that which is arbitrary and that which is limited by fixed laws, the former, viz. arbitrary, is the first and foundation of the other. . . . Even the fixing of the method and rules of the other kind of operation is an instance of arbitrary operation. . . . Therefore arbitrary operation, being every way the highest, it is that wherein God is most glorified."[130]

Edwards claims that the laws of nature are based ultimately on the arbitrary will of God. Those laws, whether in the physical realm or in the moral realms, are true laws only because God ordains them to be laws. It is the prerogative of the Creator to ordain such laws. Only God can be arbitrary in deciding what laws are true. Therefore arbitrary operation is the higher manifestation of God's glory than the laws of nature.

---

128. *Misc.* 944, *Works* 20:202
129. *Misc.* 1263, *Works* 23:212.
130. *Works* 23:202.

For Edwards, this glory of arbitrariness is part of our divine image: "So in those that are the highest order of God's creatures, viz. intelligent creatures . . . they have an image of this. They have a secondary and dependent arbitrariness. They are not limited in their operations to the laws of matter and motion, so but that they can do what they please."[131] The human will is not subject to any laws of matter. Within its own domain, human beings can act in a God-like arbitrariness. In other words, human freedom is an image of divine freedom.

Extending Edwards' argument, we may actually apply the analogy backwards. If we believe that freedom is the glory of human beings, so much more we should ascribe absolute freedom to God as God's divine glory. In this sense, human freedom is an indispensable tool for understanding the glory of God. Edwards is well-known for his polemics against free will. Here we find him actually advocating freedom, at least with respect to secondary causes, as the image of glory. Perhaps, as we shall discuss in the next chapter, freedom has a more important role in his theology than Edwards recognizes.

For now, we shall ask how arbitrariness helps us understand the beauty of hell. In its original context, *Misc.* 1263 is mainly a piece of polemic against the Deists. The Deists believes that the glory of God lies in the clockwork accuracy of the laws of nature. Edwards claims that the arbitrary work of God is even more glorious. For us, the importance lies in its application to redemptive history. The note is interesting in that this is the only place where he grades the glory of creatures according to the arbitrariness of divine operations among such creatures: "The higher we ascend in the scale of created existence, and the nearer we come to the Creator, the more and more and more arbitrary we shall find the divine operations on the creature, or those communications and influences by which he maintains as intercourse with the creature. And it appears beautiful and every way fit and suitable that it should be so."[132]

The material world is governed by physical laws, and God usually rules the physical world with those laws as instruments. Even in the material world, the divine operation is totally arbitrary in its creation at the beginning and its consummation at the end.[133] When we come to the category of human beings, the laws of the human mind "are so high above such a kind of general laws of matter, and are so singular, that they are

---

131. Ibid. 23:203.
132. Ibid. 23:203.
133. Ibid. 23:204–6.

## Eschatological Beauty

altogether untraceable."[134] When we rise higher yet to the angels, God's intercourse with them is immediate. There is no need of any laws of nature.

God's providential operation among higher beings is also arbitrary. The time of birth and death of any individual person is totally arbitrary. Even more arbitrary are the divine operations in redemptive history, such as the calling of Abraham. The climax is Christ: "Then the greatest things were done by arbitrary power, and most out of and beyond the course of nature: as the incarnation of Christ, . . . the rising of Christ from the dead to everlasting life, the alteration made in the human nature of Christ at his ascension into heaven."[135]

As Christ's work on earth is arbitrary work, so is the work of the Holy Spirit in saints: "Thus in their beginning or creation—I mean their beginning as saints or their conversion—commonly at the time of that, God's sovereign, arbitrary interposition and influence on their hearts is much more visible and remarkable than ordinarily they are the subjects of in the course of their lives."[136]

For Edwards, the electing of saints is totally arbitrary. In fact, the whole covenant of redemption is arbitrary. We have seen in the last chapter that Edwards makes a clear distinction between the ontological Trinity and the economic Trinity of the covenant of redemption. The work of redemption is totally arbitrary with respect to the inner life of God. It breaks through and surpasses all the laws of nature. For Edwards, this arbitrariness is the glory of the work of redemption. It is the prerogative of the Creator to save freely and arbitrarily. If all people finally go to heaven, the saints will not have any sensible knowledge of this arbitrariness. There will be no sensible evidence that in fact perdition could quite easily been their fate.[137]

With this perspective, we can appreciate better the purpose of Edwards' famous sermon *Sinners in the Hand of an Angry God*. The sermon is not so much a graphic description of hellfire as it is a compelling portrayal of the terrible glory of God's sovereignty.[138] Edwards reminds the

---

134. Ibid. 23:207.

135. Ibid. 23:210

136. Ibid. 23:211.

137. Holmes (*God of Grace*, 234) argues that, theologically, it only requires one person descending to hell in order that God's justice is glorified. That one person is Christ. But Christ is no longer in hell. If the saints in heaven need a continual sensible knowledge of God's terribleness, then there must be permanent occupants in hell.

138. Trueman ("Heaven and Hell," 81) rightly points out that the sermon's theme is sinner's absolute and desperate dependence on God.

sinners that they are kept out of hell by the mere pleasure of God: "By the mere pleasure of God I mean His sovereign pleasure, His arbitrary will, restrained by no obligation, hindered in no manner of difficulty any more than if nothing else but God's mere will had in the least degree or in any respect whatsoever any hand in the preservation of wicked men one moment."[139]

Therefore, the wicked have absolutely no security before an angry God: "Unconverted men walk over the pit of hell on a rotten covering, and there are innumerable places in this covering so weak that they will not bear their weight; and these places are not seen. . . . God has so many different, unsearchable ways of taking wicked men out of the world and sending them to hell."[140] Their guilt makes their existence depend desperately on the mere pleasure of God: "Your wickedness makes you, as it were, heavy as lead and to tend downwards with great weight and pressure towards hell. And if God should let you go, you would immediately sink and swiftly descend and plunge into the bottomless gulf . . . and all your righteousness would have no more influence to uphold you and keep you out of hell than a spider's web would have to stop a falling rock."[141]

The sermon aims to bring the audience face to face with the infinite might and right of God to punish them. A sinner is like "a spider, or some loathsome insect"[142] before God, liable to be dropped into the eternal inferno at any moment. For Edwards, this is not just a tactic to scare people. To portray the infinite might of God to punish is to describe the majestic beauty of God. To be sensible of God's beauty is to become a true Christian.

If hell is the manifestation of God's beauty, and if beauty is pleasurable, then the sight of hell must be pleasurable. This is the thesis of Edwards' sermon *The End of the Wicked Contemplated by the Righteous*. He uses Rev. 18:20 as his text ("Rejoice over her [Babylon], thou heaven, and ye holy apostles and prophets; for God hath avenged you on her."). His thesis is certainly provocative: "When the saints in glory shall see the wrath of God executed on ungodly men, it will be no occasion of grief to them, but of rejoicing."[143]

---

139. *Works* 22:405.
140. Ibid. 22:407–8.
141. Ibid. 22:410
142. Ibid. 22:411.
143. *Works* (BT) 2:208.

To defend this startling assertion, Edwards delineates carefully the nature of that joy. Negatively, "It will not be because they delight in seeing the misery of others absolutely considered."[144] The saints in heaven do not take delight in sufferings *per se*. Positively, "they will have *no love nor pity* to the damned as such . . . for the heavenly inhabitants will know that it is not fit that they should love them, because they will know then, that God has no love to them, nor pity for them; but that they are the objects of God's eternal hatred. And they will then be perfectly conformed to God in their wills and affections. They will love what God loves, and that only."[145]

We have seen in the section on heaven that the affections of the saints in heaven will conform to Christ completely. We have also shown that, according to Edwards, God has no regard whatsoever for the welfare of the damned. If we accept both these premises, Edwards gives us the only logical conclusion: the saints in heaven will have no regard for the welfare of the damned. If we want to reject the conclusion, we have to reject one of the two premises. In particular, we shall examine the second premise more carefully in our concluding chapter.

Returning to the sermon, Edwards argues that the saints will love God perfectly. Therefore, "they will greatly value the glory of God, and will exceedingly delight in seeing him glorified."[146] How does hell manifest the glory of God? First, the justice of God is glorified. "The sight of this strict and immutable justice of God will render him amiable and adorable in their eyes." Presumably all rational doubts about the justice of the foreordination of the *massa damnata* will be removed. Second, "the power of God will gloriously appear in dashing to pieces his enemies as a potter's vessel."[147] Third, when the saints see the agony of the damned, they "will heighten their sense of blessedness of their own state, so exceedingly different from it!" But if we should think that our joy depends on sensing the sufferings of others, Edwards immediately explains: "When they will see the dreadful miseries of the damned, and consider that they deserved the same misery, and that it was *sovereign grace*, and nothing else, which made

---

144. Ibid. 2:208.

145. Ibid. 2:209. Someone may raise the objection that the Bible encourages us to lament for the fate of the damned and to do our best to seek their repentance. Edwards replies that saints on earth do not know who is the damned. Therefore they should hope, pray and use every mean to make sure that their friends are not among the damned. Saints in heaven knows perfectly whom God loves and whom God hates. They will conform to God in his affections joyfully. (Ibid. 2:210)

146. Ibid. 2:209.

147. Ibid. 2:209.

them so much to differ from the damned . . . O how will they admire that dying love of Christ, which has redeemed them from great a misery."[148]

The saints do not rejoice in the contrast between sufferings and joy *per se*. It is the arbitrariness of God's choice, or the beauty of God's absolute sovereignty, that they rejoice in. If the saints do not have the damned to continually remind of the arbitrariness of their position in heaven, they may lose the sense of the sheer gratuitousness of God grace. Any loss of such sense of gratuitousness is a diminution of God's glory and a loss to the joy of the saints.

## *Summary*

Let us recapitulate Edwards' teaching on the glory of hell. For Edwards, hell manifests the infinity of God. This manifestation is the glory of God. First, the damned agonize upon this glory as the experience of maximal ugliness. Second, the saints rejoice in this glory when they behold hell from heaven. This enjoyment of the greatness of God has three aspects. First, hell shows that both obedient and rebellious people are tools of God's glory. God's infinity is manifested in that all must serve his purpose. Corresponding to this glory, the saints will rejoice in God's justice manifested. Lawlessness has no place in God's creation; every being must be servant to the glory of God. Second, the saints behold in the extremity of the sufferings in hell the infinite power of God. Corresponding to this glory, the saints will rejoice in God's power in annihilating all his enemies. Third, hell manifests the absolute sovereignty of God in disposing the fate of any creature. Corresponding to this is the saints' joy in the sovereign grace in redeeming them. Through the existence of hell, God is exalted as the infinite being. The saints are made sensible of their nothingness and they rejoice in it. The damned are made sensible of their nothingness and they agonize in it. Either way, God's glory is manifested.

Reading Edwards against his Puritan and Reformed background, he emerges as the most systematic thinker on the question of hell. His themes are common stock of his tradition: the greatness of God, the extremity of sufferings in hell, the justice of the damnation of the reprobate, God's sovereign passing over of the reprobate. However, Edwards holds all these themes together in a metaphysical system all of his own. In his system, the other themes are natural outworking of his greatness. They become means through which God's greatness becomes sensible to all spiritual beings.

148. Ibid. 2:209.

By building these themes into a metaphysical system, Edwards provides a formidable rational defence for these traditional doctrines.

How persuasive are the rational arguments of Edwards? We may follow the common procedure of dividing the question further into questions of logical consistency and the credibility of the premise. First, if we accept the premises of Edwards, does Edwards' conclusion logically follow? If we believe that the manifestation of God's greatness and our nothingness is the glory of God, and if we believe that the manifestation of God's glory is desirable as well as pleasurable to spiritual beings, does it follow that Edwards has shown the necessity and the pleasantness of hell? Ivan Karamazov asks whether it is ever justified to let one innocent child suffers in order to bring happiness to all people.[149] We may ask whether it is ever justified to let one soul suffers eternally in order to exhibit God's glory. If we accept the premise of Edwards, I think that the answer is a qualified affirmative. The answer is affirmative in that hell does indeed proclaim divine glory; it is qualified in that the necessity of hell is questionable. On Edwards' premise, all beings naturally agree with beings. For spiritual beings, they naturally desire their existence. They naturally assume that they have a right to exist and enjoy their existence. If a continual sensible awareness of their contingency is necessary for them to enjoy the glory of God, then an eternal sensible image of utter destruction of existence will certainly do the job. If the joy of beholding God's glory far exceeds our affections for any creatures, then it follows that the sight of hell will be pleasing to the saints. However, the question is whether hell is the only means to exhibit God's majestic glory. If, as Edwards has claimed in his musings on heaven, merely a clear vision of the infinity will drive the saints to the desire of their own annihilation, is it necessary to supplant that desire with the image of utter destruction? If the saints in heaven will be deficient in humility without the vision of hell, does that not suggest something is lacking in even the heavenly vision of God? If God's glory is perfectly manifested in the union of saints with Christ, is it necessary for God to manifest the divine glory in a terrible way? May not the power of God be also manifested in the turning all rebellious souls to repentance, rather than in punishing those souls? While Edwards provides many plausible reasons why hell is glorious, it is not clear that hell is the only way in which God can be glorified.

In the end, the arbitrariness of God is the only glory for which hell is indispensable. It is logical that an undifferentiated crowd cannot exhibit

---

149. Dostoyevsky, *Brothers Karamzov*, 276.

the prerogative of God to differentiate unconditionally. Permanent residents are needed in hell in order that the saints will eternally have sensible knowledge of their alternate fate. Even if that glory is indispensable, there is no necessary reason for more than one such resident. Of course, there is no necessary reason why God cannot send most people to hell. But how important is the glory of arbitrariness?

That question brings us to the question of the plausibility of Edwards' premise. We need to find that answer in the context of a holistic understanding of Edwards' theology. We can begin to answer that question by placing the glories of heaven and hell in the context of the totality of his whole theological aesthetics.

## Heaven, Hell, and Divine Beauty

We have indicated in the introduction to this chapter that the glories of heaven and hell are basically, though not exclusively, two kinds of glory. Heaven is mainly permeated with Trinitarian glory. In conforming perfectly to Christ, the saints participate in the intra-Trinitarian life of the Godhead. Since this intra-Trinitarian life is the glory of God, the saints become part of the glory of God. In hell, the damned are consumed by the glory of divine majesty. However, saints in heaven also experience this majestic glory. The participation of intra-Trinitarian life gives them a clear image of the infinitude of God. Consequently, the saints both enjoy their life and delight in their extinction. Conversely, the damned in hell also experience the glory of the intra-Trinitarian life, though in the inverse image of the hatred of God. The intra-Trinitarian life is the agreement of Being to Being; the agony of hell is antagonism of Being to beings. Even though heaven and hell are most distinctly marked by two different kinds of glory, both kinds of glory are experienced in heaven and in hell.

Looking back on our whole discussion of Edwards' aesthetics, we see that the two kinds of glories are intertwined throughout. In discussing Edwards' metaphysical aesthetics, we have seen that material or secondary beauty is the language for expressing spiritual or primary beauty. Our spiritual beauty is, in turn, a participation in the divine beauty. There is agreement of beings to Being in the sense that secondary and primary beauties are all types of divine beauty. There is greatness in the sense that the beauties are meant to lift us up into beauty of a higher ontological category. Thus material beauty is meant to lift us into the spiritual realm, and spiritual beauty is meant to lift us into divine beauty. Material beauty

## Eschatological Beauty

exists for the sake of spiritual beauty, and spiritual beauty exists for the sake of divine beauty. In a sense, both secondary and primary beauties have to be negated as empty without divine beauty. In the case of divine beauty, we have shown that the Holy Spirit is the glory of God and the bond of Being to Being. Yet this self-love within the Godhead is beautiful only because God is not one being among many. The infinity of God renders God's self-love into a virtuous and glorious love. In Christ, we see the perfect union between Father and Son. We also see the perfect humility of the man Jesus. The human beauty of Christ is his exaltation of the divine beauty of majesty. Yet the divine and human beauties are held together in one person in Christ, even if they are conceptually distinct. There is an existential agreement of divine and human beauties in Christ. Standing alone, neither agreement nor greatness is a sufficient explanation of beauty for Edwards. Together, they express the religious sensibilities of Edwards in vivid pictures.

For most of his theology, the two concepts of beauty work together. The infinite beauty of God is communicated to lesser beings through the participation in divine beauty. For this reason, Edwards does not need to acknowledge (perhaps even not conscious of) the fact that he is working with two different concepts. In chapter 2, we see that Edwards formally defines beauty as the agreement of being to being. This is also the definition that Edwardsian scholars usually seize upon.[150] Edwards never formally defines greatness by itself as a form of beauty. This may be the major reason why its importance has been overlooked.

Yet the two concepts of beauty do not necessarily work together. In the doctrine of hell, we actually find them working in opposite directions. On the one hand, if consent alone is beautiful, then antagonism is ugly. We have argued that the damned experience maximal ugliness in hell. Yet if there is ugliness, there is also a lack of divine beauty. If there is an eternal hell, then there is an eternal lacuna in the manifestation of divine glory. If participation in intra-Trinitarian life by creatures is the manifestation of divine glory, then only by bringing all residents of hell into this life will divine glory be manifested in all. On the other hand, if the polarization of

---

150. Two examples: "One aspect of the mind's imaginative activity in its sensation of beauty, then, is that of holding together or asserting a plurality of ideas." (Lee, *Philosophical Theology*, 151.) "The primary beauty of being's cordial consent to being and image of such beauty in the secondary beauty provide him with the surest clue to the mysteries of the things that are and the things that are good and of Him in Whom, from Whom, and to Whom the order of being and beauty are one." (Delattre, *Beauty and Sensibility*, 1)

divine infinitude and creaturely finitude alone is beautiful, then heaven is no more beautiful than hell. As long as God's greatness is perceived, the manner of perception (union or antagonism) is irrelevant. If arbitrariness is a necessary attribute of greatness, then hell is also a necessary part of divine beauty.

While the beauty of consent implies that hell is a lacuna, the beauty of infinitude suggests that hell is an essential part of divine glory. How can the tension be resolved? Is one perspective right and the other wrong? As we shall argue in our concluding chapter, the tension cannot be and should not be resolved. The tension is not a blunder of Edwards. It is a reflection of the tension found within the Bible and the church tradition.

# 7

# Conclusion

WE HAVE COME TO THE CONCLUSION OF OUR BOOK. IN THE PREVIOUS chapters, we have expounded how the concept of beauty underlies much of Edwards' theology. We have pointed out ambiguities and tensions with Edwards' theology. Now that we have given a systematic picture of his theological aesthetics, we are ready to ask questions about his theology within a larger context. His theology can be addressed either within his historical context or within our contemporary context. The first section of our conclusion tries to locate Edwards' aesthetics within his Reformed tradition. How has Edwards adopted and developed his tradition to face the challenges of his time? In the second section, we move forward to look at Reformed theology after Edwards. Edwards' aesthetics has little influence upon American Reformed theology after him. We suggest that this may be due to the shift in theological focus within the tradition. Then we cross the ocean to look at the Dutch Reformed tradition. Though it develops independently from the American Reformed tradition, its aesthetics offers some interesting comparisons with Edwards. In the third section, we move towards contemporary issues. We want to suggest questions for further studies. We pose the questions raised by philosophical aesthetics of the eighteenth century and seek for preliminary answers in Edwards' theology. We also compare Edwards' approach to other contemporary approaches to theological aesthetics. By posing questions that Edwards never intended to answer, we hope to draw out some implications of his theology for contemporary aesthetics.

## Edwards and Theological Traditions

In this section, we gather the research of previous chapters by summarizing the ways in which Edwards has both preserved and modified his theological traditions. We shall employ medieval theology for comparison and contrast where it is helpful to do so. As we have mentioned in the introduction, the rise of the new sciences and rationalism present formidable challenges to the traditional doctrines inherited by Edwards. If the physical world is governed by mechanical laws, will God become a redundant hypothesis? If the human psyche also works according to predictable regularities, where do we find a place for the work of the Holy Spirit? The Cambridge Platonists, the Scottish moderate *literati,* and other British thinkers in the seventeenth and eighteenth century offer a reasonable and gentle God. According to them, humankind should seek their salvation by using reason to guide them to live a virtuous life. These intellectuals would regard the Calvinistic God of Edwards as tyrannical and archaic. On the pastoral level, the mission of Edwards is in kindling evangelical awakenings and defending them against excess and abuse.

As McClymond[1] has persuasively argued, Edwards uses the concept of spiritual senses and rational arguments to launch a two-pronged attack against his enemies. Against various forms of deism, Edwards argues that spiritual sense is the true mark of a Christian. A spiritual sense provides us with sure knowledge that is inaccessible by ratiocination alone. Against the various beliefs on the moral self-sufficiency of humankind, Edwards offers rational arguments supporting the need for grace and special revelation. In this dissertation, we have seen how Edwards develops a rational understanding of divine beauty and the role of sensibility in participating in divine beauty.

The empiricism of Locke has argued that true knowledge starts from sensibility. Hutcheson and others enrich Locke's account to include various kinds of inner senses. Edwards extends the inner senses to include spiritual senses. If, as argued by Hutcheson, people can sense the beauty of the world, then it is reasonable to claim that they can potentially sense the beauty of God too. The Reformed tradition has long claimed that faith consists in savoring the sweetness of God. Faith is never understood as merely knowing and acquiescing rationally that Christ has died for me. Faith involves a heartfelt trust of the Savior that comes from experiential tasting of the sweetness of God. Edwards joins the two traditions together by claiming that this sweet taste of God is the empirical idea of the beauty of God. This ingenious move allows Edwards to claim that faith is based on true knowledge, as well as putting saving knowledge of God beyond the reach of mere reason. Only the presence of God through his Spirit can give

---

1. *Encounters with God,* vi–vii.

us an empirical idea of God's beauty. On this point, we concur with Miller that Edwards has dressed up Calvinism in the vocabulary of the British Enlightenment.

Theology, not philosophy, is the central concern of Edwards. However, the adaptation of traditional theology to a new philosophical language is bound to have ramifications beyond merely some changes in vocabulary. In emphasizing salvation as sensible knowledge of the beauty of God, Edwards has quietly shifted the focus of soteriology from the revulsion against sin to the beauty of the Christian life. On a personal level, this reflects the contemplative temperament of Edwards.[2] Focusing on the beauty of God is not merely an apologetic move; it reflects the heart of Edwards' piety. For Edwards, the greatest joy of a Christian is ravishing in divine beauty. On a pastoral level, Edwards moves the focus for authenticating salvation from the conversion experience to virtuous Christian living.[3] According to Edwards, those who have truly seen the beauty of the Lord will exhibit similar beauty in their lives. The genuineness of repentance can only be known through a transformed life. Unwittingly, Edwards has moved towards the Catholic understanding of piety.[4]

Christian piety is a well-trodden field in the Puritan tradition. If Edwards has subtly shifted the focus of Puritan piety, he stays safely within the conventional boundary. As a faithful citizen of the patriarchal New England society, Edwards likes to stay within traditional boundaries. However, when he starts to address unconventional questions, he gets revolutionary answers (at least from the perspective of his own traditions). The Puritans have seldom asked metaphysical questions. Metaphysical questions seem irrelevant to the practice of piety. The threat of materialism challenges Edwards to fathom the nature of the material world. If the manifestation of divine beauty is the goal of creation, it follows that the world is created in order that it may be perceived as beautiful. For Edwards, the material world has no independence apart from the constant exertion of divine power in maintaining its regular laws. The physical laws are not brute facts, but poems of praise on the constancy of the Creator. The material is created for the sake of the appreciation by spiritual beings.

2. See *Encounters with God*, chapter 3.

3. On the Puritan's emphasis and prognosis of a genuine conversion, see Morgan, *Visible Saints*, 67–75.

4. Morimoto, *Jonathan Edwards*, argues in detail for this thesis. Unfortunately, Morimoto says little about Edwards' doctrine of justification or predestination. Given the fact that Edwards subscribes to the Five Points of the Council of Dort, we need to be careful in extending this similarity of piety to the whole area of soteriology.

Edwards develops an idealistic and a thoroughly theocentric metaphysics in defense of the active sovereignty of God.[5] While the Reformed tradition has always believed that the universe proclaims the glory of the Lord, it does not formalize this belief in the form of a metaphysical system. Again, unwittingly, Edwards harks back to the medieval world of Aquinas. Edwards is not enslaved to the tenets of empiricism. Starting from his first principle (the world is created to exhibit divine glory), he does not hesitate to speculate beyond the confinement of empirical senses.

When he applies the concept of sensibility and beauty to the Godhead, again the result is revolutionary. The Reformed tradition has developed a theology of the economic Trinity in the form of covenants of redemption and grace. It has usually refrained from speculations about the ontological Trinity. For Edwards, the joy of the Christian is beholding the beauty of the Lord. By Edwards' definition, beauty is the agreement of being to Being. If God is one, in what sense can God agree with himself? How can God be beautiful? Edwards employs an Augustinian model of the ontological Trinity to solve the problem. Utilizing Lockean epistemology, Edwards argues that the Son is the idea of God within the mind of God. The Spirit is God's delight in the idea of himself. Compared with the medieval model of Aquinas, Edwards' model is more explicitly theocentric. In Edwards' model, the Son is the idea of God-self; the Spirit is the willing of God towards God-self. Using this model, Edwards achieves a very tight integration between the ontological Spirit and the economic Spirit. The ontological Spirit is God's delight in the beauty of God-self; the task of economic Spirit is to make the saints sensible of the beauty of God-self. The sensibility of beauty is the common identity between the ontological and economic Spirit. The Reformed tradition has always stressed the importance of the work of the Spirit in the covenant of grace. However, it has seldom joined the work of the economic Trinity to the nature of the ontological Spirit.

If Edwards has formed a close tie between the ontological and economic Spirit, he has made a bigger wedge between the ontological Son and the economic Son. The Son is God's idea of God-self. Why should the Son be incarnated? Why should the Son be concerned with creatures at all? The covenant of redemption is Edwards' answer. In eternity, the Son has freely agreed to take on a task alien to his ontological identity. The Son has voluntarily chosen to humble himself and become submissive

---

5. See *Encounters with God* (ch. 3) for further discussion of Edwards' theocentric metaphysics.

to the Father. There are two aspects of this submission. First, the Son becomes subordinate to the Father in the economy of salvation. Second, the Son becomes a creature in the Incarnation. In Edwards, the covenant of redemption has a subtle shift of function. In the Reformed tradition, the primary function of the covenant of redemption is to integrate the purchase and the application of salvation into a single act. In the one covenant of redemption, the Son promises to become the mediator and the Father promises to give the Son the elect saints as his reward. While concurring with this function of the covenant, Edwards has slightly shifted the focus to the humility of the Son in taking on the role of mediator.

In continuity with this focus, Edwards stresses the humility of the incarnated Son. Christ is the apex of human glory. Christ was being totally humble before God and people. While the Reformed tradition naturally regards Christ as glorious, it is not a major theme in the tradition. In the theology of Owen, Christ is glorious in his role as the mediator. He is the unique mediator between God and human beings. There is little attempt to connect the glory of Christ with the glory of humanity in general. In the medieval age, Christ is regarded as the embodiment of the highest theological virtues.[6] In stressing the glory of Christ as perfect embodiment of the virtue of humility, Edwards has moved his tradition slightly towards the Catholic tradition.

By focusing on the virtue of humility,[7] Edwards is moving towards another dimension of divine glory. The Spirit is God's delight in God-self, and this delight in God is shared by all the true saints. This delight in God is the spiritual beauty of saints. In this aspect, the spiritual beauty of the saints is an extension of divine beauty. However, the ontological Son and Spirit need not and cannot be humble before the Father. They are by nature co-equal. Humility implies subjection of one party to another. Humility can only be a creaturely excellency. By his Incarnation, Christ exhibits the beauty unique to creatures in a way impossible for the ontological Son. For Edwards, that makes Christ uniquely attractive to human beings. It is God's gracious intention to draw us to him through the human beauty of Christ. It reveals another concept of divine beauty that is not captured by Edwards' account of the person and work of the Spirit. For

---

6. Cf. Aquinas, *Summa Theologica* III.7.

7. Humility is a major part of medieval piety. However, nor the theological nor the cardinal virtues of Aquinas includes humility. Humility is subsumed under the cardinal virtue of prudence. In singling out humility as the primary virtue for human beings, Edwards leans towards the Franciscan focus on the will rather than the Dominican focus on the intellect.

Edwards, the perception of the infinite greatness of God and (by comparison) our nothingness is the perception of divine beauty. This is the awful beauty of the Lordship of God over all creatures.

This concept of beauty is developed fully in Edwards' theology of hell. In the eschaton, both the Trinitarian beauty of harmony and the awful beauty of Lordship will reach its consummation. For the saints, life in heaven is mainly a continuation and magnification of their earthly Christian joy. While on earth, they already enjoy sensible knowledge of divine beauty through the Holy Spirit. In heaven, they will be sensible of divine beauty in new ways (they shall see the glory of Christ with their physical eyes as well as with their spiritual sense) and in much greater capacity. However, it is the same kind of divine beauty. For the reprobate, they will be surprised and forced to suffer divine glory in a negative way. The immensity of God's wrath will be manifested for the first time to them. For Edwards, the extremity of sufferings in hell is a natural consequence of the immensity of God. Antagonism, the opposite of beauty and harmony, is by nature painful to spiritual beings. Since God is infinite, his antagonism towards the reprobates is also infinite. When the reprobates are made sensitive to this infinite wrath in hell, it will be infinite agony for them forever. For the saints, hell will also manifest the awful beauty of Lordship. It shows them God's sovereignty over the eternal fate of all spiritual beings. The fate of the saints and the reprobates is determined by the sheer pleasure of God. This sensible knowledge of the absolute sovereignty and sheer gratuity of God is different from the Trinitarian beauty of harmony. This will be another dimension of heavenly joy, in addition to the joy of beholding the Trinitarian beauty of God.

The Reformed tradition has long defended the existence of hell as reasonable. The Puritan tradition often employs images of the suffering of hell as tools of evangelism. Edwards continues both these heritages in his preaching and writing on hell. However, the Puritans or the Reformed schoolmen seldom speculate on the nature of the joy of heaven or the agony of hell. By formulating the joy of heaven and the agony of hell as natural expressions of the glory of God, Edwards achieves a much tighter integration between eschatology and soteriology.

Unintended by Edwards, the tightness of his theology reveals a deep tension within Reformed theology. In fact, it is a tension running through the whole history of Christianity. We may call it the tension between Neoplatonism and voluntarism. It can also be expressed as the tension between the universalism of creation and the particularism of election.

The Reformed tradition has always believed in the goodness of the universe. Psalm 19:1 proclaims: "The heavens declare the glory of God; the skies proclaim the work of his hands." In what sense do the heavens declare the glory of God? In particular, the doctrine of the image of God teaches us that there is some continuity between the Creator and human beings. All creatures, and particularly human beings, must share in some way the goodness of the Godhead. We do not have time to survey this tension in Christian tradition. To summarize the story in the shortest way possible, we may say that the medieval tradition has focused the question of this shared goodness on the divine essence. As we have shown in the introductory chapter, the medieval schoolmen consider beauty and goodness as the transcendental qualities of beings. God, being Goodness itself, has the tendency to overflow in goodness. The creation is the overflowing of his goodness into something external to him. The danger inherent in this approach is that God may then seem to be correlative to the world. The distinction between the Creator and creatures may be blurred in the general categories of being and goodness.

For the Reformed tradition, the medieval account creates too much continuity between the Creator and creatures. Calvin has only reproach for Pseudo-Dionysius,[8] the source of much of medieval Neoplatonism. In general, the Reformed tradition has avoided speculations about the reason of creation in order to avoid the danger of infringing on the mystery of God.[9] Edwards, in his effort to create a theocentric metaphysics to challenge the remote God of deism, has unwittingly brought the thread of Neoplatonism into the Reformed tradition.[10] Rather than focusing on the divine essence, Edwards put the focus on the intra-Trinitarian relationship. Creation is not portrayed as an overflowing of the goodness of being of God; it is an overflowing of the self-appreciation of God in the Trinitarian life of God. By focusing on the glory of God rather than the being of

---

8. *Institutes* I.14.4.

9. Concerning God's motive for creation, Calvin writes, "Let this admonition, no less grave than severe, restrain the wantonness that tickles many and even drives them to wicked and hurtful speculations. In short, let us remember that that invisible God, whose wisdom, power, and righteousness are incomprehensible, sets before us Moses' history as a mirror in which his living likeness glows." *Institutes*, I.14.1 (Battles' translation). Calvin contrasts how little creation by itself can teach us about God, as contrasted with the Bible. Reformed scholasticism also emphasizes creation as a free act of God. (Heppe, *Reformed Dogmatics*, 192–95.)

10. Delattre acknowledges the connection between Edwards and Neoplatonism. He believes that Edwards includes God within the category of being. This is contrasted with Plotinus, who makes God beyond being (*Beauty and Sensibility*, 28).

God, Edwards is on safer territory within the Reformed tradition. Thus Edwards avoids divinization of beings *per se*. It is not the mere existence of beings that allows beings to participate in divine life. It is the appreciation of beauty that allows spiritual beings to participate in the divine life. We return to God through ethical vision rather than anagogical religious rites. Material beings participate in the divine life indirectly when they become metaphors for divine beauty to spiritual beings. Their divinization is inseparable from the interpretation of spiritual beings. In Edwards' version of the process and return, the process of return begins and ends with the cognition of the singular beauty of God.

This brings us back to the idealism of Edwards. In the discussion on the metaphysics of beauty, we have already addressed the issue of Edwards' idealism in general. Here, we merely want to bring out that intentionality and sensibility become safeguards against pantheism in Edwards' version of process and return. When I perceive an object as beautiful, that object is different from my self-consciousness. I am conscious of something that is different from the "I" who is the subject of the consciousness. In perceiving God as beautiful, God is essentially different from the "I" who does the perceiving. On the other hand, this is the same beauty that God perceives in God-self.[11] So there is both continuity and discontinuity in the process and return. There is continuity in the object perceived (divine beauty), but difference in the subject (God vs. human beings) of the perception. Yet God remains a totally unique entity. Since God is a unique person, God cannot be grasped by reason in general. God can be grasped only insofar as God reveals himself. Not even in heaven can the saints have an exhaustive comprehension of God.[12] Thus Edwards provides perhaps the most

---

11. Edwards' theology of the intra-Trinitarian is important for avoiding another form of pantheism or panentheism. Like Edwards, Hegel conceives reality as a process through which spiritual beings come to the cognition of God. Hegel develops a form of Trinity in which the world is the objectification of the thinking process of God. God needs creation as much as thinking needs an object of thought (*The Consummate Religion*, 170–71, 191–98). For Hegel, the thinking of the finite spirits is the process through which the infinite Spirit comes to the self-consciousness of himself. By positing the Son as the perfect idea of God within the Godhead and the Spirit as divine self-love, Edwards envisions the objectification and reconciliation process as self-contained within God. Therefore, unlike Hegel, Edwards conceive creation as truly a free act of God. Secondly, the self-sufficiency of God means that God is a particular, unique entity. Unlike Hegel's God, Edwards' God cannot be reduced to concepts. As we shall see in the next section, this gives Edwards a much more robust theory of aesthetics than Hegel. The relationship between Edwards' idealism and German idealism has unfortunately received hardly any attention from scholars so far.

12. In the vocabulary of phenomenology, there is always "excess" in our encounter

complete account of the relationship between divine and creaturely glory among the Puritans, without falling into the trap of pantheism.

We shall now turn our attention to the theme of voluntarism. The Reformed tradition is well-known for its emphasis on the will of God. This is particularly prominent in its soteriology, with its doctrine of double predestination. Edwards follows his tradition in endorsing limited atonement.[13] The originality of Edwards lies in his desire to make this particularism reasonable. It is reasonable in the sense that particularism manifests the glory of the Creator. The Reformed tradition has always insisted on submission to God's will. The difficulty is the motivation for such absolute submission. What is the difference between submitting to God and submitting to a tyrant? For Edwards, the answer is that the majestic beauty of God makes it enjoyable for us to show absolute obeisance to God. Whatever God wills, the sensible knowledge of God will make us happily acquiesce to it. Even the arbitrary and eternal condemnation of people will be pleasant to us.

We shall raise two questions of Edwards' account of voluntarism. First, there is an ambiguity in Edwards' account of the majestic glory of God. On the one hand, God may be majestic in the sense that he is infinitely greater than us. God does not need us, while we are totally dependent on him. All that God gives us is based on the sheer divine gratuitousness. We may call this the glory of the metaphysical size gap between God and creatures.[14] On the other hand, God may be majestic in the sense of being inscrutable. Rather than accentuating our dependence on God, here we emphasize the mystery of God. God is glorious because he is *Deus absconditus*, the hidden God. The distinction can be illustrated by two kinds of heavenly joy in Edwards' theology. Edwards claims that when the saints behold the greatness of God in heaven, they will gladly desire for their own nothingness. This is the joy of exulting in the metaphysical size gap between God and creatures. Even Jesus beholds this kind of beauty in his human nature. Edwards claims also that when the saints behold the damned suffering in hell, they will rejoice in the arbitrary choice of God. God could equally have switched their places, sending the former group to hell and the latter group to heaven. This is the celebration of the will of

---

with God because God always appears phenomenologically as gift. Cf. Marion, *In Excess*. Edwards confines himself to Lockean vocabulary by describing the knowledge of God as sensible. We can extend his insights by reinterpreting his theology with modern philosophical vocabularies.

13. Gerstner, *Rational Theology*, 2:435; Holmes, *God of Grace*, 157–59.
14. The phrase metaphysical size gap is borrowed from Adams, *Horrendous Evils*.

the hidden God. Presumably Jesus will not celebrate this kind of divine glory in his human nature; Jesus in his human nature is the most suitable occupant of heaven. The two concepts are related: the greater the metaphysical size gap between two beings, the more the higher one will appear mysterious to the lower one. If ants can think, they will probably consider human beings as totally mysterious. Yet they are not identical. One may hold to both the greatness of God while denying the total inscrutability of God. The Old Testament emphasizes both the mysterious greatness of God and his knowability through the covenant (Deut. 29:29, 30:11–14).

Edwards is following a long tradition in pointing to the hidden God. Both Luther and Calvin acknowledge the hidden God in their theology.[15] Like Edwards, they need the hidden God to explain the fate of the damned. Is Edwards justified in glorifying in this hidden God? Do we really need him?[16] Perhaps, in the context of his polemics against the deists, Edwards has unfortunately chosen the vocabulary of *arbitrariness*. *Freedom* is more appropriate in this context. It seems more reasonable to claim that the freedom of God (rather than arbitrariness) is part of divine beauty. This is different from the beauty of the intra-Trinitarian life. While the Father necessarily loves the Son, God does not love the world necessarily. In particular, God's love for sinners is both free and gracious. Moreover, God's freedom towards creatures is undergirded by the metaphysical size gap. Since God is totally independent of creatures while creatures are totally dependent on him, his freedom regarding creatures is also perfect. This is captured by the traditional doctrine of the omnipotence of God. Yet freedom is not same as sheer arbitrariness. For example, no one compels me to pursue a doctoral degree in theology. It is a free decision. Yet it is not arbitrary. It reflects my temperament as well as my deepest convictions about reality. Similarly, we may claim that it reflects God's own nature when God freely chooses to redeem sinners.[17] Unlike Edwards, we can claim that the covenant of redemption and the economic Trinity somehow are the true images of the ontological Trinity. However, the exact relation between the ontological and economic Trinity cannot be laid out through reasoning; this is the glory of the divine freedom.

15. Gerrish, "Unknown God," 131–49.

16. For Karl Barth, this obscure God is a grave deficiency of Calvin. His theology of election is a valiant attempt to banish this obscure God from theology. See McCormack, "Grace and Being," 92–110.

17. Cf. Exod 33:19 and 20:5–6. These and similar passages show that while it is God's prerogative to punish, the Lord's name is more closely associated with mercy than with vengeance.

## Conclusion

Does that mean that we can banish the hidden God? If election to salvation is truly a free act of God, there will always be a hidden God.[18] Even on a human level, freedom implies mystery and hiddenness. If our actions are totally rule-bound, then arguably they are not truly free. If our actions are totally random decisions, then our freedom is trivial. We act freely and significantly when we act according to our deepest convictions in a way that cannot be totally explained by rules. Similarly, God truly acts according to the divine nature when God redeems sinners; yet God is free to condemn people to hell according to their desert.[19] The existence of hell is a testimony to the glory of divine freedom. Grace will not be grace without the shadow of hell.

However, will God rejoice at the sight of the damned in hell? Will saints in heaven rejoice at the sight of the damned? We enter into deep mystery in this question. On the one hand, the belief in the final victory of God seems to imply that God cannot have any regrets in the eschaton. On the other hand, if redemption is a reflection of the nature of God, then we cannot conceive God as being indifferent whether people are in heaven or in hell. We cannot follow Edwards in claiming that God and the saints will rejoice in the sight of the damned. Perhaps all we can claim is that, somehow, the shadow of hell will be overwhelmed by the heavenly beauty in the sensibility of the saints in heaven. While we may have the boldness to approach God through Christ, we shall not have the same boldness in condemning those who are without Christ, even in eternity.[20]

---

18. Barth repeats again and again in *Church Dogmatics* II.1 that God is the one who loves in freedom. Yet if, as insisted by Barth, we can only understand God through the story of Jesus, in what sense can we appreciate the Incarnation as a free act of God? According to McCormack, Barth argues that God made a primal decision to make the Incarnation and the outpouring of the Spirit constitutive of his eternal being ("Grace and Being," 100). Besides the difficult questions about the coherence of the so-called active ontology (e.g., Can God freely choose its own constitution?), one can also ask whether there is still a *Deus absconditus* behind this primal decision (cf. Helm, "Hiddenness of God," paper presented at the Rutherford House Dogmatic Conference, 2005).

19. From the viewpoint of human freedom too, we cannot dispense with hell. There is always the possibility of a final rejection of God's grace from the human side. See Fergusson, "Will the Love of God Finally Triumph?"

20. Holmes addresses a similar problem in Edwards (*God of Grace*, 239–40, 268–70). He accuses Edwards in failing to be consistently Trinitarian in his doctrine of hell. Holmes prefers Barth's doctrine of reprobation. I agree with Holmes that we cannot take the display of divine grace and divine justice as two equal and opposite ways. However, the Gospels (pace *God of Grace*, 247–50) do not uniformly portray the glory of the Messiah in terms of grace and redemption. Jesus' vehement denunciation of the Pharisees, the Olivet Discourse and other passages portray a glory of the sever judge. I have more sympathy towards Edwards in calling hell a display of divine glory. But this

## The Beauty of the Triune God

Our main criticism for Edwards is that he has too neatly segregated the harmonic beauty of the creation account and the majestic beauty of the redemption account. Both creation and redemption should reflect both kinds of beauty. We have already argued that redemption should be considered as harmonious with God's nature without denying the freedom of his grace. In creation, the majestic beauty is essential too. First, there is freedom on God's side in that God has created each particular person individually. People are not mass produced as interchangeable parts in a praising machine. God has freely and specifically chosen to create each person with her unique character (cf. Ps 139). The glory of creation includes God's freedom in creating each individual in her uniqueness. I stand in awe of the Creator for creating the unique me. On the human side, there must be some autonomy in an appreciation of divine beauty. To avoid pantheism, the subjects who appreciate divine beauty must be independent subjects. They cannot be merely a mirage or mechanical instruments through which God loves himself.[21] This does not mean that human beings have the kind of freedom championed by Edwards' opponents. We do not need to posit that people have absolute freedom to accept or reject God's forgiveness in Christ. However, people should have an analogous freedom to divine freedom, to the extent that the choice to love God is truly the decision of the individuals.

On the other hand, the redemption story must also demonstrate harmonic beauty. We have seen that Edwards is emphatic that the incarnated Christ is the archetype of the saints. In his humility and corporeality, he embodies the blessed life of the saints. However, Edwards consistently resists saying that the Incarnation and the humiliation of the Cross is a manifestation of divine beauty. Karl Barth takes the opposite position in proclaiming that only in the Incarnation and humiliation do we see the glory of God. We need both Edwards and Barth. We need a Spiritual beauty in which God, in communion with the redeemed reality, exults in the self-glory of God. We need a Christological beauty in which divine beauty is precisely manifested in God entering into the fallen world. Even in alienation and hopelessness we find the glory of God-self. The two kinds of beauty should not be harmonized, but be allowed to work in tension with one another. The working out of this tension will be a project for another day.

---

hellish glory cannot be on an equal footing with heavenly glory.

21. In the extreme case of divine voluntarism expounded in *Original Sin* III.3 (God can arbitrarily constitutes Adam and his posterity as one person), one wonders if there is any meaningful and coherent subject left to do the loving of God.

*Conclusion*

We shall summarize our evaluation of Edwards' relationship to the Reformed tradition. By focusing on the beauty of the Lord, Edwards provides an alternative and complimentary model to the forensic model of divine-human relationship. By developing complimentary models of intra-Trinitarian life and our spiritual life, Edwards provides a model where human beings can truly participate in divine beauty. By emphasizing the majestic glory of the Creator, he enriches the doctrine of election by relating election to the manifestation of the glory of God, rather than merely the stark will of God. His theology represents a genuine advance of the Reformed tradition in its philosophical sophistication. It integrates the work of the Holy Spirit in the saints with the role of the Spirit in the ontological Trinity and the purpose of creation. Its major deficiency is the lack of connection between the work of Christ and the role of the Son in the ontological Trinity. As a consequence, the glory manifested in election is exclusively the majestic glory of the Creator over the creatures. We suggest that there can be a richer interaction between the Trinitarian beauty and the Creator's glory in both the theologies of creation and of redemption.

## Edwards and Later Reformed Aesthetics

What is the influence on Edwards' on subsequent Reformed aesthetics? Unfortunately, the answer is really a study of negligence and ignorance. We'll trace briefly the development of the American Reformed theology after Edwards to suggest some reasons for this sorry state. Then we shall examine briefly the aesthetics of the Dutch Reformed tradition to suggest points of difference. The repetition of *briefly* is deliberate: we can do no more than give some indications for further research. We shall conclude with some tentative suggestions on how Edwards can contribute to the contemporary Reformed aesthetics.

We shall begin by looking at the American Reformed tradition. There are a multiple Reformed traditions in America: Old Princeton theology, Dutch schools New England theology, the Southern tradition and others.[22] Among these traditions, only Princeton theology and New England theology explicitly claim to have inherited the mantle of Edwards. Even in these two traditions, the influence of Edwards' aesthetics seems to be minimal. The influence of Edwards' theology on other Reformed traditions is negligible until the twentieth century. We shall concentrate our survey on Princeton theology and New England theology.

22. See Well, *Reformed Theology*.

## The Beauty of the Triune God

We begin with New England theology, which has the closest relation to Edwards through personal and geographical connections.[23] The founders of New England theology, Samuel Hopkins (1721–1803) and Joseph Bellamy (1719–80), were students of Edwards. Hopkins was also the first biographer of Edwards. Though the personal ties are close, the faithfulness of New England theology to the theology of Edwards is a debatable issue.[24] We claim that a shift from the theocentric vision of Edwards to a more anthropological concern is a major factor for the neglect of aesthetics in New England theology.

We have claimed in this book that Edwards' vision is driven by a theocentric metaphysics. The material world is a giant metaphor for divine beauty, and the spiritual world is an extension of the beauty of the intra-Trinitarian life. Even hell is a manifestation of the divine beauty of majesty. Unfortunately, neither his writings on the metaphorical nature of the world nor those on the Trinity attracted much attention after his death. The fact that these notes are all unpublished (during his lifetime) private notes of Edwards helps to explain their fall into oblivion.

The most important reason for such neglect is probably the fact that New England theology made a legalistic turn soon after Edwards.[25] For Edwards, the perception of divine glory is a central theme. For Bellamy and Hopkins, their central concern is the justification of the divine economy under the name of reasonableness.[26] Their quest led to significant modifications to the Calvinistic doctrines of Edwards.

In the doctrine of atonement, New England theology soon adopted Grotius' governmental theory.[27] In this theory, Christ was crucified in

---

23. The standard history of New England theology is Foster, *Genetic History*.

24. See Well, *Reformed Theology*, 41–54, for the debate between Charles Hodge (a Princeton theologian) and Nathaniel Taylor (a New England theologian) on who has preserved true Edwardsian theology.

25. "His [Edwards] disciples and later champions lacked either his profound piety, or his intellectual vigor, or both. They reverted to governmental and legalistic conceptions of Calvinism." (Haroutunian, *Piety versus Moralism*, xxx) Haroutunian argues convincingly that New England Theology soon departed from Edwards and migrated to a humanistic paradigm. Recently Sweeney (*Nathaniel Taylor*) argues that, at least with respect to Taylor, New England did consciously build upon distinctive Edwardsian ideas. However, the two themes are not mutually exclusive. One can develop Edwards in ways that depart significantly from the piety of Edwards himself.

26. "It was no longer possible to accept events as divine decrees unless they measured up to the ethical principle which had come to constitute the standards of righteous human intercourse, and to which even the Creator and the Ruler of the universe had to conform." Haroutunion, *Piety versus Moralism*, 30.

27. Bellamy may be credited as the originator of this development. See Foster, *New*

order to demonstrate God's hatred of sin. The death of Christ is not a vicarious substitution for our penalty. The death of Christ demonstrates the ultimate seriousness of the retributive justice of God. God did not spare even his Son in order to show the kind of punishment that should have befallen sinners. Christ did not literally suffer for our sins, nor is Christ's righteousness imputed directly to us. God forgives us sinners individually. Forgiveness is the prerogative of the Governor of the universe. The death of Christ demonstrates that this forgiveness is not given in a light-hearted way. After sinners receive their forgiveness, they still have to work out their own righteousness.

The quest for reasonableness in New England theory is most evident in its focus on the question of ability. In *Freedom of the Will*, Edwards makes a distinction between natural and moral ability in order to make sinners accountable for their sins. In New England theory after Edwards, natural ability becomes more and more a tool for the justification of the condemnation of sinners. Bellamy, for example, categorically denies the doctrine of limited atonement.[28] God can justly condemn only those who deliberately rejects the mercy of God, not those who never have a chance to receive mercy. The fact that human beings have natural ability to do good means that, in some vague sense, they have the ability to voluntarily accept the offer of the gospel. Nathaniel Taylor (1786–1858), arguably the greatest theologian of the New England school, argues that natural ability means that a person could— hypothetically—have been sinless throughout her life.[29] The reality is that no one has ever been able to do so, but the possibility as such should not be denied. Otherwise God would be condemning people unjustly.

We do not need to go into the details of New England theology or its demise after Taylor.[30] For our story, we need to recognize the importance of the motif of the moral government of God.[31] Edwards claims that even heathens recognize the moral government of a supreme God over human

---

*England Theology*, 113–17. See also Haroutunian, *Piety versus Moralism*, 166–76, for a general treatment of the governmental theory of New England theology.

28. Foster, *New England Theology*, 116.

29. For Taylor's theology of original sin and the controversy around it, see Sweeney, *Taylor*, 73–90. See Foster, *New England Theology*, 224–72, for the whole debate about the freedom of the will.

30. Foster, *New England Theology*, 543–53, and Sweeney, *Taylor*, 141–43, discuss its demise.

31. It is called moral government because God rules over human beings through moral persuasion rather than coercion.

affairs.[32] Against deism, he argues that the providence of God is both reasonable and commonly recognized. However, the moral government of God is not the central motif in the theology of Edwards. In New England theology, the motif grew more and more important over time. It became the central organizing theme of Taylor's theology.[33] In New England theory, conversion is our voluntary submission to the moral governance of God. The heart of New England piety is the recognition of the justice of God and our sinfulness. The relationship between God and the world is seen through the image of the ruler and its subjects. The moment of conversion is the point in our life where we submit to the moral governance of God. Seen from this perspective, Charles Finney's (1792–1875) theology of revival may be seen as a natural evolvement of New England theology.[34] Doctrinally, the Arminian Finney is far from the Calvinism of Edwards.

When we turn to Old Princeton theologians, they also have ample reasons to neglect the theocentric vision of Edwards. Fundamentally, the idealism of Edwards runs contrary to the Scottish Common Sense philosophy prevalent in both Princeton and New England theology.[35] Common Sense philosophy advocates common sense as the foundation of reliable knowledge. Theologians who adopt this approach tend to avoid speculation about the metaphysical status of substance. For example, Edwards' speculations about personal identity are rejected by both Charles Hodge (1797–1878) of Princeton and Taylor.[36] Common sense suggests that personal identity is not an arbitrary entity. This aversion to metaphysical language makes these theologians avoid Platonic language of participation.

This aversion to speculations is clearly demonstrated in the doctrine of the Trinity. As we have argued before, the aversion to metaphysical speculation is the main reason for the lack of sophistication in the Reformed doctrine of the Trinity. Edwards broke through this tradition by developing a psychological model of Trinity based on Lockean epistemology. New England theology, with its focus on the moral governance of the

---

32. *Misc.* 954, 963, etc. See especially *Misc.* 864.

33. Sweeney, *Taylor*, 91–111.

34. Ibid., 150–51.

35. For a short introduction to Scottish Common Sense philosophy, see Ahlstrom, *Religious History*, 354–56. For its relationship to New England theology, see ibid. 418–20. For its relation to Princeton theology, see Marsden, *Fundamentalism and American Culture*, 15–16, 111.

36. Hodge, *Systematic Theology*, 2:217–20. On Taylor, see Sweeney, *Nathaniel Taylor*, 83–87.

supreme God, has little to say about the Trinity.[37] Hodge follows Turretin in strenuously avoiding any speculations into the nature of the Trinity. In his chapter on the doctrine of the Trinity, the major portion is devoted to the Christology of the Nicene Council. Even for the Nicene Council, there is "a distinction between the speculations of the Nicene fathers, and the decisions of the Nicene Council. The latter have been accepted by the Church universal, but not the former."[38] Hodge classifies the psychological model of Augustine as one of the philosophical forms of the doctrine. "It may be remarked in reference to them [philosophical forms] all that they are of little value. They do not serve to make the inconceivable intelligible."

Allied with this anti-metaphysical stance is Hodge's conception of theology. For Hodge, theology is the scientific study of the Scriptures. By definition, science is the inductive study of the laws laid within the facts. "In every science there are two factors: facts and ideas."[39] Theology is the application of the scientific method to the Scriptures: "The Bible is to the theologian what nature is to the man of science. It is his store-house of facts; and his method of ascertaining what the Bible teaches, is the same as that which the natural philosopher adopts to ascertain what nature teaches." Therefore, "the duty of the Christian theologian is to ascertain, collect, and combine all the facts which God has revealed concerning himself and our relation to Him. These facts are all in the Bible."[40]

For Hodge, theology is the systematic presentation of the facts and the principles contained in the Bible. Just like physics or chemistry, it is an exercise in ratiocination. Hodge is partially reacting against what he perceived as the dangerous mysticism of Schleiermacher.[41] For Hodge, modern theology wants to build its foundation on religious experience. He insists that the only solid foundation for theology is the Bible. Theology is either the inductive study of the facts in the Bible or the explication of religious experience.

In summary, neither New England theory nor Old Princeton theology pays much attention to the question of how God can be perceived and

---

37. However, Taylor wrote a significant essay defending the Trinity against Unitarian theologians such as Henry Ware (1764–1845). Taylor's main point is that the common sense notion of the unity of God does not exclude the possibility of tripersonality within the Godhead. See Foster, *New England Theology*, 313–14.

38. Hodge, *Systematic Theology*, 1:471.

39. Ibid., 1. Bozeman's *Protestants in an Age of Science* is the standard text on this issue.

40. Hodge, *Systematic Theology*, 10–11.

41. Ibid., 65–66.

experienced in a non-rational way. In New England theory, the dominant imagery of God is the moral governor. The dominant pastoral concern is revival preaching and the moment of conversion. In Princeton theology, the dominant concern is the defense of Calvinistic orthodoxy as a scientific system. Theological explorations based on religious experience or metaphysical speculations are both rejected as dangerous and unbiblical. With the demise of New England theory and Old Princeton theology engaged in a life and death battle with modernism at the end of nineteenth century,[42] Edwards' theology was forgotten until Miller brought him back to the attention of scholars. As we have seen in chapter one, aesthetics plays a central role in this twentieth century revival of Edwards.

For Edwards, the perception of divine glory is a central theme of his theology. Not only should we assent to the notion that God is beautiful, but we must also perceive divine beauty directly. Only then do we have true knowledge of God, and only then are we truly the children of God. Being Christian means a transformed view of reality in which God's glory shines through the world and Christian experience. His theology is in many ways an attempt to understand biblically and rationally such transformation of our perception. Though Edwards knew little about medieval mystical theology, his theology continues the best of mystical theology in a Protestant framework.

Neither New England theory nor Princeton theology continues the spiritual vision of Edwards. From our perspective, this is a significant loss. While intellectually they are both impressive theological constructions, they seem to us to lack the spiritual vitality of Edwards' theology. May it not be one of the reasons for the demise of New England theology after Edwards and the gradual decline of Princetonian theology? Perhaps one of the key function of theological aesthetics is to remind us that theology is never merely an intellectual exercise. It is also an attempt to capture notionally the ineffable glory of God. In this sense, theology is always an attempt to speak intelligently about what is ultimately unspeakable.

From American Reformed traditions we shall turn now to Dutch Reformed tradition. Under the influence of Abraham Kuyper (1837–1920), Dutch Reformed tradition pays much more serious attention to a theology of culture. Since art is an important aspect of culture, Dutch Reformed tradition has its distinctive theology of art. As we have indicated before, Edwards is not interested in a theology of art. His theology is about the nature of divine beauty and its manifestation in creation. Yet, in order to

---

42. See Marsden, *Fundamentalism*, 102–23, 212–21.

develop a theology of art, Dutch Reformed theology has to say something about the nature of beauty. We shall concentrate on the nature of beauty as understood by the Dutch Reformed tradition. Our goal is not to trace any historical connections. There is no evidence that Kuyper, Bavinck, or other Dutch Reformed theologians knew anything about the aesthetics of Edwards. The comparison serves to illustrate the place of Edwards within the broad streams of Reformed tradition.

We shall concentrate on the theology of Kuyper, the founder of the nineteenth-century Dutch Reformed movement. Fundamental to Kuyper's thought is the concept of sphere sovereignty.[43] This means that different human activities have their own sphere and their own laws. Religion is one sphere, politics another sphere, art another, and natural science yet another. Each sphere is governed by its own laws: "And even so there are ordinances of God in logic, to regulate our thoughts; ordinances of God for our imagination, in the domain of aesthetics; and so, also, strict ordinances of God for the whole of human life in the domain of morals."[44]

For Kuyper, the main sin of the Roman church is the confusion of sphere sovereignty by imposing ecclesiastical authority over the other spheres: "When therefore the first education of Northern Europe was completed, and the church still persisted in swaying her absolute scepter across the entire domain of life, four great movements were started from as many different sides, *viz.*, the *Renaissance* in the domain of art, the *Republicanism* of Italy in politics, *Humanism* in science, and centrally, in Religion, the *Reformation*."[45]

Along with politics and science, art has its own sovereignty independent of religion. Kuyper believes that Calvinism represents the highest development of both art and religion in that it recognizes the independence of the two spheres: "And so, arrived at their highest development, both Relgion and Art demand an independent existence, and the two stems

---

43. We are indebted to Begbie, *Voicing Creation's Praise*, 84–101, for his discussion of the sphere sovereignty, common grace, and theology of art in Kuyper and Bavinck. Begbie give an survey of Dutch Reformed theology of art from Kuyper to Rookmaaker in part II of *Voicing Creation's Praise*.

44. Cited in Begbie, *Voicing Creation's Praise*, 85. It is interesting to note that the division into thoughts, imagination and morals sounds Kantian, though there is no evidence of any direct influence. Perhaps the concept of sphere sovereignty is more Kantian than Kuyper himself recognized.

45. Abraham Kuyper, *Lectures on Calvinism*. The book contains the six Stone lectures delivered by Kuyper at Princeton University in 1898. It is the main source for the theology of art of Kuyper.

which at first were intertwined and seemed to belong to the same plant, now appear to spring from a root of their own."[46]

In other words, art is inherently different from religion. It is only the immaturity of medieval Catholicism that led to synthesis of art and religion in the architecture of the medieval cathedrals. Some people have accused the spiritualism (the focus on spiritual realities) of Calvinism as inimical to art. They cite as evidence that no distinctive art style has risen in the land of Calvinism. Kuyper argues that this lack of a distinctive Calvinistic art form is necessitated by the liberation of art from religion: "I maintain that for the very reason of its *higher* principle Calvinism was not allowed to develop such an architectural style of its own."[47]

Kuyper appeals to Hegel to support his thesis. According to Hegel, the lower stage of religion is sensual religion, which depends on art for its expression. The higher form of religion liberates itself from the fetters of sensuality into the freedom of the spirit.[48] For Kuyper, art is essentially sensual and symbolical, while worship is a spiritual and cognitive act.

What is the purpose of the independent sphere of art? It is the reproduction of beauty. Kuyper is emphatic that beauty has an objective existence like rocks and trees: "And all these because the beautiful is not the product of our own fantasy, nor of our subjective perception, but has an objective existence, being itself the expression of a Divine perfection."[49]

Beauty, like truth and moral laws, is the creation of God. Just as natural sciences seek to discover the truth about nature, so art seeks to portray the beauty inherent in God's creation. Since beauty is an objective reality, a gift of God to everybody by common grace, both Christians and non-Christians can and do appreciate beauty. "But if, at the hand of experience and history, you become persuaded that the highest art-instincts are *natural* gifts, and hence belong to those excellent graces which, in spite of sin, by virtue of *common grace*, have continued to shine in human nature, it plainly follows that art can inspire both believers and unbelievers."[50]

By the common grace of God, everyone can potentially perceive the beauty of the universe. It follows that everyone can potentially reproduce this beauty through art. While beauty is expressed through sensual objects

46. Ibid., 148.
47. Ibid., 145–46.
48. Ibid., 148.
49. Ibid., 156.
50. Ibid., 161. Kuyper calls the pagan Greeks "the primordial nation of art" (ibid., 162). See Begbie, *Voicing Creation's Praise*, 87–89, for Kuyper's doctrine of common grace.

(e.g., paintings appeal to our sight), beauty itself is not something sensual or material. Like moral laws or truth, it is a higher dimension of reality. Thus the pursuit of art has an uplifting effect on us: "In this cold, irreligious and practical age the warmth of this devotion to art has kept alive many higher aspirations of our soul, which otherwise might readily have died, as they did in the middle of the last century."[51] Though art is independent of religion (understood as religious activities), it helps people to realize that materialism cannot be the final answer to our destiny. In that sense, art and religion are allies to one another.

More fundamentally, both art and religion are rooted in our faith commitment. Besides sphere sovereignty, the concept of faith commitment is also a central theme of Kuyper. Kuyper believes that the cohesiveness of personal identity, as well as culture identity, comes from its spiritual center. This spiritual center, or the relation to the Infinite, determines the direction of whole culture. Art, being one element of a particular culture, finds its cohesiveness only in its relationship to the spiritual center of that culture. Worship is the clearest manifestation of this center: "Divine worship furnished the tie that united the separated arts."[52] Art shows this spiritual center in a more transparent way than other activities:

> It is the central emotion, the central impulse, and the central animation, in the mystical root of our being, which seeks to reveal itself to the outer world in this fourfold [intellectual, ethical, religious, aesthetic] ramification. Art also is no side-shoot on a principal branch, but an independent branch that grows from the trunk of our life itself, even though it is far more nearly allied to Religion than to our thinking or to our ethical being.... Thus also no unity in the revelation of art is conceivable, except by the art-inspiration of an Eternal Beautiful, which flows from the fountain of the Infinite.[53]

Thus, the religious center of a culture will be reflected in the art style of that culture. Only a culture with a coherent religious center can develop a coherent art style across the different arts. A Christian culture will develop its art in relation to commitment. It does not imply that there is one distinctive Christian art style. Christians, being members of a particular culture, cannot develop an art style independent from the art styles prevalent in the society in general. Art style is always a form of historical

51. Ibid., 143.
52. Ibid., 146.
53. Ibid., 150-51.

product. Nonetheless, when Christians become the majority in a society, that society will gradually develops great art styles which reflect Christian values.[54] Kuyper does not elaborate on the process of such development. The art produced by the artists must ultimately reflect their spiritual center..

As we have said before, Kuyper has different concern from Edwards. Kuyper wants to develop a comprehensive philosophy about all human activities. Edwards is interested in a theory of spiritual perception. From these different questions, they are led to different conceptions of beauty. For Kuyper, beauty is the goal of the activity of art. Along with politics and morality, art is part of the culture mandate of God. It is primarily concerned with the divine command to Adam to have dominion over nature. The Eternal Beauty that flows from the Infinite is part of the creation of God. It is created by God and it expresses of divine perfection. Kuyper conceives beauty as a spiritual reality. It is different from both divine essence and the material world. It is a Platonic conception of beauty. Since beauty is a part of creation, both Christians and non-Christians can perceive and create true beauty. Beauty is divine in the sense that it (like moral laws) springs from divine perfection. Beauty is a gracious gift bestowed by God, but perceiving beauty is different from perceiving God.

For Edwards, beauty is the essence for God. Insofar as God is essentially triune, God is essentially beautiful. To perceive true beauty is to perceive God. The beauty of this world lies in its possibility to serve as metaphor for divine beauty. Thus the production of beauty does not merely fulfill the culture mandate; it also serves as a sensual proclamation of divine beauty. This will be the implication of Edwards' aesthetic theory. However, Edwards never develops his theory along this direction. He is not interested in a theory of art. We shall return to this implication in our last section.

The Dutch tradition continues to develop in the theology of Herman Dooyeweerd (1894–1977), Hans Rookmaaker (1922–77) and Calvin Seerveld (1930–).[55] Dooyeweerd, like Kuyper, is not a professional artist or art critic. His interest in art lies within a general theory of culture. According to Dooyeweerd, God gives human beings the cultural mandate to open up the hidden potentials of the created universe. Art has its own sphere of sovereignty within this opening process. However, Dooyeweerd is not clear

---

54. Kuyper develops this theme in the specific case of Dutch art. He extols Rembrandt as the Christian artist *par excellence*. Kuyper's main concern is to refute the claim that Calvinism is inimical to art. Ibid., 166–70.

55. Our discussion is based on Begbie, *Voicing Creation's Praise*, 106–41.

on what set the aesthetic domain apart from other domains. Rookmaaker and Seerveld devote their professional life to the study of art and aesthetics. Rookmaaker emphasizes harmony as the defining character of beauty, a theme dating back Plato and earlier. Seerveld objects to Rookmaaker and others who make the creation of beauty the defining character of art. For Seerveld, the defining character of art is *allusiveness*—"an elusive play in its artifactual presentation of meanings apprehended."[56] Despite these differences, they all adopt the Kuyperian perspective in emphasizing the independence of the aesthetic sphere within the culture mandate.

We do not need to go into the details of this story. As we have mentioned above, the Dutch Reformed school develops their aesthetics independent of Edwards. For us, the Dutch school illustrates that there is no single school of Reformed aesthetics. The fundamental belief in the absolute sovereignty of God (common to both Dutch and American Reformed tradition) does not determine how one should develop a theology of beauty. On the one hand, the Dutch school approaches beauty through the perspective of artistic activities. Their definition of beauty is motivated by the search for the essence of art. On the other hand, Edwards is motivated by a search for the vision of the Creator within creatures. It is not surprising that they develop different concepts of beauty. Even if Kuyper knew some of Edwards' writings, he would probably fail to find any relevance for his own theology of art.

However, the two approaches do have points of contact. In particular, Seerveld's concept of allusiveness bears striking similarity to Edwards' concept of image. Seerveld does not address the question whether true beauty should allude to specific objects. If we accept Seerveld's thesis that beauty is not the only goal of art, we are still left with the question when art (or nature) can be said to manifest true beauty. On the other hand, Edwards does not have an epistemological theory of spiritual perception of physical images. Seerveld's theory on the perception of allusion can enrich the theology of Edwards. Hopefully, other studies will pursue this dialogue in aesthetics among the Reformed traditions.

## The Aesthetics of Edwards for Today

In this concluding section of our concluding chapter, we want to situate Edwards' theology within contemporary scene. Our dissertation is an exercise in historical theology, and the significance of Edwards for

56. Cited in ibid., 135.

constructive theology today lies beyond the scope of our study. However, we begin our book with a short survey of the history of aesthetics. We want to return to some of the issues raised in that survey and ask some fundamental questions about the nature of aesthetics. In other words, we want to place Edwards within the history of philosophical and theological aesthetics. We believe that Edwards' theology can yield a fruitful dialogue with the issues raised in those disciplines. We want to illustrate the possible directions of such dialogue, even though a proper dialogue will be the work of another study. We conclude with a few remarks on the implication of Edwards' aesthetics for fine arts.

As we have shown in our introduction, aesthetics gradually became a separate philosophical subject in the eighteenth century. While there is general agreement on the importance of that period, there are different ways of understanding the most significant development of that time. One option is to emphasize the rediscovery of the concept of the sublime. Kant's theory of the sublime is the culmination of eighteenth century discussion of the sublime.[57] We shall cut short the discussion by going to Kant directly.

Kant lists several contrasts between the beautiful and the sublime. The former concerns the form of an object; the latter is formless and limitless. The former satisfies by its quality, the latter by quantity. The former brings a feeling of the promotion of life, the latter a feeling of a momentary inhibition of the vital powers of life. The most important difference, according to Kant, is that the former gives a sense of purposiveness, while the latter appears to be contrapurposive for our power of judgment.[58]

The sublime is divided into two kinds: the mathematically sublime and the dynamically sublime. The former is related to our faculty of cognition. Mathematically, everything else is small in comparison with the sublime. Nothing perceived by us in the world can, strictly speaking, be sublime. Everything perceived by senses has form and limitations. Therefore, "that is sublime which even to be able to think of demonstrates a

---

57. "And just as eighteenth-century literature has as its unconscious goal, in the fullness of time, the literature of the early nineteenth century, so it may be said that eighteenth-century aesthetic has as its unconscious goal the *Critique of Judgment*, the book in which it was to be refined and re-interpreted." Samuel H. Monk, *The Sublime*, 6.

58. *Critique of the Power of Judgment*, §23, 5:244–45. We give the pagination of *Kant's Gesammelte Schriften* (edited by the German Academy of Sciences), which is printed on the margin in Guyer's edition.

faculty of the mind that surpasses every measure of the senses."[59] The faculty of reason surpasses every measure of the senses. We can apprehend or conceptualize the diameter of the earth, even if our sense can never comprehend it in its actual size. Some objects provoke reason to grasp for the totality of the magnitude. Such natural objects[60] induce in us the feeling of sublimity. It is analogous to beauty in that sublimity is also a form of subjective purposiveness. This movement to grasp the totality produces "a feeling that we have pure self-sufficient reason, or a faculty for estimating magnitude, whose preeminence cannot be made intuitable through anything except the inadequacy of that faculty which is itself unbounded in the presentation of magnitudes (of sensible objects)."[61] Through the mathematically sublime, we sense the limitation of our imagination. Through this negation, we sense the unlimited capacity of our faculty of reason. The sublime arouses in us the feeling of respect, which is ultimately a respect for the vocation of reason.

The confrontation of the overwhelming power of nature arouses in us the feeling of the dynamically sublime. Kant gives examples such as thundering clouds and erupting volcanoes. Kant distinguishes the fearful from being afraid. Watching thundering clouds from a safe distance gives a fearful sight without making us afraid. If we are actually afraid that lightening might strike us, then we are in no mood to make the judgment of sublimity. Sublimity is a subjective aesthetic judgment, not an objective property of an object. The overwhelming manifestation of power in nature "makes us, considered as natural beings, recognize our physical powerlessness, but at the same time it reveals a capacity for judging ourselves as independent of it and a superiority over nature on which is grounded a self-preservation of quite another kind than that which can be threatened and endangered by nature outside us, whereby humanity in our person remains undemeaned even though the human being must submit to that dominion."[62]

Paradoxically, the sense of powerlessness in facing the dynamically sublime actually arouses in us our sense of superiority over nature. We recognize that, in the realm of practical reason, we have freedom over nature. We are not bound to sensibility. This freedom makes us superior to nature.

---

59. *Power of Judgment* §25, 5:250.

60. For Kant, only natural objects can be sublime. Artificial objects are all made according to the forms in the artisan's mind. One wonders if Kant would allow someone to call Jackson Pollock's paintings sublime.

61. *Power of Judgment* §27, 5:258.

62. Ibid. §28, 5:261–62.

Why should the overwhelming power of nature cause us to reflect on our Stoic superiority? As evidence, Kant claims that "without the development of moral ideas, that which we, prepared by culture, call sublime will appear merely repellent to the unrefined person."[63] If only morally developed people can appreciate the dynamically sublime, presumably the judgment of sublimity is a reflection of the ability to make moral judgment.

In summary, both the mathematically sublime and dynamically sublime are purposive in that they evoke in us the vocation of pure and practical reason. They do so through evoking the sense of infinity and of freedom over nature. For our purpose, there is no need to go further into Kant's theory of the sublime.

We shall now turn to Edwards. Delattre denies that Edwards has a theology of the sublime God: "The sublime is an aesthetic category appropriate to the awesome and even awful, while Edwards was very much concerned with recovering a sense of the 'lovely majesty' of God, as opposed to the 'awful majesty' of God so much emphasized by many of his contemporaries among evangelical Christians. . . . Beauty and light and joy rather than terror and darkness are what he found at the heart of God and being-in-general, whereas the sublime, unlike beauty, has about it always at least a touch of terror."[64]

If our thesis is correct, then Delattre is *totally mistaken*. Can God be described with more awful majesty than *Sinners in the Hand of an Angry God*? Delattre depends on Edwards' early musings on the definition of beauty, and totally ignores Edwards' teaching on the glory of election and hell. We have shown that the awful majesty of God is equally important to Edwards as the lovely majesty of God. Moreover, the awful majesty of God in Edwards is similar to the sublime in Kant.

First, the awesome God confronts us as the infinite being. This corresponds to Kant's mathematical sublimity. Edwards would agree with Kant that physical senses can never comprehend infinity. Edwards, disagreeing with Kant, believes that we can sense (without comprehending it completely) divine infinity through other spiritual senses. For Edwards, infinity is not merely a construct of reason. It is a spiritual reality that God freely chooses to reveal to the saints (for their enjoyment) and to the damned (for their torment). Second, the awesome God of Edwards confronts us as the one who has absolute power over us. This corresponds to Kant's dynamic sublimity, understood as power dominating over us. For Kant,

63. Ibid. §29, 5:265.
64. Delattre, *Beauty and Sensibility*, 146.

sublimity can be felt only in safety from danger. True terror is contrary to sublimity. For Edwards, true terror can be part of the experience of sublimity. The arbitrary decision of election and damnation is the ultimate display of divine dynamic sublimity. The elect will enjoy the sublimity of the electing God in gratitude; the damned will encounter this sublimity in terror. Edwards asserts that there will be no tragic hero in hell; the damned will be crushed both physically and spiritually. This dynamic power will leave no space for human autonomy. While, for Kant, the dynamically sublime is an aesthetic judgment reflecting human freedom, for Edwards it is an aesthetic judgment reflecting divine freedom. In contemplating the thundering clouds, Edwards claims that we sense the sovereign power of God over us.

If the experience of sublimity in Edwards and Kant bears striking similarities, the origin of such experience is radically different. For Kant, we do not literally perceive a sublime object. Neither infinity nor freedom can be perceived in a space-time framework. Sublimity is a free-play of the imagination. Our imagination goes beyond our perception in a harmonious play with the faculty of reason. Sublimity is a totally subjective condition. For Edwards, sublimity is perception of a particular objective reality. Sublimity is a relationship between God and creatures. It is not objective in the sense of "being an object in space-time." God is not such an object. In Edwards' theology, no spatial-temporal object can be sublime in the strict sense. They are neither infinite, nor do they have infinite power over us. Natural objects become sublime when they serve as metaphors for divine sublimity. The thunder clouds are just noisy without spiritual discernment. They become sublime when we see the power of God epitomized in the roaring thunders.[65] For both Kant and Edwards, human imagination is engaged in going beyond sensible perception. For Kant, this going beyond is also a turning inwards into our subjectivity. For

---

65. Delattre claims that "beauty provides the first and fullest and most adequate way of filling in the right-hand side of the equation 'being is x' or 'being consists in x'" (*Beauty and Sensibility*, 28). In other words, beauty is a transcendental and objective property of being. Farley (*Faith and Beauty*, 49, fn. 15) claims that Delattre is ambiguous on this point. While claiming beauty is a property of beings, Delattre also insists that beauty is a disposition of the heart. Thus it is both objective and subjective in Delattre's account. Our discussion of sublimity suggests the solution. The sublime in spatial-temporal phenomena is an attitude and interpretation of the human subject, but it is universal validity because it is based on divine interpretation. God intends whose phenomena to be a metaphor of himself. We may note here that Kant claims that while the sublime is a subjective judgment, it is universally valid because it is based on the universal structure of subjectivity. Thus he distances himself from the psychological theory of Burke. (*Power of Judgment*, "General remark," 5:277–78)

Edwards, this going beyond is reaching out through the spiritual sense to the divine reality undergirding spatial-temporal reality.

Kant spends considerably more time in addressing the nature of beauty. To stay within our purpose, we can merely give a hint of how our discussion of sublimity can be extended to the issue of beauty. Both Kant and Edwards resist a merely psychological theory of beauty. We do not just happen to enjoy beauty; we enjoy beauty because beauty is the sensible presentation of our deepest convictions. Our delight in beauty reflects a deeper level of reality. Kant and Edwards diverge radically on the nature of that reality. For Kant, that reality is our vocation to impose self-legislated lawfulness upon the sensible world.[66] For Edwards, that reality is the return to God through the sensibility of divine beauty. Edwards has a much richer account of the symbolic function of material beauty. It tells of God's wisdom and power, as well as sin and redemption. Kant's account is limited to the principle of free lawfulness. However, they both agree that the significance of beauty lies in its symbolic function. Similar to the discussion of sublimity, the question of how symbols function and what they represent can become the channel for a dialogue between Edwards and Kant.

We now turn to case of aesthetics in a specifically theological context. In our introduction, we present Aquinas' theology as the epitome of medieval approach to theological aesthetics. In his theology, the Son is the source and archetype of all forms. Beauty is the perception of forms in all their integrity and clarity. For medieval theologians like Aquinas, the perception of forms is not merely a cognitive event. It is a perception of divine presence within creation. McGinn calls this paradigm of divine presence the metaphysics of flow.[67] "Flow is the emanation of form from the First Source that is the font and origin of all forms."[68] God is not merely the efficient cause of the universe. The efficient cause can be categorically different from the effect (e.g., a cook and the hamburger she cooks.) In the metaphysics of flow, the effect bears resemblance to the cause because the effect participates in the nature of the cause. In this paradigm, the universe is a natural but freely-chosen emanation from God. Therefore

---

66. The way that beauty can symbolize the vocation of practical reason is a complicated story that we cannot go into now. See the helpful discussion in Guyer, *Value of Beauty*.

67. Bernard McGinn, *Harvest of Mysticism*, 14–17.

68. *Alberti Magni: De Causi et processu universitatis a Prima Causa* I.4.1, cited in ibid., 16.

we can behold the glory of the cause through the effect. For Aquinas, the beauty of the world is an exhibition of the beauty of the Son.

The Thomistic vision is a creative integration of Neoplatonism and Aristotelianism. It is a compelling vision for the medieval age, but it is a foreign vision for the modern age. Yet we find attempts to construct a similar vision for modernity. For the twentieth century, Balthasar has resurrected a large-scale theory of form. Roberts summarizes Balthasar's aesthetic vision as following: "Beauty is concerned with form (*formosus, speciosus*) and with the splendor that radiates faith. It is the form, the *Gestalt*, which is the expression of the artistic vision, and yet the glory that shines forth is nowhere present except in the form." "Aesthetics, therefore, is concerned with form, shape, composition, expression, and seeing such forms *as they are*. . . . What is seen is the *doxa* of the form, but this glory is the glory of being."[69]

Balthasar does not subscribe to an Aristotelian theory of form; his theory is not tied to some definitional essence of particular objects. His concept of form is closer to the Thomistic concept of clarity. It is based on both the objectivity of being and the subjectivity of perception. Being has an inherent splendor and integrity, which is called its form. When this form is perceived by people, they recognize it as the beauty of the world. Beauty is still a transcendental property of being. In Balthasar's vision, all beings—insofar as they are existents—emanate the glory of form.

In what sense is this vision of glory a theological aesthetics? For Balthasar, being speaks of divine beauty because it proclaims the free love of God.[70] In his account, the fatal turn of Western philosophy began with the deconstruction of metaphysics in Duns Scotus and the worship of being itself in Meister Eckhart. Instead, the study of metaphysics should tell us that being can never be a sufficient ground for itself. Being can be realized only through concrete existents, yet concrete existents presuppose the being as its ground. This mutual dependence suggests, for Balthasar, that neither being-in-general nor concrete existents are self-sufficient. They both depend on free love of the self-sufficient God. God freely creates in order that God may have the objects of love. Even the most hideous creature "has a shattering grandeur when it is the language of a love who wishes to perceive the reflected glory of the first miracle in all Being's

---

69. Roberts, *Theological Aesthetics*, 234.

70. See Balthasar, *The Realm of Metaphysics*, 613–56, the two sections entitled "The Site of Glory in Metaphysics" and "Love as Custodian of Glory."

forms."[71] This miraculous love is God's free creation of being. The fact that something—rather than nothing—exist suggests a self-sufficient Love as its *a priori* ground. The form is the concretization of this divine love in particular objects.[72]

Richard Viladesau, building on the work of Rahner and Lonergan, takes an alternative approach to theological aesthetics. Viladesau accepts the Enlightenment critique that we cannot have unmediated knowledge of being. He begins with the structure of our knowing, and asks whether the very possibility of knowing implies an openness to the revelation of God.

Viladesau believes such openness is implied because any knowledge is always implicitly an attempt to comprehend reality as a totality: "When the mind grasps an object through understanding and judgment, in the very process it transcends that grasp: it is tacitly aware that the object is more than what is grasped, and at the same time it recognizes the provisional character of its own insights. This *excusses* points to the a priori condition of possibility for the mind's knowing sensible objects as objects and of differentiating them from itself—namely, the pre-apprehension (*Vorgriff*) as "being" as such: the total horizon of knowledge and its dynamism."[73]

When we grasp an object with our mind, it is always grasped as an object-within-the-world. Implicitly, we have an unthematical understanding of reality in its totality. Such implicit grasping for totality is the basis for the possibility of knowledge about spiritual reality.

What is the role of beauty in this transcendental theory of perception? Beauty is the joy we experience when the world apparently conforms to our pre-apprehension of reality as a harmonious and intelligible whole: "Objectively, beauty is the order of reason in things, their truth and goodness, their 'rightness'—that is, their intelligibility, their accord with the dynamism of the human person toward being and being-well."[74]

Beauty is the joy of experiencing the world as corresponding to the well being of our psyche. In this theory, order and harmony are also the

---

71. Ibid., 648.

72. We present only one side of Balthasar's aesthetics. The other side is his focus on Christ being the unique expression of the form of God. Balthasar is challenged by the theology of Barth to make Catholic theology more explicitly Christocentric. Whether he has successfully integrated the two sides of his aesthetics is an open question. See Chia, "Theological Aesthetics or Aesthetic Theology?" 75–95. Our purpose here is to bring in Bathasar where he can serve as a contrast to Edwards.

73. Viladesau, *Theological Aesthetics*, 81–82.

74. Ibid., 131.

criteria for discerning beauty. In Thomistic theory, harmony is an indication of the simplicity of the undivided Cause of all things. The reason here is that our intellect, in its desire to grasp the world through reason, naturally desires the world to be orderly and harmonious. When the world corresponds to the dynamism of our psyche, we experience the joy of existence or the joy of being part of this world.

How is beauty a mediation of divine reality? For Viladesau, God is regarded as an asymptote of finite experience of beauty. All our sense of beauty is accompanied by a sense of tragedy: "the rejoicing in existence (or in "form") that characterizes it is simultaneously tied to an acute awareness of finitude: the gratuitous joy of beauty and its delight in form arise precisely out of contrast with the abyss of nonbeing experienced in the fragile, threatened character of human existence, for which it is possible not to be."[75]

Our experience of beauty is always marked by the awareness that it could have been otherwise. The world is not inherently harmonious, and it is often marked by the most grotesque disharmony. In our panting for the infinitude, we are implicitly affirming the existence of ultimate Beauty, "a reality the apprehension of which would be unmixed and unlimited joy in existence, and which in itself—that is, as self-apprehending—is self-conscious Beauty or infinite Bliss."[76] This self-conscious and infinite Beauty is God.

In both the accounts of Balthasar and Viladesau, being as experienced by us is found to be lacking in completeness. It requires an absolute ground to sustain and affirm it. In the approach, beauty is the perception of this affirmation and the joy accompanying this perception.

Edwards' theological aesthetics represents a different approach. Edwards is not interested in presenting God as the completion of our finite beauty. It is not the finitude of our experience that points to the infinitude of God. The starting point of our experience of divine beauty in Edwards is the theology of revelation. God reveals God's own beauty through the imparting of the Spirit in us. Therefore, our experience of divine beauty is a participation in the intra-Trinitarian life of God. Divine beauty is not perceived through a mystical view of the world; it is the perception of divine beauty that leads to our altered sense of reality.[77]

---

75. Ibid., 136.

76. Ibid., 138.

77. Thus Miller and Elmwood have misread Edwards by equating the altered view of the world as the essence of divine beauty in Edwards. See Introduction above.

Edwards' aesthetics is an idealistic reinterpretation of Calvin's dogma of the world as theatre of God's glory. For Calvin, the world truly proclaims the glory of God, though sin hinders us from appreciating the true nature of earthly beauty. Yet Calvin does not provide an epistemology of sin and regeneration. In Edwards' scheme, sensibility and affections provide the epistemological connection. Only with sensible knowledge of divine beauty can our affections be changed. Only with renewed affections can we have sensible knowledge of the true earthly beauty.

Shall we start our aesthetics with a general theory of being or cognition, and discern how our experience of finite earthly beauty is correlated with the infinite ground of beauty? Shall we start with explicit Christian doctrines and ask how they are mirrored in our earthly experience?[78] For us, the evaluation of the merits and the pitfalls of these two approaches would seem to be a major question of theological aesthetics. This is work for another study.

Finally we come to the question of how Christian aesthetics may contribute to the general culture mandate.[79] If we ask what Edwards' aesthetics may say to the culture of arts in general, the answer will be pretty short. Since non-Christians cannot have sensible knowledge of divine beauty, they will pursue a different kind of beauty in their fine arts. That does not mean Christian and non-Christian art have no commonalities. As we have indicated in the last section, both a Kantian artist and a Christian artist may have aesthetic experience of free lawfulness and sublimity. To that extent, their fine arts may both engage in these themes. Yet they will interpret these aesthetic experiences differently. The Kantian artist may even understand rationally the Christian artist's worldview, but such notional knowledge will not lead to a change in the affections of Kantian artist. The Christian understanding of arts will have no persuasive force for the Kantian artist. For both the Kantian and the Christian artists, their arts will present in a sensible form their understanding of reality. The Christian artist has no right, even within his own theology, to demand the Kantian artist to present reality as he does.

Is that a problem? I do not think so. By now it is a cliché to claim that the Enlightenment project is bankrupt. There is no self-evident and universal structure of human consciousness. The postmodern paradigm teaches us that reality actually appears differently to different people. We

---

78. Among recent writers of theological aesthetics, Patrick Sherry represents the Protestant approach.

79. This is Dyrness' question to Edwards. See Introduction above, p. ?.

construct our worlds with our presuppositions, language and culture. The postmodern paradigm can be regarded as an indirect verification of the Edwardsian understanding of sensibility. We are not sensible of the world in the same way. Moreover, the ways we are sensible of the world are often pre-critical and meta-cognitive. If the postmodern paradigm is correct, then we should not expect a Christian paradigm, or any particular paradigm, to become the general culture mandate.

Does that mean that Christian artists cannot contribute meaningfully to the cultural of fine arts in general? Of course not. The fact that different artists begin with different sensibilities of the world does not mean that their sensibilities are incommensurable. Both a Christian and a Kantian may enjoy the beauty and pathos of Bach's *St. Matthew Passion*, though the Christian will presumably identify with the libretto in a more literal way. The Christian artists contribute to the general culture precisely by presenting their sensibility of the world in their work. They do not need to insist that their arts are the only legitimate arts. Theologically, if the Christian God is indeed the Creator of the world, then they can trust that their arts will create echoes in other people's heart. God will not cease to reveal his beauty.

The theological aesthetics of Edwards may indeed provide important resources for a Christian in dialogue with postmodernity. The reason is not that Edwards is a postmodern theologian disguised in seventeenth-century theology.[80] The reason is that the postmodernism has taught us that our construction of reality is often motivated by pre-apprehensions of reality. These pre-apprehensions cannot be defined or subsumed under the roles of reason. Our perception of reality cannot be reduced to mere rules. The theological aesthetics of Edwards is based on the sensible encounter of unique entities—between God and human beings, between different human beings. The material world is a sensible metaphor of such encounters. Based on this understanding, fine arts can be regarded as deliberate and sensible metaphors of such encounters. It may persuade where reason fails to reach. It may conjure up divine realities for the postmodern mind that is weary of the tyranny of universal reason. Such an aesthetic vision focuses on the unique encounter of the subject and her world. The postmodern celebrates such unique encounter. This suggests a new imperative for theologians and Christian artists to work together in the postmodern era.

With this tentative note on Edwards and postmodernism we shall conclude our study.

80. Daniel, *Philosophy of Jonathan Edwards*, represents this kind of distortion.

# Bibliography

## Primary text by Jonathan Edwards:

*The Works of Jonathan Edwards*. Founding editor: Perry Miller. 26 volumes published:
Works 1: *Freedom of the Will*. Edited by Paul Ramsey. New Haven: Yale University Press, 1957.
Works 2: *Religious Affections*. Edited by John Smith. New Haven: Yale University Press, 1959.
Works 3: *Original Sin*. Edited by Clyde A. Holbrook. New Haven: Yale University Press, 1970.
Works 4: *The Great Awakening*. Edited by C. C. Goen. New Haven: Yale University Press, 1972.
Works 5: *Apocalyptic Writings*. Edited by Stephen J. Stein. New Haven: Yale University Press, 1977.
Works 6: *Scientific and Philosophical Writings*. Edited by Wallace E. Anderson. New Haven: Yale University Press, 1980.
Works 7: *The Life of David Brained*. Edited by Norman Petit. New Haven: Yale University Press, 1985.
Works 8: *Ethical Writings*. Edited by Paul Ramsey. New Haven: Yale University Press, 1989.
Works 9: *A History of the Work of Redemption*. Edited by John Wilson. New Haven: Yale University Press, 1989.
Works 10, *Sermons and Discourses 1720-1723*. Edited by Wilson H. Kimnach. New Haven: Yale University Press, 1992.
Works 11: *Typological Writings*. Edited by Wallace E. Anderson and Mason I. Lowance. New Haven: Yale University Press, 1993.
Works 12: *Ecclesiastical Writings*. Edited by David Hall. New Haven: Yale University Press, 1994.
Works 13: *The "Miscellanies," a-500*. Edited by Thomas A. Schafer. New Haven: Yale University Press, 1994.
Works 14: *Sermons and Discourses 1723-1729*. Edited by Kenneth P. Minkema. New Haven: Yale University Press, 1997.
Works 15: *Notes on Scripture*. Edited by Stephen J. Stein. New Haven: Yale University Press, 1998.
Works 16: *Letters and Personal Writings*. Edited by George S. Claghorn. New Haven: Yale University Press, 1998.
Works 17: *Sermons and Discourses, 1730-1733*. Edited by Mark Valeri. New Haven: Yale University Press, 1999.

The Beauty of the Triune God

Works 18: *"The Miscellanies," 501–832.* Edited by Ava Chamberlain. New Haven: Yale University Press, 2000.
Works 19: *Sermons and Discourses, 1734–1738.* Edited by M. X. Lesser. New Haven: Yale University Press, 2001.
Works 20: *The "Miscellanies," 833–1152.* Edited by Amy Plantinga Pauw. New Haven: Yale University Press, 2002.
Works 21: *Writings on the Trinity, Grace and Faith.* Edited by Sang Hyun Lee. New Haven: Yale University Press, 2003.
Works 22: *Sermons and Discourses, 1739–1742.* Edited by Harry S. Stout and Nathan O. Hatch, with Kyle Farley. New Haven: Yale University Press, 2003.
Works 23: *The "Miscellanies," 1153–1360.* Edited by Douglas Sweeney. New Haven: Yale University Press, 2004.
Works 24: *The Blank Bible.* Edited by Stephen Stein. New Haven: Yale University Press, 2006.
Works 25: *Sermons and Discourses, 1743–58.* Edited by Wilson H. Kimnach. New Haven: Yale University Press, 2006.
Works 26: *Catalogues of Books,* edited by Peter Thusen. New Haven: Yale University Press, 2008)

## Other published works of Edwards

*The Works of Jonathan Edwards.* Edited by Edward Hickman. 2 vols. 1834. Reprint. Edinburgh: Banner of Truth, 1974.
*The Wrath of Almighty God: Jonathan Edwards on God's Judgment against Sinners.* Edited by Don Kistler. Morgan, PA: Soli Deo Gloria, 1996.
Unpublished manuscript:
*Catalogue,* MSS 151, box 15, folder 1202, Beinecke Library, Yale University.

## Other sources

Adams, Marilyn McCord. *Horrendous Evils and the Goodness of God.* Ithaca, NY: Cornell University Press, 1999.
Addison, Joseph. *Selections from Addison's Papers Contributed to the Spectator.* Edited by Thomas Arnold. Oxford: Clarendon, 1879.
———. *The Spectator,* vol. 4. Edited by G. Gregory Smith. London: Dent, 1898.
Ahlstrom, Sydney E. *A Religious History of the American People.* New Haven: Yale University Press, 1972.
Aldridge, A. Owen. "Edwards and Hutcheson." *Harvard Theological Review* 44 (1951) 35–52.
Allison, Henry. *Kant's Transcendental Idealism: An Interpretation and Defense.* New Haven: Yale University Press, 1983.
Ameriks, Karl. *The Cambridge Companion to German Idealism.* Cambridge: Cambridge University Press, 2000.
———. "Introduction: Interpreting German Idealism." In *The Cambridge Companion to German Idealism,* edited by Karl Ameriks, 1–17. Cambridge: Cambridge University Press, 2000.

# Bibliography

Ames, William. *The Marrow of Theology*. Translated by John Dystra Eusden. Grand Rapids: Baker, 1968.
Aquinas, Thomas, *Summa Theologica, Ultimate Christian Library*. CD-Rom. Ages Software, 2000.
Ariew, Roger, and Marjorie Green. "Ideas, in and before Descartes." *Journal of the History of Ideas* 56 (1995) 87–106.
Balthasar, Hans Urs von. *The Glory of the Lord: A Theological Aesthetics*, vol. 5: *The Realm of Metaphysics in the Modern Age*. Translated by Oliver Davies et al. Edinburgh: T. & T. Clark, 1991.
Barth, Karl. *Church Dogmatics* II.1. *The Doctrine of God*. Translated by T. H. L. Parker et al. Edited by G. W. Bromily and T. F. Torrance. Edinburgh: T. & T. Clark, 1957.
Beardsley, Monroe C. *Aesthetics from Classical Greece to the Present: A Short History*. Tuscaloosa, AL: University of Alabama Press, 1966.
Begbie, Jeremy S. *Voicing Creation's Praise: Towards a Theology of the Arts*. Edinburgh: T. & T. Clark, 1991.
Beiser, Frederick C. *The Sovereignty of Reason: The Defense of Rationality in the Early English Enlightenment*. Princeton: Princeton University Press, 1995.
Berkeley, George. *Philosophical Works: Including the Works on Vision*. Edited by Michael Ayers. The Everyman Library. London: Dent, 1975.
Boland, Vivian. *Ideas in God according to Saint Thomas Aquinas: Sources and Synthesis*. Studies in the history of Christian Thought, 69. Leiden: Brill, 1996.
Bowie, Andrew. *Schelling and Modern European Philosophy: An Introduction*. London: Routledge, 1993.
Bozeman, T. D. *Protestants in an Age of Science: The Baconian Ideal and Antebellum American Religious Thought*. Chapel Hill, NC: University of North Carolina Press, 1977.
Broadie, Alexander. "Art and Aesthetic Theory." In *The Cambridge Companion to The Scottish Enlightenment*, edited by Alexander Broadie, 280–97. Cambridge: Cambridge University Press, 2003.
―――. "The Human Mind and Its Powers." In *The Cambridge Companion to The Scottish Enlightenment*, edited by Alexander Broadie, 60–78. Cambridge: Cambridge University Press, 2003.
Bush, Michael David. *Jesus Christ in the Theology of Jonathan Edwards*. Ph.D. diss., Princeton Theological Seminary, 2003.
Caldwell, Robert. *The Holy Spirit as the Bond of Union in the Theology of Jonathan Edwards*. Ph.D. diss., Trinity Evangelical Divinity School, 2003.
Calvin, John. *Institutes of Christian Religion, Ultimate Christian Library*. CD-Rom. Ages Software, 2000.
Chai, Leon. *Jonathan Edwards and the Limits of Enlightenment Philosophy*. New York: Oxford University Press, 1998.
Chappell, Vere. "Locke's Theory of Ideas." In *The Cambridge Companion to Locke*, edited by Vere Chappell, 26–55. Cambridge: Cambridge University Press, 1994.
Chia, Roland. "'Theological Aesthetics or Aesthetic Theology?' Some Reflections on the Theological Aesthetics of Hans Urs von Balthasar." *Scottish Journal of Theology* 49 (1996) 75–95.
Cohen, Charles Lloyd. *God's Caress: The Psychology of Puritan Religious Experience*. New York: Oxford University Press, 1986.

Copan, Paul. "Jonathan Edwards's Philosophical Influences: Lockean or Malebranchean?" *JETS* 44 (2001) 107–24.
Crisp, Oliver. "How 'Occasional' was Edwards's Occasionalism?" In *Jonathan Edwards: Philosophical Theologian*, edited by Oliver Crisp and Paul Helm, 61–77. Aldershot, UK: Ashgate, 2003.
———. "Jonathan Edwards on the Trinity and Individuation." Paper presented at the Rutherford House Dogmatic Conference, 2005.
Daniel, Stephen H. *The Philosophy of Jonathan Edwards: A Study in Divine Semiotics.* Bloomington, IN: Indiana University Press, 1994.
———. "Postmodern Concepts of God and Edwards's Trinitarian Ontology." In *Edwards in Our Time: Jonathan Edwards and the Shaping of American Religion*, edited by Sang Hyun Lee and Allen Guelzo, 45–64. Grand Rapids: Eerdmans, 1999.
Dear, Peter. "Method and the Study of Nature." In *The Cambridge History of Seventeenth-Century Philosophy*, edited by Daniel Garber and Michael Ayers, 147–77. Cambridge: Cambridge University Press, 1998.
Delattre, Roland André. *Beauty and Sensibility in the Thought of Jonathan Edwards: An Essay in Aesthetics and Theological Ethics.* New Haven: Yale University Press, 1968.
Donagan, Alan. "Spinoza's Theology." In *Cambridge Companion to Spinoza*, edited by Don Garrett, 343–82. Cambridge: Cambridge University Press, 1996.
Dostoyevsky, Fyodor. *The Brothers Karamzov.* Translated by David Magarshack. London: Folio Society, 1964.
Dyrness, William A. *Reformed Theology and Visual Culture: The Protestant Imagination from Calvin to Edwards.* Cambridge: Cambridge University Press, 2004.
Eco, Umberto. *The Aesthetics of Thomas Aquinas.* Translated by Hugh Bredin. London: Radius, 1988.
———. *On Beauty: A History of a Western Idea.* Translated by Alastair McEwen. London: Secker & Warburg, 2004.
Elwood, Douglas J. *Philosophical Theology of Jonathan Edwards.* New York: Columbia University Press, 1960.
Emerson, Roger L. "Science and Moral Philosophy in the Scottish Enlightenment." In *Studies in the Philosophy of the Scottish Enlightenment*, edited by M. A. Stewart, 11–36. Oxford: Clarendon, 1990.
Erdt, Terrence. *Jonathan Edwards: Art and the Sense of the Heart.* Amherst, MA: University of Massachusetts Press, 1980.
Farley, Edward. *Faith and Beauty: A Theological Aesthetic.* Aldershot, UK: Ashgate, 2001.
Fergusson, David. "Will the Love of God Finally Triumph?" In *Nothing Greater, Nothing Better: Theological Essays on the Love of God*, edited by Kevin J. Vanhoozer, 186–202. Grand Rapids: Eerdmans, 2001.
Fiering, Norman. *Jonathan Edwards' Moral Thought and Its British Context.* Chapel Hill, NC: University of North Carolina Press, 1981.
———. "Rationalist Foundations of Jonathan Edwards' Metaphysics." In *Jonathan Edwards and the American Experience*, edited by Nathan O. Hatch and Harry S. Stout, 73–101. New York: Oxford University Press, 1988.
Flower, Elizabeth, and Murray G. Murphey. *A History of Philosophy in America.* 2 vols. New York: Capricorn, 1977.

Foster, F. H. *A Genetic History of the New England Theology*. Chicago: University of Chicago, 1907.
Gaut, Berys, and Dominic McIver Lopes. *The Routledge Companion to Aesthetics*. 2nd ed. London: Routledge, 2005.
Gerrish, Brian. "'To the Unknown God': Luther and Calvin on the Hiddenness of God." In *The Old Protestantism and the New: Essays on the Reformation Heritage*, 131–149. Edinburgh: T. & T. Clark, 1982.
Gerstner, John H. *The Rational Biblical Theology of Jonathan Edwards*. 3 vols. Orlando: Ligonier Ministries, 1991.
Gregory of Nyssa. *On "Not Three Gods."* Nicene and Post-Nicene Fathers, series 2, vol. 5, edited by Philip Schaff, 649–53. *The Ultimate Christian Library*. CD-Rom. Ages Software, 2000.
Guyer, Paul. "Absolute Idealism and the Rejection of Kantian Dualism." In *The Cambridge Companion to German Idealism*, edited by Karl Ameriks, 37–56. Cambridge: Cambridge University Press, 2000.
———. *Value of Beauty: Historical Essays in Aesthetics*. Cambridge: Cambridge University Press, 2005.
Hamilton, Edith, and Huntington Cairns. *The Completed Dialogues of Plato, including the Letters*. Bollingen Series LXXI. Princeton: Princeton University Press, 1961.
Hardman Moore, Susan. "For the Mind's Eye Only: Puritans, Images and 'The Golden Mines of Scripture.'" *Scottish Journal of Theology* 59 (2006) 281–96.
Haroutunian, Joseph. *Piety versus Moralism: The Passing of The New England Theology*. 1932. Reprint. New York: Harper and Row, 1970.
Hatch, Nathan O., and Harry S. Stout. *Jonathan Edwards and the American Experience*. New York: Oxford University Press, 1988.
Hegel, G. W. F. *Lectures on the Philosophy of Religion*, vol. 3: *The Consummate Religion*. Edited by Peter Hodgson. Berkerly: University of California Press, 1985.
Helm, Paul. "A Forensic Dilemma: John Locke and Jonathan Edwards on Personal Identity." In *Jonathan Edward: Philosophical Theologian*, edited by Paul Helm and Oliver Crisp, 45–60. Burlington, VT: Ashgate, 2003.
———. "John Calvin and the Hiddenness of God." Paper presented at the Rutherford House Dogmatic Conference, 2005.
Henry, Caleb. *Jonathan Edwards as Lockean Puritan? Epistemology and Natural Law in Jonathan Edwards*. Ph.D. dissertation, Claremont Graduate School, 2002.
Heppe, Heinrich. *Reformed Dogmatics Set Out and Illustrated from the Sources*. Edited by Ernst Bizer, translated by G. T. Thomson. London: Allen & Unwin, 1950.
Hodge, Charles. *Systematic Theology*. Reprint. Grand Rapids: Eerdmans, 1989.
Holmes, Stephen R. "Does Jonathan Edwards Use a Dispositional Ontology? A Response to Sang Hyun Lee." In *Jonathan Edward: Philosophical Theologian*, edited by Paul Helm and Oliver Crisp, 99–114. Burlington, VT: Ashgate, 2003.
———. *God of Grace and God of Glory: An Account of the Theology of Jonathan Edwards*. Edinburgh: T. & T. Clark, 2000.
Hutcheson, Francis. *An Inquiry into the Original of our Ideas of Beauty and Virtue*. 1726. Reprint. no loc.: Elibron Classics, 2003.
———. *Philosophical Writings*. Edited by R. S. Downie. London: Dent, 1994.
Jenson, Robert W. *America's Theologian: A Recommendation of Jonathan Edwards*. New York: Oxford University Press, 1988.

Kant, Immanuel. *Critique of the Power of Judgment*. Edited by Paul Guyer. Cambridge: Cambridge University Press, 2000.

Kistler, Don. *The Wrath of Almighty God: Jonathan Edwards on God's Judgment against Sinners*. Morgan, PA: Soli Deo Gloria, 1996.

Kivy, Peter. *Blackwell Guide to Aesthetics*. Oxford: Blackwell, 2004.

———. *The Seventh Sense: A Study of Francis Hutcheson's Aesthetics and Eighteen-Century British Aesthetics*. 2nd ed. Oxford: Clarendon, 2003.

Knight, Janice. "Learning the Language of God: Jonathan Edwards and the Typology of Nature." *William and Mary Quarterly*, 3rd series, 48 (1991) 531–51.

———. *Orthodoxies in Massachusetts: Rereading American Puritanism*. Cambridge: Harvard University Press, 1994.

Kristeller, Paul Oskar. "The Modern System of the Arts: A Study in the History of Aesthetics." *Journal of the History of Ideas* 12 (1951) 496–527; 13 (1952) 17–46.

Kuyper, Abraham. *Lectures on Calvinism*. Grand Rapids: Eerdmans, 1931.

Lee, Sang Hyun. "Edwards on God and Nature." In *Edwards in Our Time: Jonathan Edwards and the Shaping of American Religion*, edited by Sang Hyun Lee and Allen C Guelzo, 15–44. Grand Rapids: Eerdmans, 1999.

———. *The Philosophical Theology of Jonathan Edwards*. Princeton: Princeton University Press, 1988.

Locke, John. *An Essay concerning Human Understanding*. Edited by Peter H. Nidditch. Oxford: Clarendon, 1975.

Malebranche. *Dialogues on Metaphysics and on Religion*. Edited by Nicholas Jolley and David Scott. Cambridge Texts in the History of Philosophy. Cambridge: Cambridge University Press, 1997.

Marion, Jean-Luc. *In Excess: Studies of Saturated Phenomena*. New York: Fordham University Press, 2002.

Marsden, George M. *Fundamentalism and American Culture: The Shaping of Twentieth-Century Evangelicalism, 1870–1925*. New York: Oxford University Press, 1980.

———. *Jonathan Edwards: A Life*. New Haven: Yale University Press, 2003.

Matless, Sally I. *Jonathan Edwards' Relational Metaphysics of Love*, Th.D. diss., Harvard University, 2002.

McClymond, Michael J. *Encounters with God: An Approach to the Theology of Jonathan Edwards*. New York: Oxford University Press, 1998.

McClymond, Michael J., and Gerald R. McDermott. *The Theology of Jonathan Edwards*. New York: Oxford University Press, 2012.

McCormack, Bruce. "Grace and Being: The Role of God's Gracious Election in Karl Barth's Theological Ontology." In *The Cambridge Companion to Karl Barth*, edited by John Webster, 92–110. Cambridge: Cambridge University Press, 2000.

McGinn, Bernard. *The Harvest of Mysticism in Medieval Germany (1300–1500)*. The Presence of God: A History of Western Christian Mysticism, vol. 4. New York: Crossroad, 2005.

———. "Love, Knowledge and *Unio Mystica* in the Western Christian Tradition." In *Mystical Union in Judaism, Christianity, and Islam: An Ecumenical Dialogue*, edited by Moshe Idel and Bernard McGinn, 59–86. New York: Continuum, 1996.

Menn, Stephen. "The Intellectual Setting." In *Cambridge History of Seventeenth-Century Philosophy*, edited by Daniel Garber and Michael Ayers, 9–32. Cambridge: Cambridge University Press, 1998.

Miller, Perry. *Jonathan Edwards*. Plymouth, MA: Sloane, 1949.

———. *The New England Mind: The Seventeenth Century.* Cambridge: Harvard University Press, 1939.

———. *The New England Mind: From Colony to Province.* Cambridge: Harvard University Press, 1953.

Mitchell, Louis J. *The Experience of Beauty in the Thought of Jonathan Edwards.* Studies in Reformed Theology and History, N.S. 9. Princeton: Princeton Theological Seminary, 2003.

Monk, Samuel H. *The Sublime.* 1935. Reprint. Ann Arbor, MI: University of Michigan Press, 1960.

Morgan, Chris. *Jonathan Edwards & Hell.* Fearn, UK: Mentor, 2004.

Morgan, Edmund. *Visible Saints: The History of a Puritan Idea.* Ithaca, NY: Cornell University Press, 1963.

Morimoto, Anri. *Jonathan Edwards and the Catholic Vision of Salvation.* University Park, PA: Pennsylvania State University Press, 1995.

Muller, Richard A. *Post-Reformation Reformed Dogmatics: The Rise and Development of Reformed Orthodoxy, c.a. 1520 to ca. 1725, vol. 3, The Divine Essence and Attributes.* Grand Rapids: Baker, 2003.

———. *Post-Reformation Reformed Dogmatics: The Rise and Development of Reformed Orthodoxy, c.a. 1520 to ca. 1725, vol. 4, The Trinity of God.* Grand Rapids: Baker, 2003.

Owen, John. *The Death of Death in the Death of Christ, Works of John Owen, vol. 10.* Ultimate Christian Library. CD-Rom. Ages Software, 2000.

———. *Meditations and Discourses on the Glory of Christ, Works of John Owen, vol. 1.* Ultimate Christian Library. CD-Rom. Ages Software, 2000.

———. *PNEUMATOLOGIA: A Discourse Concerning the Holy Spirit, Works of John Owen, vol. 4.* Ultimate Christian Library. CD-Rom. Ages Software, 2000.

Pauw, Amy Plantinga. *The Supreme Harmony of All: The Trinitarian Theology of Jonathan Edwards.* Grand Rapid: Eerdmans, 2002.

Plantinga, Alvin. *The Nature of Necessity.* Oxford : Clarendon, 1974.

Pseudo-Dionysius. *Pseudo-Dionysius: The Complete Works.* Translated by Colm Luibheid. Mahwah, NJ: Paulist, 1987.

Reid, Jasper. "Jonathan Edwards on Space and God." *Journal of the History of Philosophy* 41 (2003) 385–403.

Roberts, Louis. *The Theological Aesthetics of Hans Urs von Balthasar.* Washington, DC: Catholic University of America Press, 1987.

Ross, James F. *Philosophical Theology.* Indianapolis: Hackett, 1980.

Schreiner, Susan. *The Theatre of His Glory: Nature and the Natural Order in the Thought of John Calvin.* Studies in Historical Theology 3. Durham, NC: Labyrinth, 1991.

Shaftesbury, Anthony Ashley-Cooper, 3rd Earl of. *Characteristics of Men, Manners, Opinions, Times.* Edited by Lawrence E. Klein, Cambridge Texts in the History of Philosophy. Cambridge: Cambridge University Press, 1999.

Sher, Richard B. *Church and University in the Scottish Enlightenment: The Moderate Literati of Edinburgh.* Edinburgh: Edinburgh University Press, 1985.

Sherry, Patrick. *Spirit and Beauty: An Introduction to Theological Aesthetics.* 2nd ed. London: SCM, 2002.

Stewart, M. A. "Religion and Rational Theology." In *The Cambridge Companion to The Scottish Enlightenment,* edited by Alexander Broadie, 31–59. Cambridge: Cambridge University Press, 2003.

———. *Studies in the Philosophy of the Scottish Enlightenment*. Oxford: Clarendon, 1990.
Stolnitz, Jerome. "Beauty: Some Stages in the History of an Idea." *Journal of the History of Ideas* 22 (1961) 185–204.
———. "On the Significance of Lord Shaftesbury in Modern Aesthetic Theory." *Philosophical Quarterly* 11 (1961) 97–113.
Stout, Harry S. *The New England Soul: Preaching and Religious Culture in Colonial New England*. New York: Oxford University Press, 1986.
Strader, Ronald Edwin. *The Chronological Development of the Spiritual-Aesthetic in the Philosophical Theology of Jonathan Edwards and its Relationship to Seventeen- and Eighteenth-Century British Philosophy*. Ph.D. diss., Claremont Graduate School, 1981.
Studebaker, Michael. *Jonathan Edwards' Social Augustinian Trinitarianism: A Criticism of and an Alternative to Recent Interpretations*. Ph.D. diss., Marquette University, 2003.
Sweeney, Douglas A. *Nathaniel Taylor, New Haven Theology, and the Legacy of Jonathan Edwards*. New York: Oxford University Press, 2003.
Tillich, Paul. *Systematic Theology, vol. 1*. Chicago: University of Chicago Press, 1951.
Turretin, Francis. *Institutes of Elenctic Theology*. 3 vols. Translated by George M. Giger, edited by James T. Dennison. Phillipsburg, NJ: Presbyterian and Reformed, 1992–97.
Townsend, D. "Lockean Aesthetics." *Journal of Aesthetics and Art Criticism* 49 (1991) 349–61.
Trueman, Carl R. *The Claims of Truth: John Owen's Trinitarian Theology*. Carlisle, UK: Paternoster, 1998.
———. "Heaven and Hell: (12) In Puritan Theology." *Epworth Review* 22.3 (1995) 75–85.
Tuveson, Ernest Lee. *The Imagination as a Means of Grace: Locke and the Aesthetics of Romanticism*. Berkeley: University of California Press, 1960.
Vetö, Miklos. "Spiritual Knowledge according to Jonathan Edwards." Translated by Michael McClymond. *Calvin Theological Journal* 31 (1996) 161–81.
Viladesau, Richard. *Theological Aesthetics: God in Imagination, Beauty, and Art*. Oxford: Oxford University Press, 1999.
Von Rohr, John. *The Covenant of Grace in Puritan Thought*. Atlanta: Scholars, 1986.
Walker. D. P. *The Decline of Hell: Seventeenth-Century Discussions of Eternal Torment*. London: Routledge & Kegan Paul, 1964.
Weir, David A. *The Origins of the Federal Theology in Sixteenth-Century Reformation Thought*. Oxford: Clarendon, 1990.
Well, David. *Reformed Theology in America: A History of its Modern Development*. Grand Rapids: Eerdmans, 1985.
Zakai, Avihu. *Jonathan Edwards's Philosophy of History: The Reenchantment of the World in the Age of Enlightenment*. Princeton: Princeton University Press, 2003.

# Index

Addison, Joseph, 17, 32, 36, 43–55, 58, 60–62
affection, 29–31, 39–41, 43, 49, 54, 61, 63, 65, 82, 85–94, 105–7, 110, 111, 151, 152, 158, 179, 181, 216
Ames, William, 29, 30, 102, 104, 126
Anderson, Wallace, 34, 35, 56, 69, 70, 78, 80
Aquinas, Thomas, 22–28, 31, 41, 65, 67, 72, 73, 75, 83, 84, 87, 92, 95, 96, 101, 106–9, 113, 114, 154, 155, 188, 189, 212, 213
Aristotle, Aristotelian, Aristotelianism, 5, 20, 21, 23, 32, 40, 65, 67, 72, 213
Augustine, Augustinian, 21–22, 99, 100, 104, 107, 188, 201
atom, 5, 71–73, 77, 90, 147, 148

Balthasar, Hans Urs von, 213–15
Barth, Karl, 137–41, 194–96, 214
beauty
    awful, 138, 160, 173–75, 190, 210, 212
    clarity, 23, 25, 27, 212, 213
    complex, 58
    equality, 58, 116
    general, 7, 60, 98
    particular, 21, 26, 27, 60, 110
    primary, 56, 59, 66, 83, 182, 183
    secondary, 56, 59, 66, 68, 75, 83, 182, 183
    Trinitarian, 15, 16, 190, 197, 215
Begbie, Jeremy, 203, 204, 206
being in general, 9, 60, 66, 83. 97, 98, 109, 110, 210, 213
Bellamy, Joseph, 102, 198, 199
Bush, Michael David, 118, 123, 125, 126, 131, 132, 136

body
    beauty of, 20, 81, 82
    in heaven, 145, 147–53, 156, 160
    in hell, 163, 167

Calvin, Calvinism, Calvinistic, 12, 23, 27–29, 36, 37, 86, 97, 121, 144, 145, 170, 186, 187, 191, 194, 198, 200, 202–204, 206, 216
cause and effect, 5, 6, 8, 15
Christ
    abasement, 129–32, 136
    divine glory of, 128, 130, 131, 133, 138, 139, 157, 174, 175
    human glory of, 138, 140, 157, 161, 162, 174, 175
    humility of, 133, 135–38, 157, 159, 161, 174, 175, 183, 189
Covenant of
    Grace, 119–25, 131, 188
    Redemption, 118–25, 127–32, 137, 138, 141–43, 177, 188, 189, 194
Consent, 9, 11, 13, 56, 57, 59, 60, 64, 81–83, 98, 110, 116, 183, 184

damnation, 116, 165, 169–72, 180, 211
Daniel, Stephen H., 11, 12, 15, 79, 82, 217
Delattre, Roland, 2, 3, 7, 9–11, 13, 15, 56, 64, 66, 68, 73, 82, 83, 94, 97, 183, 191, 210, 211
deposition, 10, 64
Dooyeweerd, Herman, 206
Dyrness, William, 14, 27–29,

Eco, Umberto, 21–26
Elwood, Douglas, 8, 9, 16

227

*Index*

Enlightenment, 1, 10–12, 15, 17–19, 26, 30–32, 34–36, 55, 63–67, 79, 84, 91, 187, 214, 216
epistemology, 2, 7, 11, 26, 67, 86, 106, 107, 188, 200, 216
Eriugena, 8, 23
Excellecny, 4, 6, 8, 57, 81, 82, 88, 89, 96, 99, 125, 126, 132–38, 153, 160, 169, 189

faculty, 25, 37, 62, 86, 87, 149, 208–11
Farley, Edward, 9, 13, 211
Fiering, Norman, 64, 65, 69, 70, 136, 162–64, 166, 169, 171
fine arts, 18, 19, 45, 51, 208, 216, 217
Flower, Elizabeth, 33, 64, 70, 95
Foster, F. H., 198, 199, 201

Gerstner, John, 2, 97, 193
glory of God, 14, 29, 30, 37, 39, 60, 63, 87, 88, 109, 136, 138, 145, 153, 154, 162, 163–67, 169, 172–74, 176, 177, 179–83, 190, 191, 193, 196, 197, 202, 216

heaven
  glory of, 29, 144, 145, 147, 150, 162
  joy of, 16, 143–45, 147–49, 151–53, 156–58, 160, 167–69, 179–82, 187, 188, 190, 193, 210, 211
Hegel, G. W. F., 60, 69, 192, 209
hell
  agony of, 167, 168, 179, 182, 190
  glory of, 166, 168, 175, 180
Heppe, Heinrich, 119, 120, 144, 161, 163, 191
Hodge, Charles, 97, 198, 200, 201
holiness, 38, 80, 89, 94, 110, 144, 147, 149, 151, 159, 160, 162, 169
Holmes, Stephen, 12, 13, 73, 107, 163, 164, 166, 170, 171, 177, 193, 195
Holy Spirit, 9, 13, 14, 16, 21, 83, 89, 91, 101, 103, 104, 107, 108, 110, 112–16, 121, 125, 129, 162, 177, 183, 186, 190, 197
Hopkins, Samuel, 35, 198
Hume, David, 33, 36, 37, 51, 66, 67

Hutcheson, Francis, 1, 6, 7, 17, 18, 32, 36–38, 43, 47–62, 77, 186

idea (in epistemology), idealism, 4–6, 8, 11, 14, 25, 27, 32, 39, 44, 46–48, 50–54, 57, 61, 62, 66–74, 76, 77, 81, 84–86, 90, 135–38, 173, 183, 186–88, 192, 198, 200, 216
image, 13, 20, 26–29, 37, 45, 46, 68, 74, 78, 79, 81–83, 99, 100, 104–8, 121, 140, 145, 146, 153, 154, 167, 168, 173, 176, 181–83, 190, 191, 194, 200, 207
Incarnation, 121, 123, 124, 128, 130, 132, 134, 135, 137–41, 152, 159, 174, 175, 177, 189, 195, 196

Kant, Kantian, 17, 55, 62, 66, 74, 106, 203, 208–12, 216, 217
knowledge
  sensible, 86–88, 94, 149, 150, 166, 170–72, 175, 177, 182, 187, 190, 193, 216
  speculative/ notional, 40, 86, 87, 89, 94, 107, 175, 202, 216
Kuyper, 203–7

law of nature, , 10, 31, 34, 35, 59, 65, 68, 72–75, 77, 80, 89, 90, 112, 149, 175–77, 180, 186, 187
Lee, Sang Hyun, 10–12, 64, 68, 73, 74, 78, 99, 107, 108, 111–14, 155, 183
Locke, Lockean, 2, 4–7, 11, 17, 32, 35, 37, 38, 46 48, 50, 53, 61, 65, 66, 68–70, 83–86, 88–92, 136, 107, 126, 132, 138, 164, 186, 188, 193, 200
Luther, 27, 28, 194

McClymond, Michael J., 12, 14, 17, 70, 72, 84, 115, 166, 186
Marsden, George, 1, 19, 35, 81, 166, 200, 202
Mather, Cotton, 33, 34, 37
Matless, Sally I., 64, 65, 69, 70, 73, 108, 116

## Index

Miller, Perry, 12–17, 37, 70, 84, 102, 187, 202, 215
Mitchell, Louis J., 7, 12, 132
Morimoto, Anri, 118, 130, 187
Muller, Richard, 101, 102, 104, 119
music, 24, 49–51, 55, 149

Newton, Isaac, 2, 4, 7, 10, 17, 31, 32, 34, 54, 65, 67, 68, 70, 164
Neoplatonic, Neoplatonism, 21–23, 27, 30, 31, 43, 75, 80, 82–84, 97, 116, 131, 190, 191, 213

Owen, John, 30, 103, 122, 123, 145, 146, 152, 162, 189

Pauw, Amy Plantinga, 14, 99–101, 107
Plato, Platonic, Platonism, Platonist, 8, 18–21, 23, 25, 30, 31, 35, 36, 39, 40, 42, 65, 69, 70, 200, 206, 207, 212,
predestination, 10, 22, 26, 30, 191
proportion, 20, 21, 23–27, 30, 31, 39, 40, 42, 45, 47, 56–61, 63, 64, 75, 76, 81, 139, 157, 158, 163, 166, 170, 171, 175
Pseudo-Dionysius, 10, 22, 26, 30, 191
Puritan, 1, 2, 8, 10, 12, 14–18, 29, 31, 33–36, 55, 63, 66, 68, 79, 80, 86, 101–4, 118, 119, 121, 122, 125, 145–48, 152, 162, 165, 180, 187, 190, 193

religious experience, 12, 201, 202
reprobation, 169, 175, 195
Rookmaaker, Hans, 203, 206, 207

Schelling, Friedrich W. J. von, 9, 10
Seerveld, Calvin, 206, 207
self-love, 53, 107–11, 114–16, 126, 139, 183, 192

sense
 spiritual, 61, 62, 86–88, 92, 186, 190, 210, 212
 moral, 32, 49, 50, 62
 internal/ inner, 7, 48–51, 54, 61, 62, 86, 186
Shaftesbury, Earl of, 17, 18, 32, 33, 36, 38–43, 46, 48, 55, 60–62, 70, 80, 164, 165
Sherry, Patrick, 13, 15, 21, 216
sign, 12, 23, 30, 46, 54, 77, 82–89
Studebaker, Michael, 99–101, 104, 107, 109
subject (the human ego), 10–12, 25, 26, 30, 62, 106, 192, 196, 217
Sweeney, Douglas A., 198–200

taste, 18, 39–41, 44, 50–52, 55, 61, 086, 91, 186
Trinity
 intra-Trinitarian life 15, 113, 116, 118, 137, 153, 155, 161, 182, 183, 191, 194, 197, 198, 215
 psychological model, 14, 99, 104, 112, 116, 200, 207
 social model, 14, 99–102, 104, 111, 112, 116, 118, 126
Trueman, Carl R., 122, 123, 145, 163, 164, 177
Turretin, Francis, 102, 103, 119, 201
type, archetype, 15, 24, 26, 27, 30, 78–80, 82, 94, 104, 110, 182, 196, 212

Viladesau, Richard, 18, 214, 215
virtue, 7, 11, 18, 20, 38–42, 48, 56, 57, 67, 98, 109, 110, 115, 130, 133, 134, 136–38, 153, 165, 177, 189, 204

www.ingramcontent.com/pod-product-compliance
Lightning Source LLC
Chambersburg PA
CBHW051637230426
43669CB00013B/2342